PRAISE FOR

THE SECOND-BEST
BUSINESS BOOK EVER WRITTEN

"Well written, timely, and incredibly relevant for anyone who practices thought leadership, consumes thought leadership, or is curious about thought leadership. Buy it! Read it! Embrace it!"

—Peter Winick, founder and CEO, Thought Leadership Leverage

"Much of what passes for thought leadership these days are provocative ideas packaged in a pithy way designed to generate clicks. That is most definitely NOT what Tom Marks writes in his *The Second-Best Business Book Ever Written*. Rather, Marks identifies three key sources of human behavior—desire, emotion, and knowledge—and links thought leadership around these ideas to three areas of influence—Wisdom, Trust, and Ethics. Of course, none of these ideas are new, which is why Marks traces them back to the classic Greek scholars Socrates, Plato, Aristotle, and the lesser known Aspasia. Deriving lessons from these original thought leaders, as well as from the worlds of sports and Broadway musicals, Marks makes the compelling case that market leadership, as well as thought leadership, is predicated upon these eternal truths. Having experienced living and working in non-Western cultures, I can say that whether your world view is rooted in ancient Greek philosophers, or the Eastern teachings of Buddha or Confucius, these truths that have stood the test of time can be wonderful guides to business and personal success."

—Jonathan Gartner, advisor, mentor, investor

"Over the many years I've known Tom as both friend and mentor, I've learned more about business thought leadership from him than I have from the many books I've read. Each page of this book is crammed with wisdom and insight, and I guarantee that you will underline, highlight, and dog-ear it. By his own definition, Tom cannot call himself a 'thought leader,' but there is nothing that prevents me from bestowing that name. I take exception to just one thing about this book—it is not 'the second-best business book ever written'—it is the best! You can put away all the other business books on your list and read this one—it's that good. Tom is the ultimate storyteller, and this book underscores that. What Tom brings in this book is rare: He both entertains and educates—two principles that are critical to getting through a book about success in business."

—**Alan Bergstrom,** CMO and brand consultant

"Business goals are necessary, but sometimes they get in the way. You want to be a leader? You want to make a difference in your company, your community? The secret from this book is that leadership—thought leadership—starts and ends with not trying to be different but simply being more of yourself. Be human. Be honest. Plan your business strategy around that and success won't be far away."

—**Joe Pulizzi,** best-selling author of seven books including *Content Inc.* and *Epic Content Marketing*

"From the teachings of Aristotle in the halls of Lyceum to wisdom-based pitches made by sales executives in the corporate boardroom, Tom blends history, data, science, psychology, and personal experience into a well-conceived methodology delivering fact-based instruction sure to improve sales and overall business results. Focusing on the customer, developing critical insights from industry trends, and mastering the art of storytelling form the foundation of thought leadership—the pinnacle of positioning in the corporate office, and in the market. I found Tom's writing to be reflective, insightful, inspirational, informative, amusing, and challenging. I trust you will as well."

—Doug Deardorf, CEO, NiSoft™

"Admittedly, I had only barely heard of thought leadership prior to reading Tom Marks's *The Second-Best Business Book Ever Written.* Thanks to Tom's caring, creative, and curious new book, thought leadership will help guide and influence both our organization and my leadership throughout our future endeavors. Tom's ability to clearly articulate difficult and insightful business concepts in a humorous and positive way will be helpful to any reader—whether you're early in your career or a seasoned CEO. It's truly a great read."

—Jason Ilstrup, JD., president, Downtown Madison, Inc.

"Based on the wisdom of ancient philosophers, Tom Marks presents a straightforward process for developing the competency of thought leadership. Most notably, his process is as relevant for selling products and services to prospective clients as it is for selling individual competencies and know-how to a potential employer. It's a great read!"

—Dr. Ron Glickman, author, *Lead for a Change: Proven Strategies to Clarify Expectation, Foster Growth, and Achieve Breakthroughs*

"This isn't just one of the best sales and marketing books I've had the pleasure of reading; it's one of the best business books."

—Adam Eberle, private equity consultant, entrepreneur

"It's important to treat yourself to every chapter in this book . . . there's something for all of us to learn on virtually every page . . . It's delightful, educational, and will take you away to places you can only imagine."

—Jill Adams, CMO, El Pollo Loco

THE SECOND-BEST BUSINESS BOOK EVER ✓ WRITTEN

THE SECOND-BEST BUSINESS BOOK EVER WRITTEN

THE PURSUIT *of* THOUGHT LEADERSHIP
IN SALES, MARKETING, *and* LIFE

TOM MARKS

AN INC.
ORIGINAL

An Inc. Original
New York, New York
www.anincoriginal.com

HELLO IN THERE
Words and Music by JOHN PRINE
© 1970 (Renewed) WALDEN MUSIC, INC. and SOUR GRAPES MUSIC, INC.
All Rights Administered by WALDEN MUSIC, INC.
All Rights Reserved
Used by Permission of ALFRED MUSIC

This work is being published under the An Inc. Original imprint by an exclusive arrangement with Inc. Magazine. Inc. Magazine and the Inc. logo are registered trademarks of Mansueto Ventures, LLC. The An Inc. Original logo is a wholly owned trademark of Mansueto Ventures, LLC.

Distributed by River Grove Books

Design and composition by Greenleaf Book Group
Cover design by Greenleaf Book Group
Cover Image from Adobe Stock

Publisher's Cataloging-in-Publication data is available.

Print ISBN: 978-1-63909-038-9

eBook ISBN: 978-1-63909-039-6

First Edition

To my wife, Kathy. Her decades of support have been uninterrupted, unwavering, and unmatched by humankind.

CONTENTS

FOREWORD

To the best of my recollection, I met Tom Marks in 1999 when we were working together at a software company in the financial services industry, me as a sales rep and Tom as a consultant. From that day forward, we've never looked back. Although I haven't said this directly to Tom, I've told many people that he's always been my "secret weapon."

For decades my career has been deeply rooted in sales. I started as a sales rep in pharmaceuticals and have been a sales manager, a business development director, a vice president of sales, an executive vice president of sales, a chief revenue officer, and a chief commercial officer. In most cases, my career has been working with private equity firms including, but not limited to, Vista Capital Partners, Rakuten, New Mountain Capital, The Riverside Company, and Serent Capital. I've been fortunate to have recorded several billion dollars in successful exits.

Just the other day, I posted a personal update on LinkedIn, and not surprisingly, Tom was one of the first to congratulate me on my latest career announcement. He's that way. Thoughtful about others, long before being thoughtful of himself. But that's not really the point of this story. When I thanked Tom and wrote for all the public to see, "I learned everything from you," it caused a bit of a kerfuffle as people started responding humorously, "I thought it was me," or "So, now we know who's ass you've been kissing," or my favorite, "So when you said it was me, you were really cheating."

For as long as I can remember, Tom has been fascinated by Greek philosophers. One night over dinner, he asked me to do an online search on thought leadership and the Greeks. I was an unsuspecting dupe in his amusing gambit when I came to find out that Tom was number one on Google. He didn't say he was—that's something he would never do just as he'd never say he's a thought leader—but I'll tell you this: The dude is where thought leaders go for their thought leadership.

Over the years, I've read plenty of business books. Some by choice and others by force. In both cases, it's difficult for me to read a business book in a session or two. Let's face it, they're just not page-turners. Most often, I'll opt to read a chapter here and there, perhaps make a notation or two, and then move on to a business magazine or a trade publication that is more to my liking. But Tom's *The Second-Best Business Book Ever Written: The Pursuit of Thought Leadership in Sales, Marketing, and Life* is a 100-percent exception. This is a business book that is literally rule breaking, and no one who knows Tom should ever suspect anything less than that. To be fair, Tom is not a rule-breaker because he's really the one person in America who has set the rules about thought leadership.

Sure, many people have written about thought leadership, but very few have taught us how to become a thought leader, the steps we need to take—in exacting detail, I might add—and how we can be better professionals and better people along the way. And, of course, no one has ever done it through the lens of the great Greek scholars.

Sprinkled in for good measure, you'll see Tom's brain working overtime as he amuses us and educates readers with tangents that provide added context and some lighthearted oddities that help us understand the human side of his thinking. You'll also see how all this fits together in his glorious expression of how thought leaders connect the dots when there are no dots to connect. Thankfully, he shows us how to do that.

What I really like about Tom's book, and his entertaining musings, aside from the fact that this isn't just one of the best sales and marketing books I've had the pleasure of reading this century—it's one of the best business books—is that it's for everyone, absolutely everyone who is in business, or is thinking about going into business as a profession.

It doesn't matter if you're in sales or marketing, operations, leadership at the C-suite level, or anything in between. Thought leadership is for all of us; it's aspirational, achievable, and of tremendous value regardless of where you are in your career, or what positions you have held. As corny as it sounds, this *is* a must-read for anyone who wants to be a thought leader, or for any company that wants to be known as a thought leader.

And there's one last thing I'd like to share with you because you rarely see this in business, at least I haven't. Certainly, Tom is a marketing, corporate ethics, and thought leadership consultant, but is he? I'm still torn between if he's all of that or if he's a really terrific salesman. Perhaps he's one giant bundle of everything. The fact remains I've never seen or worked with any marketer who was so concerned about sales, so fascinated by the process, so attuned to the importance of lead generation and closing rates that my one career wish has always been to find the next person to be the *Tom Trifecta*. Sales, marketing, and thought leadership all in one. Let me know when you find that person.

All the best and sincerely,
Adam Eberle
Private equity consultant, entrepreneur, and sales leader
Cleveland, Ohio

ACKNOWLEDGMENTS

I got a pretty significant head start on this book. That's because my parents, Melvin and Mary Marks, both deceased, gave me, my older brother, Bill, and my younger sister, Pam, the lifelong gifts of education, curiosity, and purpose. It sure sounds to me that they took their cues from Socrates, Plato, Aristotle, and Aspasia.

I also got a head start on happiness. How on earth can a woman be married to an ad man and a writer? Two professions that can grind a person down to nibs. But somehow Kathy Marks found the magic potion, not that I have a clue what the formula is, but my hunch is it has something to do with a healthy dose of patience and a sidecar of affirmative head-bobbing.

To my editor, Jeffrey Curry, whose life I made miserable, but who, like the Greek Stoics, never let on and probably never gave it much thought. He's a machine, a rule-follower to my rule-breaking tendencies, and a counterbalance of politeness to my saltiness and abrasion.

Hats off to the publishers and the publishing team. Mansueto Ventures, *Inc.* magazine, River Grove Books, and Greenleaf Book Group. They wore so many hats just to make this happen—with special condolences to the entire team that made it through the process without shedding too many tears and hopefully laughing at some bad jokes, tasteless stories, and my own Socratic Questioning because times have changed, the processes, too, and the old dog needed extra time to learn the new tricks.

And to all the writers in the world, at least the purest of them, who understand that the A in AI still stands for artificial, that AI is not always a viable shortcut, that it's more often a short-circuiting of what matters on the inside, our heartbeat, and that someday, maybe on the outside some good can come from AI. Thank you for taking the time to read this book. We all have a bit of the Greek scholars inside us, and I'm really glad we do.

My very best to you,
Thomas R. Marks
Madison, Wisconsin, and Tucson, Arizona

INTRODUCTION

O f all the sales and marketing positions a company or an individual can own, provide relevant differentiation in, and win the day with, thought leadership is at the very top. In my *21st Century Disciplines of Market Leaders*, which I wrote around the turn of the century, I added thought leadership to the mix; it already included the disciplines of price/value leadership, customer service leadership, technology and innovation leadership, and now thought leadership. In order to be a market leader, you must attain one—or perhaps even more than one—of these disciplines to be a market winner.

Because honesty, in its purest form, is a key characteristic of all thought leaders, I'm going to hit you with the truth. Many business books today are written for the purpose of winning more business for an author, or acquiring new speaking gigs, or upping hourly rates, and anyone who fits into that camp is A-OK with me. It's a smart move. But after more than four decades in the sales and marketing business, I'm beyond those goals. And frankly, I'm damn glad I'm not anchored to those intentions, although I must admit it took decades. I have only one intent, and that's to teach the ins and outs of thought leadership to as many people as possible because that's how corporations, and the individuals who run them, succeed.

There's a process to becoming a thought leader; it's methodical, detailed, rewarding, and enjoyable in an enlightening sort of way. After all, where's the amusement in being a price-chopper? Or even a technology leader where the tenure is as short as my nephew's attention span? The greatest thought leaders started sharing their thinking 2,500 years ago through the teachings and writings of my four favorites: Socrates, Plato, Aristotle, and the high priestess of just about everything, Aspasia.

I'm going to travel with you down the thought leadership road, known as the Via Egnatia, from the foothills that rise above Athens to the skyscrapers that tower above Madison Avenue. And all along the way, I'm going to show you how I did it for Fortune 500 companies, and for small and midsize businesses, with a few wild detours that will make time fly. Even though thought leadership is the most bankable and desirable discipline a company can embrace, it's taken the sales and marketing industries a while to get there.

In fact, for several decades, professionals were enamored with the five Ps, which were introduced in the 1960s by Edmund McCarthy, a professor at Michigan State University—one of the first universities to offer a four-year degree in advertising. At the time, it was quite possible that a degree in advertising probably scared the shit out of parents who were hoping their child would attend Michigan State for a more traditional degree in, say, engineering, education, pre-med, or accounting. But a degree in advertising? My child? For God's sake.

God and advertising aside, McCarthy brilliantly categorized what he called *the marketing mix strategy* into five distinct groupings that we all know today as product, price, people, promotion, and place. In actuality, McCarthy initially introduced the concept as the four Ps; the people category was added later. Of course, by today's standards, it's an oversimplification of the complexities of business: the data decision-making that is part of any winning business strategy; the need for segmentation, and segmentation within segmentation; the interplay of competition—local, regional, national, and global; the introduction of e-commerce that has transitioned the meaning of *place* to *any place*; the innovation of digital that has made every aspect of the five Ps completely granular and personal on almost every level; and the list continues to grow.

Nevertheless, McCarthy went on to lay the groundwork for a stellar career in marketing and advertising, notching awards and accolades for his freethinking and his insights, including the Trailblazer Award from the American Marketing Association (AMA), our highest honor.

As trends come and go, my advice to anyone, and that includes corporate leaders, sales reps, marketing specialists, and most particularly individuals who want to get into these professions, is to hitch your wagon to what stands the test of time, not what you stand to gain from a timely trend that tests your limits of patience. If you learn how to be a thought leader, or your company embraces a thought leadership position, you'll be set for years. And so will your team, your culture, and your success.

Nothing comes easy anymore; it just doesn't. We know that shortcuts, workarounds, and mortgaging the future on a quick sale today is no approach to long-term success. Avoid these at all costs and stick with what's stickiest. It might take a little bit of work to be a thought leader, maybe some added costs to help you get started, but over the long term—and by that I mean no more than one or two years—you'll actually save a lot of time, money, and massive aggravation that will amount to incredible savings. Plus, you'll avoid chasing trends, losing messaging consistency, confusing customers, and turning your brand inside out.

After I crisscrossed the country conducting thought leadership workshops and talking on the professional speakers' circuit, three observations continue to stay with me several years later. These observations fall into the framework of what Plato told us about the way we behave: "Human behavior flows from three main sources: **desire, emotion**, and

knowledge." I have witnessed a real **desire** by people from all stripes to quickly embrace, integrate, and launch a thought leadership campaign. That's fantastic, but like many sales and marketing disciplines, thought leadership is not a footrace; it requires a well-defined progression of steps and checklists, and I'll be your guide for that.

I have also seen and felt the **emotion** from people who can't wait to start selling, particularly when mastering my proprietary *Critical Insight Selling* technique, which is the actual pitching of thought leadership. Frankly, it's great to see, but *Critical Insight Selling* is as advanced a sales technique as there is, and its mastery is not a two-part video series that ends with the words "Go out there and sell like hell." However, I can assure you that conquering this sales approach will turn you from an order-taker to the order of merit for being a top producer.

And finally, if our human behavior ultimately flows into and through **knowledge**, I've been amazed at the amount of interest there has been to expand people's knowledge about the historical perspectives regarding thought leadership. In particular how Greek scholars and their sense of ethics play so closely into what's good and bad in our lifetimes, how dialed in Socrates, Plato, Aristotle, and Aspasia were to the importance of listening, asking questions, pushing ethical behavior, and pursuing an existence steeped in honesty and trust. For me, and I'm hoping for you, it's part eye-opener and part head-scratcher. The head-scratching part is how a gap of 2,500 years can seem so expansive while at the same time so narrow. I keep thinking, *Did this dude really think this way more than two thousand years ago?*

Throughout my forty-seven-year career, I've consistently taught the steps and mechanics of how to become a thought leader, the progressions—and there is an exacting chronology to these progressions—the research, the insights, and the selling of those insights that can result in increased revenue and incremental sales. For me, the *how to* will always be important because it provides us with the knowledge of how to succeed, but so is the *context*, the way all the parts fit together and drive our emotions; the *history*, because we should never lose sight of the historical perspectives of what got us here, and where we went straight or afoul; and finally the *people* who played a role in how we arrived at where we are today, and where we might go tomorrow.

I like to think of thought leadership as the one discipline in the *21st Century Disciplines of Market Leaders* that can apply to any company regardless of its size or industry, and also the one discipline that's applicable to an individual who wants to be a thought leader in their space and practice. I'll explain both, at times in numbing detail, but there will be breaks and digressions, there will also be historical highlights along the way, perhaps not too different from the historical markers your parents pulled off the highway to see, much to your annoyance, and there will be the occasional expression of my ideologies just to keep things sassy and scrappy.

And if you find yourself asking what the best business book ever written was, I have three answers for you. Choose one or choose them all. For me, it's either *How to Succeed in Business without Really Trying* written by Shepherd Mead (the play version won the Pulitzer Prize for Drama and seven Tony Awards and later became an entertaining movie starring Robert Morse, Michele Lee, and Rudy Vallée), or Peter Drucker's *Management: Tasks, Responsibilities, Practices*; I'm still in possession of my first-edition copy, which is dog-eared, underlined, and highlighted, and I continue to refer to it even fifty years after its publication. But if it's success you're after, the best business book ever written is the book that motivates you to become a successful thought leader.

And speaking of the best ever, and also the first ever, you'll see in chapter seven, titled "You Can't Be a Thought Leader without Voice-of-Customer Research," there's a "spoiler alert" in the lead-in to this chapter. That's because there's never been a published, step-by-step guide on how to conduct Voice-of-Customer (VOC) research to determine critical insights, until now. Have fun with it, dog-ear the pages, underline the paragraphs, and highlight the takeaways.

Here's to you and your **desires**, **emotions**, and **knowledge** that you'll embrace in the pursuit of thought leadership.

1

BUT FIRST, THE BASICS

There are so many complications that surround business principles, approaches, theories, philosophies, and ultimately business books. They are, through no fault of their own, snapshots in time that can't possibly track the real-time movements of an ever-changing economy, let alone all the business nuances and trends that change faster than the styles at Paris Fashion Week. But there is one business principle that does not change, and will not change.

Thought leadership.

My guess is that thought leadership won't become utterly meaningless until every company becomes a thought leader, and when that happens, which will not be in our lifetime, a good part of the disciplines of market leaders won't matter either. And that'll be about the same time you can kiss goodbye branding and whatever strategy and tactics we practice today.

As we know, thought leadership started with Socrates, Plato, Aristotle, and Aspasia, who, incidentally, was by far the better orator than the three men. Their principles of thought leadership are more in demand today than a ticket was for Taylor Swift's Eras Tour. (Actually, probably not, although Ticketmaster didn't help the situation or the affordability of those tickets for the Swifties.) By nature, latching on to the most current trend is our version of marketing shrewdness, that we know what's hip, that we understand the most relevant goodness, and that we are the card-carrying source of intelligence. Until we aren't. Trends are fleeting at best. Like SEO specialists who recommended stuffing, or telemarketers who have the inside track on the latest come-back, or mass marketing in favor of data-driven personalization, or spray and pray in public relations, and, of course my personal favorite, the Yellow Pages, where the budgets were enormous and the returns puny. If you could measure them at all.

In my *21st Century Disciplines of Market Leaders*, I noted there is a tendency for people to believe that the largest companies have the greatest abilities to embrace these disciplines, and then have a death grip on a particular discipline because they have the resources to dominate a position, and the megaphone to convince you that they are who they are. For the most part, that's probably true. But when the truth isn't exactly the truth, a discipline can crumble faster than a house of cards in a Florida hurricane.

That's what bothers me about business theories and approaches. They tilt unfairly in the direction of the bigger players, who aren't always the best players. The big companies hog the oxygen in the business school classroom, absorb more pages in business books, and consume more space in business magazines. But along the way, we've lost sight of small and midsize businesses. And those are the companies that incubate the bigger behemoths. What we're missing is more than the boat; we're missing the fact that the principles of market leadership shouldn't be exclusive to the Fortune 500 just because a small business is defined as having 500 employees or less, or $500 million in sales, which isn't exactly chump change. The disciplines should be far-reaching and not discriminatory, and they should be available to everyone.

Thought leadership turns a blind eye toward all of that nonsense. If you want to be a thought leader, be a thought leader without worrying about market share, head count, and customer count. I've worked with some big players like McDonald's for thirteen years, Foot Locker, Honeywell, Finish Line Sports, FIS Global, Rakuten, American Family Insurance, and plenty of others. But the more I talk about them, the greater a disservice I do to smaller organizations. My preference is to include some supporting examples from very fine businesses where teams are busting their asses every day, where they're doing it right and making an impact in their industry and in their communities, and where hard workers have put in place market-leading disciplines that might not have captured the fancy of the fanciest business schools. But they have, in some cases, changed the world, made it a better place to inhabit, and added to a life of quality for many people, without much fanfare.

The lessons from Socrates, Plato, Aristotle, and Aspasia also have none of the boundaries that we typically set in our writings and teachings about thought leadership. From your personal perspective, you will either be a thought leader or not. The choice will be yours. Your company will either be a thought leader or it won't be; honestly, it's that simple. This is as conclusive and definitive as the sun rising and setting. That's why thought leadership is my favorite of all the disciplines in the *21st Century Disciplines of Market Leaders*. Once you arrive at the station, you have a first-class ticket to wherever you want to go. And not even a huge business can take your ticket away from you.

Of course they'll try, but they won't succeed—unless they want to buy you out, and that can be its own form of success. When Plato said, "A good decision is based on knowledge, not on numbers," we know he wasn't speaking in chief financial officer dark mode. He was talking about what every Greek philosopher taught us: There's nothing more important than knowledge, and we must do everything we can to curate it, both inside and outside a company, and that has nothing to do with a company's size and resources. That's why I'm flipping the switch from dark mode to daylight by shining the spotlight on some businesses that have excelled at various types of corporate philosophies, not always thought leadership, but certain necessary disciplines within disciplines. They include Marten Machining, WEA Trust, Mister Car Wash, Avante Properties, M3 Insurance, ArbiterSports, Rakuten OverDrive, and a handful of others that have two common distinctions: They chose to do it right, and they preferred to provide a life of quality to everyone in their orbit. And that's the philosophy of our original Greek thought leaders who taught us that the pursuit of a life of quality is what we need to be tracking toward. It must always remain in our sights.

There's an old joke on the professional speaking circuit that goes something like this: "How do you know so-and-so is a thought leader?" asks one person.

And the other responds, "Oh, just ask him."

That everyone thinks they're a thought leader is the biggest singular problem thought leaders are challenged by, and it's really the only problem. Imposters, posers, wannabes, and pretenders walk the earth. Aside from that, everything else is clear sailing. Who doesn't want to be a thought leader; who wouldn't want to grab the influencer podium and stand confidently behind it? It sure beats being disrespected in the industry, being mocked by your competitors, and being cast aside as irrelevant in the space you're operating in.

There's something else that's discussed behind the scenes at speaking events, in the green rooms, the coffee bars, and the back of the conference center. We joke about the promotional copy that reads, "If you only learn one thing from his speech, it's worth every penny." Who the hell writes that crap? True professional educators on the circuit will respond, "Yeah, one thing in sixty minutes sounds pretty thin." Of course, that's mainly in reference to the speakers who shill their topics, such as "Thank God It's Monday," "Harnessing Your Inner You," and "Thriving on Overload." These are all valuable speeches to the correct audiences, but probably not an audience that wants to learn about market leadership and the processes to get there. There's a huge difference between educating and entertaining, and thought leaders aren't much for theatrics, and therefore aren't always very entertaining. In fact, they're probably a little dry, but you'll learn a lot and be able to apply even more. Perhaps, you'll learn something every sixty seconds, not every sixty minutes.

And that's the purpose thought leaders serve: to teach a lot, to help you apply wisdom easily and affordably, and to drive thought leadership's success regardless of your company being a multibillion-dollar enterprise, or a manufacturer that's just becoming enterprising.

Now, let's load up and start our travels down the road to thought leadership with some history lessons tossed in for good measure, along with a handful of side trips about Greek philosophy, the concepts of branding, a few rules to follow, and, of course, some rules to break.

2

THOUGHT LEADERSHIP TAKES ROOT: FUMBLES, STUMBLES, AND LESSONS FOR ALL

B y all accounts, the Green Bay Packers (and thereafter the New York Jets) future Hall of Fame quarterback Aaron Rodgers was born with a rock-solid throwing arm and an annoying chip on his shoulder. I'm no Rodgers fan; after all, I was born and raised in inner-city Chicago and have been a Bears fan since birth, but I recognize and acknowledge greatness, and Aaron Rodgers is a great football player. Some of his other qualities?

Not so much.

But these aren't lessons about tackle football. They're insights about leadership; about what happens off the football field, and on a more important playing field; about greatness in sales and marketing, and more broadly greatness in business; and about the lessons that Rodgers,

Socrates, Plato, Aristotle, and my favorite female Greek scholar, Aspasia, can teach us about thought leadership, the single most important and relevant differentiator in the business playbook.

Or, as Plato not so recently said, obviously unaware of Aaron Rodgers's famous retreat into darkness, "We can easily forgive a child who is afraid of the dark; the real tragedy of life is when men are afraid of the light."

And now, I'd like to shed some light on what's required in business, but frequently misunderstood. What every salesperson needs to know, but doesn't always know how to achieve. And what every marketing expert wishes they had in their bag of tricks, but often lacks the tricks of the trade to employ it. To simply say that thought leadership is an essential part of the disciplines of market leaders is like saying a stick is an essential part of a Popsicle. Well, it is, assuming you're not interested in taste, color, packaging, name, price, quality, and the beat goes on.

Thought leadership caught fire in the sales and marketing world shortly after the turn of the century and it continues to be a flame-thrower if you're looking for results and success. However, it can still remain elusive to many companies, and even more elusive to their leaders. In a way, it reminds me of the sales and marketing concept we know as *solution selling*, far more difficult to implement than to understand. And that's usually because people tend to speak around sales and marketing concepts—not logically through them—making the concepts easier to acknowledge, but their implementation difficult. Part of that is because of our tendency to revert to "sales and marketing speak," a lexicon so fraught with bullshit and exaggeration that we cross the line from a certain truth into feigned authenticity. Again, we claim to understand these concepts because we're all bobbing for the same apples, but mastering the approach is never easy, and sometimes downright embarrassing.

So why is thought leadership important in business today, why is it easy to achieve, and why is it completely authentic without the usual sales and marketing blather? We'll get to that in high time, and that's a promise I will keep, which is one stick in the thought leadership Popsicle, keeping promises, of course.

And telling the truth.

Patrick Justin McAfee was born in Plum, Pennsylvania, in 1987. He was known for his kickoff and punting skills and played eight seasons in the NFL for the Indianapolis Colts. During that time, and afterward, he dabbled in professional wrestling and became known for a damn good head of hair and wearing muscle T-shirts without showing many muscles. Presumably, that's the life of a kicker, equal time in the weight room and the bakery aisle.

Giving credit where credit is due, McAfee then punted and switched careers to become a top-notch sports broadcasting analyst with his own shows on SiriusXM, Westwood One, YouTube, and ESPN. For many years, McAfee has been a favorite of Aaron Rodgers—or perhaps it's the other way around—and Rodgers has become a regular on McAfee's shows. Today, McAfee has become better known for his mouth than his leg.

But a bizarre turn of events occurred on *The Pat McAfee Show* when Rodgers was a guest on November 5, 2021. Rodgers claimed, in multiple instances, that he's a "critical thinker" during a fifteen-minute stream of consciousness that was focused on whether he was telling the truth, or misleading the public about being vaccinated at an earlier presser. At that time, he wouldn't definitively say if he was vaccinated, but most people assumed he was when Rodgers claimed he was "immunized." His vaccination beliefs are completely irrelevant to becoming a thought leader or, in Rodgers's case, a critical thinker, but telling the truth, as I mentioned before, is non-negotiable; it's a pre-existing condition of thought leadership, and anyone who falls short of truth telling cannot be a thought leader, or a critical thinker for that matter.

A writer and editor friend of mine asked me if I really believed that Aaron Rodgers was a critical thinker, and if I would be interested in authoring an article about that.

I told him no, to which he responded, "No to what?"

"No, dude, I'm not interested in writing about it, and no he's not a critical thinker, which is the end of the story."

Of course, my friend wanted to know more about my disinterest, so I told him, "Look, critical thinkers don't call themselves critical thinkers just as thought leaders never call themselves thought leaders."

Period.

And there you have it, two introductory lessons for the price of one. Thought leaders tell the truth and they don't call themselves thought leaders. And that ends our discussion of Aaron Rodgers, Pat McAfee, football, punting, and sports talk broadcasting.

But not about telling the truth.

AND NOW A SMALL AMOUNT OF CONTEXT

Thought leaders date back to the classic Greek scholars and philosophers spanning the years of 450 BC to 325 BC. That was the origin of thought leadership, and it's worth everyone's time to study Socrates, his pupil Plato, and Plato's ace student, Aristotle, to understand the depths and primers of what thought leadership is today. But also, let's not forget Aspasia, one of the most important scholars and thought leaders in Athens, and more than likely the world's first feminist. There will be plenty of enlightening stories about Aspasia, and why I believe, without question, she was our first feminist—and I can't wait to share those stories with you.

If you want to become a thought leader, or put your company in the enviable and profitable echelon of thought leadership, then you'll need to read on and learn how to become a thought leader yourself, how to evaluate my *21st Century Disciplines of Market Leaders* to see if thought leadership has a place for you, how to become a great storyteller just as the Greek scholars were, and ultimately journey down the Via Egnatia, the ancient cobblestone road carved from the hillsides that surround Athens, which paved the way for unimaginable riches and rewards.

Hopefully, you'll reach the pinnacle of all sales disciplines, my proprietary Critical Insight Selling, that puts solution selling back in the cobblestone age where it belongs and teaches sales reps how to sell wisdom before they sell anything else. And along the way, you'll also learn about corporate ethics, a pivotal part of thought leadership; the human characteristics of thought leaders; and my seven rules that every thought leader needs to honor. When they say in the movies, "We ride at dawn," that's nonsense. Our ride starts now.

GIDDY-UP

For purposes of easy digestion and chewability, let's turn our attention to the modern-day origins of thought leadership in general, and the definition of thought leadership in a sales and marketing context, in particular.

Thought leadership's rise to preeminence didn't occur until the turn of this century, perhaps a few years later. In relation to sales and marketing concepts like solution sales; branding; the five Ps; disruption marketing; feature/benefit selling; and inbound, outbound, and rebound marketing—and the endless list of names we assign to concepts that make us feel important as if it were a notch in our belts—thought leadership is actually an infant, but it's growing like a weed. Unfortunately, its growth spurt has been more of an act of self-aggrandizement and bravado than an actual disciplined approach to knowledge creation and the understanding of thoughtfulness.

In all likelihood, most of this chatter began in 1980 with the publishing of Michael Porter's superb book *Competitive Strategy: Techniques for Analyzing Industries and Competitors*, where he reasoned that businesses needed to focus on a single act of brinkmanship and positioning. To that end, Porter determined that a business needed to be either driven and dominant across a wide swath of products and services, or more niche-driven toward various segments like low-cost offerings or consultative services.

In its time, Porter's reasoning was quite innovative. His finite thinking isn't overly relevant today, but much to his credit, he did attempt to categorize what had previously been a mishmash of categorically uncategorized business philosophies. In turn, his rationale did give way to a landmark 1995 book authored by Michael Treacy and Fred Wiersema, titled *The Discipline of Market Leaders*. Treacy and Wiersema's book was brilliant and provided context and clear reasoning to continue with the categorization of what companies needed to aspire to in order to be market leaders. Unfortunately, the book didn't provide much of an actionable step-by-step process of how to get there, wherever there might be.

In their premise, Treacy and Wiersema promoted the disciplines of market leadership as operational excellence, product leadership, and customer intimacy. By today's standards, that might seem pretty ho-hum, but in its day it was a humdinger.

However, there were two aspects about *The Discipline of Market Leaders* that shaped, for better or worse, the business climate of the 1990s. The first, and most obvious, was the introduction of *customer intimacy* into our corporate lexicon, a neologism coined by Wiersema himself, and one of those notch-in-the-belt labels that probably meant a lot to him and his pupils at Massachusetts Institute of Technology. In many respects, customer intimacy has been a hanger-on with an enduring shelf life where other customer service terms have been one-hit wonders and faded like "Video Killed the Radio Star"—which was somewhat true but, most interestingly, a song recorded simultaneously by two English rock bands, the Buggles and Bruce Woolley & The Camera Club.

Wiersema correctly reasoned that next-level customer service needed to be more strategic between two companies where the lines were blurred between vendor and customer; in this case, customer service would be the star and customer intimacy would be the level to which a customer and the supplier were partners, where the supplier understood their customer so intimately that the relationship was predictive, and where the supplier knew their customer better than the customer knew themselves. This was really breakthrough thinking that was creative, innovative, and true.

But in 1995, the year before Wiersema published his own book on customer intimacy, a scandal arose among the publishing elite, and Treacy and Wiersema, along with several others, were at the center of the firestorm. Their involvement was creative and innovative, but the firestorm couldn't have been further from honest and true. And in that regard, some business scholars believed it chipped away at both men's reputations as innovators and educators, and might have temporarily exiled them to a land far, far away.

It was reported in a 1995 article written for *Bloomberg Businessweek* that the creative and innovative part of this publishing firestorm was concocted by Treacy, and although that might have been true, most parties were found to be liable for the dustup. At that point in time, as it remains today, being listed on the *New York Times* best-seller list was more than a feather in your cap. It was a gold mine, a hall pass to selling thousands more books, a way to be noticeably more than a blip on the publicity radar, and a ticket to higher speaking and consulting fees. Back then, the only real requirement to get on the list was to sell 5,000 books in one week, but that was a somewhat arbitrary number controlled by the editors of the list. Treacy and Wiersema reasoned that selling 10,000 of their books in the first week would be sufficient to be absolutely certain of etching their name on the coveted list of best sellers, and would be like winning the British Open golf tournament and having your name etched indelibly on the claret jug literally seconds after your victory, just as it was done for John Daly, the mullet-wearing, hard-drinking, ever-partying, chain-smoking, dice-rolling American golfer only months before.

So, in their quest for fortune, but also misfortune, Treacy and Wiersema, it is said, spent a tidy $250,000 of their own stash and purchased more than 10,000 copies of their book by placing orders at random booksellers mostly in New York City.[1] If true, in an incredulous act of audacity, they must have figured it would be better to be as close to the scene of the crime as possible than to be, say, at bookstores in San Francisco, 3,000 unsuspecting miles away. This way, they would allegedly be certain of more than a shot at the title; they'd be guaranteed champs.

It didn't take long for the *New York Times* to speculate that our champs might be, in fact, chumps who gamed the system for their own reward and celebrity. Not long after, the *New York Times* changed their requirements for authors to be named on the best-seller list, and even to this day, the newspaper continues to adapt and rework those requirements as they struggle to combat digital downloaders, as well as politicians who have political action committees purchase 10,000 books at a time, only to hand them out like lollipops at campaign stops in Iowa and New Hampshire.

In order to backtrack on their publishing nightmare, Treacy and Wiersema claimed they had ordered the books to ultimately provide them to their vast array of clients, probably at discounted prices, and their intentions were not to cross the one-week *New York Times* best-seller list finish line in the allotted seven-day period, but to distribute the books quickly in an effort to curtail any copycat theorists. Nevertheless, the damage was done.

THE PROBLEMS WITH BOOKS ABOUT BUSINESS

Although this supposed workaround by Treacy and Wiersema hardly qualifies as a deep, dark secret, the reality of business book publishing is often understood, but rarely discussed. Take, for example, the 1562 oil painting by Pieter Bruegel, *The Suicide of Saul*, which is part of the permanent collection at the Kunsthistorisches Museum in Vienna: It depicts Saul's death by falling on his own sword when his armor-bearer refuses Saul's request to stab him to death. To that end, why would business writers fall on their own sword and reveal the most inherent problems with business books?

That's a tad bit rhetorical because thought leaders will always be honest, they'll always speak the truth, not muddy the waters with self-inflicted workarounds that game the system, and they'll never be apologetic for discussing what few people feel comfortable discussing. And that speaks to the simplest of all notions that business books are like photographs: They're dated the day we take the snapshot.

And that applies to Michael Porter, Michael Treacy, Fred Wiersema, and even Jim Collins, the immensely talented thinker, writer, and theorist of *Good to Great*, and other terrific books.

It's not the fault of our own thinking and writing. We can't help but be driven by business examples that are here today and perhaps gone tomorrow. After all, those are the dynamics of business—change is inevitable, theories and approaches evolve and dissolve in real time, and leaders find success pushing forward, but also find regret and loss, and even embarrassment, when times change and tables turn.

In *The Discipline of Market Leaders*, the corporations that were analyzed included Airborne Express, Intel, and Universal Card, a company established in 1990 and long ago defunct that was a combination of a credit card and a long-distance calling card. In *Good to Great*, the great companies included Wells Fargo, one of the most fined and penalized companies in the history of the United States;[2] Circuit City, a business that has gone in and out of business; Pitney Bowes, an enterprise that has transformed itself frequently and was mostly acquired by another company named Syncsort along with some private equity firms; Philip Morris, the tobacco company that has been scolded more times than Dennis the Menace; Nucor, a steel-producing corporation that has paid enormous environmental fines;[3] Fannie Mae, the organization that was at the heart of the subprime disaster that led to the horrific recession in 2008; and the list goes on. What on earth is a business writer to do?

I guess the promise, and the disclaimer at the bottom of the page, needs to be that *these companies are great at this moment in time, but I can't promise that they'll be great tomorrow, next year, or the next few years.* Again, business writers can write only in the context of a company being a time-stamped photograph, a snapshot of what it is today, not even tonight.

THE DEFINITION OF A THOUGHT LEADER

So what is a thought leader other than a truth-sayer, a private sector ombudsman hired to separate fact from fiction, perhaps a finger-pointer at those who favor a workaround as opposed to hard work, and a person who understands that the best interests of a company aren't always the self-interests of management? Let's define thought leadership, not in general terms as many already have, but in regard to the disciplines of sales and marketing, where few have even attempted to.

A sales and marketing thought leader is a person who focuses on three distinct areas of influence: **Wisdom and Insights**, **Trust and Honesty**, and **Ethics and Causes**. Each one of these areas of distinction is applicable to an individual or a company, and each has its own nuances and shadings that require forethought, introspection, and ongoing examination. In the end, all of these purposeful activities work confluently to drive a company's revenue and incremental sales.

And each one of these distinct influences forms a canvas that becomes a colorful and enduring representation of thought leadership that has assumed the coveted fourth position in the *21st Century Disciplines of Market Leaders* that I developed over my forty-seven-year career in sales and marketing, which, by the way, does not make me an expert, but it does make me, well, experienced.

This is why the lessons of the past five decades, which brought us from business categorization to market leadership disciplines and from customer intimacy to the need for unbridled truth and honesty, were the precursors to what thought leadership is today. It's why Porter, Treacy, Wiersema, and Collins are so important. They're part of recent history, which tells us to be mindful of the past and resourceful about the future. Which is exactly why the great Latin American writer Eduardo Galeano said, "History never really says goodbye. History says, 'See you later.'" And we'll certainly see more of that in our discussions about Socrates, Plato, Aristotle, and Aspasia.

But we'll also see why thought leadership is the future of sales and marketing. And no one could be more on the money about that, particularly about the future, than one of my favorite rappers, Future, who, in his own brand of mindfulness, said that when everyone is all in one place, magic happens.

That's what thought leaders do with their clients: They make magic, and it brings everyone together all in one place.

3

THE DISCIPLINES
OF MARKET LEADERS

The more we look back, the more you'll understand the fundamentals of thought leadership and how it can drive revenue and profitable transactions in the sales and marketing motion. That's because even as troubled as they might have been, the ancient Greek philosophers understood the power of **Wisdom and Insights**, **Trust and Honesty**, and **Ethics and Causes**. And surprisingly, as twisted as their ethics were, particularly in voicing their opinions about the inferiority of women, there are dozens of examples of remarkably forward-thinking beliefs when you analyze the attributes of deontological, teleological, and *Nicomachean Ethics*.

In my *21st Century Disciplines of Market Leaders*, I've dramatically updated the findings and conclusions of the works of Porter, Treacy, Wiersema, and others, not just bringing their approaches into a more contemporary framework, but also keeping an arm's length from diving too deeply into companies and organizations that, as we have learned, date business books faster than you can say Peter Drucker. Most importantly, you'll discover the step-by-step processes of how to become a thought leader, how to implement thought leadership into your company, how to sustain it, and how it can drive revenue and incremental sales through Critical Insight Selling that promotes your thought leadership wisdom ahead of anything else. This works in tandem with building trust and solid relationships for decades into the future. Almost universally, this has been absent from the most superlative business books.

There are four essential components to the *21st Century Disciplines of Market Leaders*. Every business that aspires to be a market leader must embrace at least one of these disciplines, but unlike the opinions of Porter, Treacy, and Wiersema, who believed that putting all your eggs into one discipline basket was all that was required, this type of thinking has become a relic in today's multi-segmented, more highly competitive business climate where options are plentiful and failures are, too. In fact, it's not unusual, be it planned or coincidental, that some market leaders are actually adept at more than one market-leading discipline. Let's tackle the first three disciplines.

THE PRICE LEADER

The first discipline of market leaders is being a price and value leader. I'm not a fan of this position or anything similar to it mainly because it's one part commodity and one part unsustainable, except in a handful of well-documented circumstances. The price/value relationship has always been troublesome for sales and marketing leaders. And it's been that way for decades. The belief that you are a commodity provider when you sell on price alone has a lot of relevancy behind it, but to also assume that you're a valuable resource when you're a price machete is turning a blind eye to the particulars of the sales cadence.

If anyone doesn't believe that price is an important part of many transactions—but certainly not all—they're disregarding research that is irrefutable. In a study conducted in 2022 by First Insight during the holiday shopping cycle, it was determined that price and deals were the top consumer influencers for purchasing, followed by quality and value. Although price and value are not the same influencers, they are hopelessly intertwined.[1]

When consumers are removed from the equation, and we focus on B2B transactions, the waters are characteristically muddy. That's because far more factors play critical roles in B2B purchases. These factors, and plenty of others, all have some sort of comportment in purchasing decisions including sales cycles, supply chains, product guarantees and efficacy, research, interdisciplinary and cross-departmental feedback and reporting, training programs, road maps for sustainability, volume discounts, quality controls, and the list goes on. Of course price is an integral component, but B2B pricing models and theories are far from cut-and-dried.

Let's be real. Price will almost always be a consideration no matter who the audience is or what the industry manufactures or distributes. If, for instance, you admire a 2023 Rolls-Royce Phantom that lists for $450,000, you might readily pass on tying a bow on it and driving it home, but if you were approached to buy the same car for $70,000, you might actually consider it, for whatever reason, and that still calculates to price being a consideration, as implausible an example as that might be.

Thankfully, the modern world is filled with people who addressed pricing challenges head-on and succeeded beyond their wildest imaginations. However, most salespeople, and the companies they represent, find overcoming cost objections difficult and tough sledding. If they didn't, then pricing would never be an issue and value would no longer be the exit ramp for pricing obstacles. And we wouldn't need sales training that focuses on alleviating pricing challenges let alone learning the ins and outs of the Columbo Close or the Puppy Dog Close.

I'm intrigued, and have been for many years, by Erica Feidner, who grew up in Vermont and became a piano prodigy at the age of nine, if not before. She was raised in a household of musicians that also included twenty-six pianos, and attended the Julliard School (preparatory high school) in New York. She made her orchestral debut at age eleven and later went on to earn a BFA and MBA from top-notch colleges. The milestones since her college days have been, well, far from the black-and-white keyboard she spent hours tickling.

That's because Erica has been named by many organizations as one of the ten greatest salespeople of all time, joining a coveted list of others including David Ogilvy, Dale Carnegie, Zig Ziglar, Mary Kay, and Ron Popeil, the inventor of Chop-O-Matic, Mr. Microphone, Pocket Fisherman, Buttoneer, the Electric Food Dehydrator, Showtime Rotisserie, and many others. In fact, Popeil might be considered the greatest salesman of all time . . . before his passing, he would have enthusiastically confirmed his standing.

But my money's on Erica Feidner.

Shortly after college, Feidner joined the sales team at Steinway & Sons and became their top worldwide salesperson for more than ten straight years. Consider for one moment how difficult it can be to sell a Steinway piano. The sales cycle is probably agonizingly long as prospects need to test the action of the keys, listen to tonal qualities, play new pianos as they move off the assembly lines, look for deals on used pianos, assess the many Steinway models that might or might not fit their needs, and, of course, because price is always a consideration, determine if the piano is worth $240,000, much more, a little less, or should the customer consider a Baldwin, Yamaha, Kawai, or forty-seven other manufacturers? And let's not forget the TAM (total available market size); how big is the market for a Steinway piano? It can't be huge. After selling more than $40 million worth of Steinways,[2] Feidner retired from sales, founded her own company called Piano Matchmaker, and has been featured on CNN and PBS, in *Inc.* magazine and *The New Yorker*.

In any event, the first discipline available to market leaders will always be the ability to be a price leader. And make no bones about it; there are plenty of successful price-cutters. Walmart has owned the category for decades, but other players have been successful, too, including Aldi, Spirit Airlines, Dollar General, and Kia Motors. However, attempting to be the price leader is a tough row to hoe, and there are so many factors that can turn you sideways, if not upside down. Cost of materials, supply chain hiccups, foreign manufacturing threats, uncertain labor demands, to name a few. The price leader discipline is a risky bet fraught with wafer-thin margins and vast uncertainties. My advice to our clients is a cautionary tale, as many companies fail, rather than succeed, when they embrace this discipline. Whether my clients heed my advice or not, price leadership has always been a market leadership discipline available to all.

THE CUSTOMER SERVICE LEADER

The second discipline of market leaders is customer service—that is, you can be a customer intimacy or customer service champion. For some, a business that provides exceptional service is table stakes, or the price of entry, for being a successful company. Providing marginal or poor service just doesn't cut it in nearly any business environment. Make no mistake about it, there's a significant difference between providing really good customer service and providing legendary service. For me, it's a discipline that's more solid than being a price leader if only because management has more control over their destiny. Further, you can tell a more compelling story about service than you can about price. This couldn't be more evident than in the grocery trade's love affair with EDLP (everyday low pricing) in the eighties and nineties, which has all but vanished like D. B. Cooper.

Like Walmart owning the price leader category, for years I might add, Nordstrom has owned the customer service category. In fact, whether it was urban legend or not, the story of a person returning automobile tires to a Nordstrom store and receiving their money back, even though Nordstrom never sold tires, is a public relations bonanza. But was this tale really true, or was it a sales and marketing story that grew to epic proportions with some of the truth and details lost in the translation? Actually, as I discovered, there's quite a bit of truth in the play-by-play. And here's the truth right from the horse's mouth, from Peter Nordstrom, the company's president:

Almost everywhere I go, this story follows us around, and someone says, "Well there's no way that's true. You guys have perpetuated this myth as kind of a metaphor to talk about your service culture." And I say, "No, it's actually true."

The story starts almost forty years ago at a Nordstrom store in Fairbanks, Alaska, where Craig Trounce was a store associate. One day, Craig noticed a customer rolling a pair of tires into the store. When Craig asked how he could help, the customer asked to return the tires, insisting that he bought them at that very location with a guarantee that he could bring them back to the store at any time.

Of course, Nordstrom never sold tires. But in 1975, it purchased three stores from a company that did—Northern Commercial of Alaska. The Northern Commercial Company offered an eclectic mix of goods—everything from towels and linens to automotive supplies. When Nordstrom took over the locations, it narrowed the merchandise mix to apparel and shoes.

Instead of turning the tires away, Craig wanted to do right by the customer, who had driven more than fifty miles with the intention of returning these tires. Knowing little about how tires are priced, Craig called a tire company to get their thoughts on how much the tires were worth. He then gave the customer the estimated amount, took the tires, and sent him on his way.

Lost over the years is the exact dollar amount the customer received in exchange for those tires, but no doubt it's been earned back a thousand times over when you consider the scope and resonance of the story today. In fact, the tire story has become so important to our culture, we even hang tires in some of our stores and break rooms as a reminder of our commitment to our customers.[3]

But lest we forget, there are many, many superior customer service providers that have staked their claim on this market leadership discipline. A few of these include The Ritz-Carlton, Trader Joe's, Disney, Zappos, Costco, and so on. But these are name players, and it's important to remember that not a day goes by when small- and medium-size businesses (SMBs)—from a local manufacturer to the corner doughnut shop—aren't providing millions of customers with terrific one-on-one service that the biggest companies can only wish they were able to provide. Where the largest companies often talk of their commitment to customer service, the smaller companies talk about topflight service being habitual, cultural, ingrained as part of their nature, and an organic sense of who they are. As Aristotle said, "More excellence comes about as a result of habit. We become just by doing just acts, temperate by doing temperate acts, brave by doing brave acts."

He was right. Owning a discipline of market leadership will always be a brave act. Thought leaders need to be brave because they serve up insights and opinions that aren't always popular (but are almost always true), that might go against the grain, that could lead to doubt among people who always think they're right, but seldom are. It's what I call the *consultant's curse*, interacting with a group of people, usually of the middle manager variety, who will always shoot for the old gunslinger, who might be faster on the draw but slower on intellect, and who shield their shortcomings by amping up their chest thumping. The truth can hurt, but it can also resolve, and you'll know with speed and certainty who's hiding from it. I learned this from someone whom I admired for a lifetime.

My father, a formidable consultant in his own right, was fond of defining a consultant as someone who borrows your watch to tell you what time it is; when the gig is over, sometimes they'll even return the watch. It was tongue in cheek, but it was based on some realities. And those realities are that quite often the solution to what ails us is what's in front of us. That's why part of the process of becoming a thought leader, or a company that practices thought leadership, starts with Voice-of-Customer (VOC) research, always and without any exceptions. We'll learn about VOC in a short time, but it can validate what's in front of us while revealing what we can't see in back of us or around the next corner.

In addition to being brave, here's another fact: All thought leaders are consultants, but not all consultants are thought leaders, not by a long shot. And if any consultant tells you they're a thought leader or, good golly, a critical thinker, run away and don't look back. That's bad form and plainly disingenuous. Others can call people thought leaders, but thought leaders never call themselves thought leaders. It's akin to mouthing off and saying, "I'm a genius," or, even worse, "I'm a member of Mensa." That sort of bravado has no place in thought leadership and hopefully no place in your business.

Our second discipline of market leaders, the customer service position, can be strong, until it isn't. But don't fret. People on both sides of the transaction aisle will have bad days, point fingers, pass the buck, and behave poorly. Never let those moments of lousy behavior derail you; they're temporary and many times without merit. None of the disciplines are a footrace; they're a long haul that pays dividends well beyond the finish line. And here's what I mean.

You Don't Need to Be Big to Be Great: A Car Wash Customer Service Story

Again, a prevailing thought is usually centered on the notion that all large companies can buy their way into almost any discipline of market leadership. But let's not forget there are many huge companies that act irresponsibly, that don't necessarily own a particular discipline and might not particularly care.

That would never have been the case for one of my clients, Mister Car Wash, that began, humbly enough, as a small car wash operator in 1969 with a handful of locations in Houston. From there, they grew. And grew some more. And like the saguaros native to Arizona, the company maintains a rich tradition of continued growth from their current headquarters in Tucson. As of this writing, Mister Car Wash operates about 500 locations in twenty-one states and trades on the New York Stock Exchange. I've never worked with Mister Car Wash on the *21st Century Disciplines of Market Leaders*, rather spending my consulting time on VOC, creative processes, market strategies, and growth opportunities. However, known to me, but unknown to them, this company started as a small business focused on the second discipline, customer service, although they're fonder of calling it hospitality. They are not a price leader, or a technology and innovation leader, although they keep current with the advances that are needed in the industry. And they do not produce billions of dollars in revenues or profits like Walmart, Target, Microsoft, Oracle, and the like.

The first car wash in the United States opened, not surprisingly, in Detroit around 1914. The car wash was called Automated Laundry, for who knows what reason, but none of it was automated, and unless you somehow had trouble differentiating your T-shirts from your Model T, it had nothing to do with cleaning your clothing. In fact, three guys pushed the car through a makeshift tunnel and washed it with soap and water, refilling their pails for rinsing. How this was any different from washing your car in a driveway is anyone's guess, aside from that the washing was done by others. And speaking of washing your car in your driveway using soap, a garden hose, and pails of water, this is something you should never ever do unless you don't give two shits about the environment and water sustainability.

The innovation of car wash automation didn't take hold until 1940 in Hollywood, California. Upon closer inspection, it really wasn't that automated; a primitive winch system, attached to the car, moved it through the tunnel, but attendants still washed and rinsed the car as the winch pulled it down the line. Partial automation occurred six years later, as the winch was still in place, but overhead sprinklers served to wet down cars, and rudimentary brushes and blowers helped to automate the process.

Full automation finally found its footing in 1951 in Seattle, Washington, at a place called Elephant Car Wash known as much for innovation as for its iconic pink rotating elephant sign. Located on Fourth and Lander, the "super wash" integrated sprays, nozzles, brushes, and large-scale blowers for drying. And then the floodgates opened. The industry gained some traction, if not its mojo, and became a business opportunity for hundreds of investors and owners across America. As the industry grew, so did the mythology, and with it a devastating stigma. Aided by no shortage of car wash movies, TV shows, rollicking scenes, and oddball references, car washes hit the big time that unfortunately relegated them to the small time. Seedy characters, jokers, chauvinists, and gadflies laid the groundwork for the stigma that the industry fought for decades.

At the top of the list was the 1976 movie *Car Wash* that unwittingly damaged the industry with portrayals of employees who were loose cannons, ne'er-do-wells, and nitwits, but the movie was hilarious and boasted an exceptional cast. It was fronted by two of my favorites, Richard Pryor and George Carlin, and supported by wonderful character actors including Otis Day (yes, that Otis Day of Otis Day and the Knights in *Animal House*), "Professor" Irwin Corey, Antonio Fargas (yes, that Antonio Fargas who played Huggy Bear in *Starsky & Hutch*), and Ivan Dixon (yes, that Ivan Dixon of *Hogan's Heroes*). The movie was a romp of dreams, mostly shattered, hopes, disappointments, and eccentric personalities who shed light on the daily life at a car wash.

Most surprisingly, however, was that *Car Wash* was written by Joel Schumacher, who went on to forge an illustrious Hollywood career as a director, producer, and writer with credits including *The Lost Boys* (quite good), *The Client* (even better), *St. Elmo's Fire* (the Brat Pack), and *Batman & Robin* (a clunker). The point is, we all need to start somewhere, but with hard work and a thoughtful approach to life, there's no finish line we can't cross.

And boy oh boy did Mister Car Wash cross the finish line of success. For them, it wasn't through being a price-chopper (like many other car washes), or trying to out-innovate the competition (you might win the day, not the year), but by being a customer service leader, not just a front-runner, but a forerunner.

After I completed my internal VOC with the company's general managers as the respondents, this is what I wrote to Mister Car Wash's leadership as the prologue to my initial findings:

I have completed more than 125 Voice-of-Customer projects for companies in disparate industries over the last 45 years. Although it *wasn't titled VOC before the turn of the century, one-on-one inter-views were always an inherently valuable part of any marketing strategy, including the disciplines and principles of branding. These companies and organizations have numbered name brands and organizations including McDonald's, Foot Locker, Eastbay, Lady Foot Locker, Honeywell, CUNA Mutual, California Avocados, Rakuten, Finish Line Sports, the National Mango Board, American Family Insurance, Fresh Markets, Tenneco, Power School, Lion Apparel, FIS Global, University of Wisconsin, to name a few. During this time, I have interviewed over 4,000 people, been sub-ject to complaints about my clients, praise in many cases, and only once was I hung-up on by a customer who denounced the CEO of a $40B company. And never, in a career spanning 45 years, have I written a Prologue to a VOC initiative.*

Until now.

Many of my clients are admirable companies, some are less than that, while others, even after decades of service, are still finding their footing, and their voice. I don't think Mister Car Wash fits comfortably into any of those categories. On the contrary. Mister, from my point of view, is in its own class, standing shoulder-to-shoulder with other companies that have elevated admiration to higher levels. Patagonia, Adobe, Salesforce, and Zappos are entries into a "raise-the-bar" genus that's almost unimaginable; except it's not, it's authentic, absolute, and straight from the horse's mouth.

A negative word wasn't spoken, complaints were benign, attempts at identifying weaknesses were met with long pauses, and suggested changes to the company were prefaced with "can we circle back to that question?" Who describes work as "home?" Who, in the context of change, wants the perception of their job to be aligned with the highest respected job titles around? And who will go to the mat for a team member, just as we do the same for a family-member? A Mister Car Wash General Manager, that's who.

So, what's Mister Car Wash's customer service and hospitality secret? In an industry that's riddled with unprofessional employees, dressed more for a day at the beach than a day at work, where a wave and a smile is like pulling teeth, and the biggest source of pride is closing time, Mister Car Wash has breached the unheard-of. They single-handedly changed the industry's stigma from bad boy to goodness gracious, from uninformed to uniformed, and from unpleasant to polite. It didn't happen overnight; in fact, it was a slog. But they stuck to their spray guns and turned a job of last resort into a job of first choice. They pay benefits, managers haul down six figures complete with stock options, there are opportunities for advancement around every car wash tunnel, and they treat people like humans, not like shit. That's easy to say, but far more difficult to achieve. They also have an accomplished CEO; his name is John Lai, a Tucson guy who turned the bad boy car wash image into a hospitality juggernaut. Lai's greatest strength is most CEOs' greatest weakness: He's passionate about compassion, or perhaps it's the other way around, but in the end, what was probably a roll of the dice turned into a jackpot.

At every Mister Car Wash location, they wave hello and smile. At every Mister Car Wash location, they wave goodbye and hope to see you soon. They dress in uniforms that are straight and professional, maybe a little uptight, but you need to go to extremes when you need to change an extreme. They are polite like a Girl Scout and caring like a social worker, and in some regards, particularly with older patrons, they *are* like social workers, and that's because Mister Car Wash customers frequently go there to visit with the crew.

Remember the Nordstrom tire story? I know Mister Car Wash stories that are shinier than their revolutionary tire shine application.

There's the one about the crew member who taught a customer how to use their cell phone; the countless anecdotes of staff helping mothers babysit their children while the moms used the free vacuums to clean the french fries, cornflakes, and Gummy Bears from between the seats; and, oh, the time when a car was driven through a half-acre, mud-soaked parking lot and the only thing filthier than the car was the driver's shoes. He rolled down his window, politely asking the even more polite kiosk attendant if they could wash his shoes at the same time they washed the car mats. When my slip-ons went flying from the force of the power washer, and staff and customers took cover, the only noise louder than the blowers was the laughter from the patrons.

I can only imagine what happened when the crew went home and told their families about the guy who had his shoes washed. Little did they know that the original car wash, Automated Laundry, wasn't wrongly named after all.

You don't need to be a huge corporation to be a market discipline leader, and particularly a customer service leader. Of course, you do need to be committed, and it helps to break through the traditional table stakes of customer service. Mister Car Wash documents this culture and these disciplines to the T, which also means no T-shirts. There's an entire manual on how to dress, what to wear, and how to smile and wave, and comprehensive training guides on how to succeed, become a great leader, and why hospitality is so critical to success.

THE TECHNOLOGY AND INNOVATION LEADER

Which brings us to our third discipline. And that is being a technology and innovation leader. This is one of my favorite disciplines because it's a position that you have definitive control over. Not 100 percent control by any measure, but more control than, say, price leadership. If you have a product that's truly innovative, which is also the same as a technology breakthrough, you'll probably look with fondness toward this discipline. But be aware: It can be fleeting if other competitors either mimic or improve on your innovation and technology. You're on the hamster wheel for sure, but if your company is committed to R&D, this is a powerful position to capitalize on.

For decades, the blue-chip software and technology companies have grabbed this discipline and had a stranglehold on it. IBM, Oracle, SAS, Intuit, Microsoft, Google, and plenty of others are at the forefront of this leadership. But confusion still exists among marketers who believe you need to be a software or technology platform provider to own this discipline. That's not true.

The greatest technology company in the world isn't Microsoft; it's an online retailer. Amazon isn't only the leader in e-commerce, warehousing operations, supply chain logistics, and predictive analytics, but they're also a price leader, at least in their innovation of the use of Amazon Prime, a service that generates more than $40 billion in annual subscription sales.[4] And let's not forget Amazon's single-day sales of over $12 billion during their annual Prime Day. Those one-day sales would place them around number 300 on the top 500 US companies in revenue alongside DuPont, Textron, and Norfolk Southern, with the minor exception, of course, that those three companies generate sales over the course of 365 days, not one day.

And this has nothing to do with Amazon Web Services (AWS). AWS stands alone in the category of technology companies by offering cloud computing platforms for storage and archives, content delivery, and computer and server support, among many other services that dominate the market with $80 billion in revenue in 2022 and enormous profits of $23 billion.[5]

And there's little reason to exclude Walmart from the list, too. They are a technology behemoth from a supply chain innovation perspective, and they're at the top of the endcap when it comes to any big-box retailer in e-commerce sales. In fact, in 2022, it was estimated that Walmart's online sales would top $70 billion. For the worthless sake of comparison, America's second-largest big-box retailer, and no slouch themselves, Costco, had shown a steady decline in online sales throughout 2022.[6] As fine a company as Costco is, their online efforts are falling so flat that they no longer report online sales in their monthly earning calls. And if we look further down the list of similar big-box retailers to Walmart, let's say Target, their online sales have topped out at approximately $20 billion,[7] a far cry from Walmart's more than $70 billion.

Obviously, these are all huge corporations with enormous resources to be almost any type of company they want to be. But they've all succeeded where other large businesses have failed because they were steadfast in their commitments to choosing more than one discipline of market leadership and riding it beyond the finish line, in glorious fashion, I might add. So, it's important to remember that being a technology and innovation leader is not limited to tech and software companies; there are plenty of other product and service offerings that are innovative and groundbreaking.

And let's get real: There are plenty of other companies where revenues weren't the deciding factors about market leadership. Here's a second case where my horse also won the derby.

You Don't Need to Be Big to Be Great: A Technology and Innovation Story

In the small town of Stevens Point, Wisconsin, population 25,000, nestled between the even smaller twin cities of Iola-Scandinavia and Plover-Whiting, sits a community best known as the corporate headquarters of Sentry Insurance (a mutual with assets nearing $30 billion that I did some work for many years ago); the University of Wisconsin–Stevens Point, a college with the best natural resources department in the country; and the birthplace of Suzy Favor Hamilton, one of the most decorated US female track athletes of all time, who appeared in three Olympic Games, and a woman I knew and wrote about because her life was a confusing blend of triumph and tragedy.

Not too far from Sentry Insurance and the university, and what would have been a short jog for Favor Hamilton, stands a small company with the biggest ambitions any publicly traded company could ever hope to equal. Marten Machining was founded in 1984 by a fellow, not surprisingly named Alan Marten, who fits splendidly into the classic story of a man who founded a successful company in a garage that housed his car, assorted odds and ends, and probably some lawn and garden equipment. Except he never cared much for the garage part of the story, preferring to focus on the present.

Marten is a company that grabbed the technology and innovation bull by the horns, and like the cowboy who rode that notorious bucking bull, Bodacious, they have steadfastly refused to let go of the innovation leadership discipline. No matter who tried to pilfer it. To say the Martens are the David to the dreaded Goliath is a tiny footnote on a 141st page of annotations. They are, more fittingly, the glue that makes many of the devices in the medical, aerospace, manufacturing, semiconductor, and energy industries work together beautifully so our very existence is remarkably so much better. In the vernacular, they manufacture *stuff*, sometimes microscopic *stuff*, that lots of other bigger *stuff* relies on to function properly. They are a small company that owns the innovation discipline in spite of competitors that are a dozen times larger. They are, and you'll hear more about this later when we explore Greek ethics, a company that promotes a life of quality.

They are so passionate about technology and innovation that most of the time I don't know what the hell they're even talking about. Perhaps you might, but all this talk about nitinol, carbide, Inconel, titanium, tungsten, Elgiloy, and molybdenum will make your head spin, and that's just watercooler conversations about what materials these scientists will be working with today. The truly heady stuff doesn't happen until the metrology lab opens up for the day. It's a laboratory so advanced it requires certification from the National Institute of Standards and Technology, which states as their mission that they "promote US innovation and industrial competitiveness by advancing measurement science, standards, and technology in ways that enhance economic security and improve our quality of life."[8]

So please allow me to follow the logic chain for one brief moment. Okay, we have a government agency that certifies innovation and technology standards that ultimately improve our quality of life while concurrently certifying the laboratories where all this occurs. One of which just happens to be in Stevens Point, Wisconsin, which also happens to be the home of the Marten family, who started the business in a garage (sorry, Alan), not a metrology lab, who are now certified by the government's certification arm to be innovation leaders competing with global companies far larger than they are, all in a town known for the Green Circle cycling and jogging trail, as well as a featured stop on the Ice Age National Scenic Trail that runs a total of 1,200 miles mostly through Wisconsin.

Makes perfect sense to me.

So what the hell is metrology anyway, and why is Marten Machining so incredibly good? Or put another way, in the context of small companies being market discipline leaders, why is Marten Machining an innovation leader when other companies many times their size are not? Well, first off, remember the big guys are big, but they're not always that smart. The Martens are smart and their values are timeless:[9]

The foundation of our company is built on our core values that are incorporated in everything we do.

- *Commitment to Quality*

- *Continuous Improvement*

- *Sustainable Growth*

- *Community*

- *Opportunity*

- *Authenticity*

- *Respect*

- *Communication*

Over the course of the last four decades, every expansion, each purchase of new high tech equipment, and every skilled employee was added to satisfy the growing and complex demand of our customers' needs.

What makes these values different from the values of other companies? The Martens mean it; these aren't just words on a mission statement plaque in the lobby. They're words spoken to their college recruits at the local job fair and to their engineers training in Germany. When the parts you manufacture fly in space, help transmit images from Mars, and save a human life on a surgical table, you're in a business that's pretty damn serious, so no small details can be dismissed, not even a single word that could be disingenuous or superfluous. And that's the beginning of the meaning of metrology; it's pretty damn serious.

Metrology is actually the scientific study of measurement, which drives precision, perfection, and performance in advanced manufacturing. But that serves only as a definition, hardly the actual practice of the innovation. In order to perform metrology, you need to build a lab, and here's the part that's somewhat amusing in a non-amusing way. Imagine building a laboratory that has a sole purpose of measuring to the most exacting standards in the universe. Who the hell is going to put their ass on the line to do that? If you think about it, what if the floor is sloped by a fraction of a millimeter, or a wall isn't level by a whisker, or what if the entire building settles after a few months? The fact is, you can't settle for settling. It brings new meaning to the carpenter's ode: Measure twice and cut once.

Well, apparently, there are a few craftspeople in the world who actually do this. As it's explained on the company's website (https://martenmach.com/metrology), the physical measuring of parts is done by way of this process:

> *The Zeiss Prismo 9/12/7 and Zeiss Prismo Ultra 9/13/7, both equipped with fixed and articulating probe sensors and coupled with an Erowa Compact 80, reduce measurement uncertainty and provide proof of compliance in an unattended environment. The Zeiss Prismo Ultra coordinate measuring machine (CMM) is one of the most accurate CMMs produced and is certified according to ISO 10360-2 to have a maximum volumetric measurement error of 0.5+L/500 μm.*

Precisely. This is exactly what I was thinking. And you should also be thinking that it's very possible, even likely, that you can be a technology and innovation leader even if you're a small company.

So let's take a step back for one moment. You can be a price leader, a customer service leader, and now a technology and innovation leader. At this moment, you'll need to begin practicing the first phases of introspection and examination. Are you, or your company, any of these? Can you in good conscience objectively answer *yes* to any or some of these three disciplines? If not, I strongly suggest you move through the process of *market discipline determination*. You'll need to determine if you can support any of these claims. You can try this yourself, or more appropriately in a group exercise or workshop. In short order, we'll learn how to do this.

SMALL BUSINESS IS A LARGE BUSINESS

There are more than 33 million small businesses in the country.[10] These companies represent about 99 percent of all businesses in America. The Small Business Administration defines a small enterprise, and they should know, as any company with less than 500 employees, which doesn't sound so small to me, but that's not the point. What's most important is that business books, college textbooks, and business courses in college and grad schools breeze past these 33 million companies and focus on the 1 percent. The problem with theories, anecdotes, case studies, and the admiration we have for big business is that they marginalize the fact that SMBs deserve the same amount of attention and access to the same theories, anecdotes, and principles for success as the large companies. Because these theories and strategies don't always fit SMBs, they're frequently not applicable to a business like Marten Machining because they're not scalable, or the approaches require financial investments and resources that aren't necessarily available.

What good are these business strategies if they don't neatly apply to 99 percent of the businesses in the country? In actuality, they're not much good at all. That's the backbone of the *21st Century Disciplines of Market Leaders*. Your ability as a company to lead has little to do with size, reach, or number of employees, and everything to do with finding your discipline, holding on to it, and sustaining it—and if the next stage of your succession is selling your company, your market leadership disciplines transfer with the sale. It's an annuity that protects you, helps build your brand, strengthens your messaging—mostly what branding is anyway—and provides relevant differentiation from your competitors, which you'll need more than ever.

Try to focus on being a price/value leader, a customer service leader, or a technology and innovation leader. But don't constrict your thinking. Technology and innovation do not need to be software applications; they can be systems, delivery methods, e-commerce solutions, an app, one of many generative or chat-specific AI solutions, and the list goes on. The same rings true for customer service. Think beyond the traditional call centers, the help desks, to providing assistance that's top-notch. If you serve up a type of service that few others in your area provide, like services to seniors, a type of guarantee or warranty, volume rebate programs, or loyalty and rewards platforms, these are all examples of types of customer service approaches that can be unique and even revolutionary to an industry.

In Plato's words, "As the builders say, the larger stones do not lie well without the lesser." That's because small businesses need larger ones, and larger businesses need smaller ones. That's how all the pieces fit together regardless of the business ecosystem you're part of. Why then do theories, dictums, philosophies, and strategies need to be different according to a company's revenue, number of employees, square footage, and the like? They do not. And should not. The *21st Century Disciplines of Market Leaders* will always apply to your business no matter if you're Mister Car Wash or Marten Machining, and regardless of your company being larger than these two or smaller.

The actions and the steps to get you to your chosen discipline are all embraceable and straightforward to implement, regardless of industry type or the size of your company. Now's the time to be the leader you want to be. And I know the odds will be in your favor.

ASPASIA BUCKED THE ODDS

You can be that leader even when the odds are against you as they were with Aspasia. Aspasia was brilliant with a tremendous intellect. We're not certain as to her date of birth, or death for that matter, but she was practicing thought leadership in Greece around 470 BC. In fact, Socrates, arguably the smartest man in Athens at the time, if not the entire world, chilled at Aspasia's house and found her to be chock-full of wisdom with a razor-sharp wit.

From my research, and arguably not much is known about Aspasia, she reminds me of Dorothy Parker, the New York–bred poet, writer (as if poetry isn't writing), satirist, and one of only two founding female members of the Algonquin Round Table. The round table, which featured its own litany of literary thought leaders, also included the likes of George S. Kaufman, Robert Benchley, Harpo Marx, Herman J. Mankiewicz, and Heywood Hale Broun, one of my favorite sports columnists who famously said, "Jack Nicklaus will never be happy until he shoots an 18 for an entire round."

Aspasia's thoughts, as well as her thought leadership, can be found in some of the teachings of not only Socrates, but also Plato. Plutarch, probably Greece's most famous historian, and also no slouch when it came to mathematics, philosophy, and thought leadership, said of Aspasia, "She managed as she pleased the foremost men of the state, and afforded the philosophers occasion to discuss her in exalted terms and at great lengths." Plutarch, it was purported, had a crystal clear mind that many attributed to his vegetarian diet at a time when livestock was the centerpiece of virtually every meal.

Aspasia was probably the world's first feminist at a time when feminism was all but forbidden. In part, that's why little is known, or even discussed, about the great women philosophers of the day, who also included Arete of Cyrene, Themistoclea, Hipparchia, Leontion, and

Hypatia. Unfortunately for us, we can only imagine the greatness of these women philosophers, in part because they were typically muzzled by many of their male counterparts, including one of the greatest philosophers of the ancient world, Aristotle, who said, "As regards the sexes, the male is by nature superior and the female inferior, the male ruler and the female subject." But the Greek women philosophers, like Aspasia, laid it on the line and defied traditions, which, in turn, had an everlasting impact on Western civilization and the origins of thought leadership.

Not surprisingly, thought leaders are individuals of great character, and oftentimes they find their path by finding a light—not retreating into darkness—that guides them to objectivity, honesty, and keen insights. Aspasia found her lighted pathway through her comedic quick wit, which no one has denied, and her lofty intellect that was admired by Socrates, Plato, and the statesman Pericles, with whom she had a romantic relationship. It is that type of admiration that remains a characteristic of thought leaders today. Interestingly enough, the terrific feminist artist, art historian, thought leader, and trailblazing art educator, Judy Chicago, who was born in my hometown and took the city's name as her own, portrayed Aspasia in her most famous work, *The Dinner Party*, which depicted some of the artist's favorite feminists, including some well-known writers, artists, and instigators like Georgia O'Keeffe, Emily Dickinson, Virginia Woolf, and Anne Hutchinson.

What discipline will fit you best? It's not difficult to determine what that will be. But more times than not, it won't be the disciplines of price, customer service, or technology and innovation leadership. Like Aspasia, those will be disciplines where you'll need to buck the odds, but the fourth discipline of market leaders is the obvious favorite because it welcomes everyone, at any time, and never suffers even in economic downturns, or hostile environments. And we'll learn more about the odds-on favorite in the fifth chapter.

4

DETERMINING WHAT DISCIPLINE FITS YOU BEST

I n my workshops that usually include no less than eight people, but no more than fifteen, I set up one easel for each of the three disciplines of market leaders—again, one easel for being a price leader, one for customer service leadership, and the third for technology and innovation leadership. Prior to my workshops, I provide a deck that explains the *21st Century Disciplines of Market Leaders*, why it's of critical importance, how it influences prospecting and lead generation, its impact on increasing sales revenue, why VOC research is an important starting point, and the inner workings and alignment of the disciplines with Critical Insight Selling. I also include sections about our Greek philosophers, the importance of storytelling, and why thought leadership is a critical differentiator between the mediocre and the exceptional. I believe, after decades of conducting these workshops, that nearly every participant has thought long and hard about the deck beforehand.

We circle the room three times. I ask each participant to prove why they're a price leader. Then I ask each member of the group to prove they're a customer service leader, and so forth and so on. Within a short period of time, it becomes obvious to me if the proof points are supporting the claims, are lackluster, or even falling flat. Each proof point is written on the flip chart no matter how ridiculous or incredulous it might sound. It's important to do this because the end-of-day recap can be pretty lively as we read through some of the initial findings, almost as if they were a blooper reel.

When writing a messaging composite, which every company needs to develop regardless of size, we typically structure our composites in a taxonomy or hierarchy that's organized by level 1, level 2, and level 3 narrative pitch flows. Each pitch flow is an overwhelming and compelling story that ultimately works in alignment with your brand and supports, and proves, your market leadership discipline. Under each pitch flow are proof points, some of which can be factual and statistical, and others of which can be emotional, but all the proof points need to provide the fuel that supports your narrative pitch flows. When we circle the room in determining a company's strongest disciplines, I ask for the proof points, not necessarily the narrative pitch flows, as those will be written at a later date when we determine where the company's strengths really are, assuming they have a strength.

For instance, a level 1 narrative pitch flow for a former client, WEA Trust, a health insurance provider to municipal employees that's been gobbled up by other insurers, was stated this way:

With keen eyes on budgets, municipalities need to be resourceful, and that requires a health insurance company that is solely focused on local cities, towns, and village employees, which makes WEA the knowledge and thought leader, as well as the leading provider of customized information and insights about your municipality that will help you make informed decisions about your next health plan.

The proof points that supported this proposition included:

- Benchmarking or insight benchmarking findings
- Annual decision-maker perception and attitude research reports
- Municipality VOC diagnostics
- Case statements
- Interactive white papers
- Websites customized for each municipality with valuable healthcare-related content

These were the proof point differentiators that distanced WEA Trust from other insurance providers who were offering healthcare plans to a wide variety of industries without specializing in one particular segment. Their second narrative pitch flow was this:

What makes WEA Trust both a service innovator and a technology leader, far in front of everyone else in this business, is our commitment to providing solutions that are based on your exact and personalized wants and needs—that's why we're the only company that has implemented a consumer-as-innovator approach to product and customer service development; you have a strong voice in product design and customized service protocols and processes.

And the proof points were as follows:

- Municipality VOC diagnostics
- Annual consumer-as-innovator case statement/report
- Case statements
- Interactive e-books with links to customized content including videos, infographics, and white papers
- Feedback loops and surveys for customer service and product designs and road maps

And the third narrative pitch flow was this:

What works for one municipality won't always work for another. Truth be told, developing customized health insurance programs for each local government is too much work for most insurance companies. But not too much for WEA Trust. It's our view that we need to go to work for the people who make local governments work for us.

And the proof points were as follows:

- Video case statements
- *Voices Magazine*
- New local government status alert
- Localized blogs

And the fourth narrative pitch flow was this:

WEA Trust is the only health insurance company that provides insight benchmarking to municipalities that serve as a true source of knowledge for the municipality's health plan administrators. You'll know the most authoritative trends, from real decision-makers like yourself. This is information that goes beyond statistics and reaches the heart of the matter—what people are really thinking—which is why many administrators refer to WEA Trust as the industry thought leader.

And the proof points were as follows:

- Biannual reporting
- Insight benchmarking alerts
- Case statements
- Interactive case statements
- Online resource center with log-in

The fifth narrative pitch flow went like this:

Many insurance companies are helping millions of people with sensible products and diligent customer service; but at WEA Trust, that's our starting point—we bring new products and innovations to you every year, more information to make better decisions, and unmatched input from you in developing insurance plans that are yours, not someone else's.

And the proof points were as follows:

- Diagnostic survey of software filtering
- Case statements
- Interactive video demo

In all, there were seven different pitch flows and sets of proof points. You won't need that many, and I'm not quite certain why we drafted seven to begin with, but you can see what pitch flows look and read like.

So, after the flip charts are full, or possibly somewhat empty, you'll know if you're a price leader, a customer service leader, an innovation and technology leader, or none of these. This isn't a game of horseshoes where you score two points for a "leaner," or one point for a shoe within six inches of the stake. The glass needs to be overflowing, not merely full. If you have four or five solid proof points of both varieties, statistical and emotional, then you can begin working on your narrative pitch flows. Obviously the more proof points the better.

Examples of factual or statistical proof points could be a metrology lab (just like Marten Machining that proves they're a technology leader), first to market software releases, number of app downloads, number of customers, locations and distribution centers, worldwide offices, production output, manufacturing space square footage, R&D investment, quantitative research findings, market share, website analytics, ISO certifications, loyalty club members, customer service perception and attitude research surveys, and so on.

These are different from emotional proof points that are more human-centric. Emotional proof points almost always include testimonials and customer quotations, case studies, customer videos and spotlights, perception and attitude research findings, and VOC research results. In both cases, statistical and emotional proof points are used to support your level 1, level 2, and level 3 narrative pitch flows, which, in turn, are used to help determine your company's market leadership positions by way of *market discipline determination*. Here, you need to assess as objectively as possible what you have written on the flip charts. You'll know rather quickly if there's overwhelming support of a leadership position for price, customer service, or technology and innovation. But let your participants make that determination. Far more than half the time, you won't see enough support to be a market leader in any of these three disciplines. That's just the way it is, and that's fine. You're in the vast majority of US companies that can't make a discipline leadership claim in good faith.

And that's okay. Not every company can be a market leader, and if all businesses were, then there'd be no leaders; we'd all be dealing from the same deck, and all fifty-two cards would be identical. It is interesting, in today's context, to think about what Aristotle said: "In making a speech, one must study three points: first, the means of producing **persuasion**; second, the **language**; third, the proper **arrangement** of the various parts of the speech."

Thinking in terms of a speech as Aristotle suggested, what if we composed an oral presentation to determine your chosen discipline? If that's the case, the **persuasion** would be your discipline, the **language** your pitch flows and proof points, and the **arrangement** a combination of your brand, the messaging taxonomy, and its delivery. If your proof points are persuasive, if the language is compelling, and if you have them arranged in an order that provides unwavering support for your discipline of choice, then you might be on to something. Leave it to Aristotle; he's still relevant in sales and marketing, but so are Plato, Socrates, and Aspasia. Again, history never really says goodbye.

WHAT'S REALLY, REALLY OLD IS NEW AGAIN

In spite of his enormous intellect, or perhaps because of it, Socrates was one messed-up dude. We all know how his story ends, and for the most part, whether it was factual or fictional Greek political chest thumping, Socrates stuck to his convictions. His death occurred relatively quickly, but his life was a lesson that all thought leaders need to be intimately familiar with, not only because he was forthright, immensely respected, and pursued by many for his wisdom and critical thinking, but also because his insights were penetrating, his disposition stoic, and his beliefs were principled beyond praise, even by his enemies.

Those are a few of the essential existential characteristics of being a thought leader. They are the characteristics you'll need to embrace, and then integrate into a corporate culture. Being honest, respected by your antagonists, insightful, even-keeled to the point of being stoic, and committed are the fundamentals that will define you. And what could possibly be wrong with any of those?

Not a thing.

What we know about Socrates isn't from Socrates. His philosophies, teachings, and insights were analyzed and written about by Plato. What we do know is that by all accounts the dude was not much to look at, large, and overweight. He reminds me of a professional fake wrestler with a face like André the Giant and the body to go with it. We also know he was married to Xanthippe, who bore him three sons. His children, it is said, did not inherit Socrates's penchant for an unkempt manner that included a bath only when citizens retreated in his presence in search of cleaner air, not changing his clothing, and refusing to wear shoes. At least Socrates understood the importance of having a good wife when he said, "By all means marry. If you get a good wife, you'll be happy. If you get a bad one, you'll become a philosopher." It was during his first marriage to Xanthippe that he became a philosopher.

In 399 BC, thirty days after Socrates was found guilty by a jury of his peers, most likely on trumped-up charges, but, according to Plato, charges nevertheless for not obeying the Greek gods and influencing Grecian youth regarding his beliefs, Socrates was sentenced to death. After the reading of the verdict, Socrates famously exclaimed, "And if again, I say that to talk every day about virtue and the other things about which you hear me talking and examining myself and others is the greatest good to man, and that *the unexamined life* is not worth living, you will believe me still less." The words *the unexamined life is not worth living* are imperative for future thought leaders to understand. Their meaning is that a human life lacks a certain amount of purpose if we don't examine ourselves, or attempt some sort of introspection. For Socrates, his belief was that we need to use our faculties of reason to elevate our existence above that of animals, and perhaps the Greek gods, who were mythological creatures, for us to be wholly human.

Today, *the examined life* is a famous concept that asks us to become deeply conscious of our existence and our place in the world so we can be more meaningful and more purpose driven. To a large extent, this was also what Plato and Aristotle believed, although Aristotle's *Nicomachean Ethics* took it a step further, which will be discussed later. This is part of the battle cry of today's thought leaders, or, if you're Aaron Rodgers, today's critical thinkers, which, as a reminder, he's not part of.

Thought leaders adhere to an examined life because they understand that in order to grow and be useful to a company, they need intro-spection and examination to become knowledgeable about their own experiences, the sensibilities and proficiencies of their business, their career, and the insights into what makes people tick. This is precisely why we need to tackle which disciplines of market leadership you can own, if there are any. If the disciplines of price, customer service, and technology and innovation leadership don't fit hand in glove with your business, start considering the thought leadership discipline that every one of us can snag because we all possess the characteristics of reason-ing; if we did not, we would all be the beasts and animals that Socrates believed we were not.

After Socrates had gulped down the executioner's hemlock-laced cocktail, he fell to his knees and then to his death. Plato recalled that Socrates had been accepting of his fate and spent the day of his death with friends. His demeanor was stoic and resolved in a way that reminds me of Sir Thomas More's conflict with Henry VIII in one of the most brilliant plays ever written, *A Man for All Seasons*, by Robert Bolt. After refusing to take an oath of approval about the king's second marriage, More was convicted to death at the Tower of London, but before he gently laid his head on the stone for the beheading, More said, "I die His Majesty's good servant, but God's first."

The point is, all thought leaders are principled and stick to their beliefs. Although, by today's standards, a hemlock potion or a behead-ing are pretty extreme measures if you disagree with a consultant who's a bona fide thought leader.

Our story about Socrates doesn't end here; in fact, it's best to go back about thirty years before the cocktail of death ended his life. Interestingly, Socrates was known as the smartest man in Athens, not so much for what he knew, but more for what he did not know. Even as a young man, he would stroll the streets of Athens speaking with elders, asking them questions, debating their logic and beliefs, and even examining their life philosophies. You are correct if you're thinking that parts of the concept of the unexamined life found their foundation in Socrates's early years in his walks around town. Socrates questioned where others kowtowed to the Greek gods du jour. Where others preferred to lead a life of moral shortcuts, Socrates chose to lead his life in a vise grip of high morality, and where others evangelized, our very first thought leader listened. And when he was done listening, he listened some more.

In regard to Socrates being the smartest man in the world, he famously said, "True knowledge exists in knowing you know nothing." And that is part of the thought leader's credo: *The more you know, the more you need to know.* So, in addition to listening from here on out, I ask my clients to be curious, ask questions, find out why, and try to rationalize and make sense of the behavior of others—which, in some cases, will be impossible, but that's what will formulate your insights and lead to a deeper understanding of purchasing behaviors. Without understanding those behaviors, you'll never fully know how to sell and how to market.

Socrates understood that knowledge, and very much education, were important disciplines in much the same way as our *21st Century Disciplines of Market Leaders*. He referred to the ability to achieve knowledge through *disciplined conversations*, which I refer to as *disciplined listening* and which we know today as the preliminary lead-up to VOC. The disciplined conversations that Socrates referred to are actually the framework for not just asking **why**, but also asking **what if** as Socrates asked us to do.

That's the framework today's philosophers refer to as *Socratic Questioning*. If you choose to make your proof points nearly 100 percent bulletproof, you can use these questions to fortify your claims.

I don't always practice Socratic Questioning (particularly if there's a challenging deadline), but in the few instances I do, it's almost always because the proof points seem to lack the validity that supports the chosen discipline. In those cases, I typically choose four categories of questioning: high-level, follow-up, alternative, and consequential questions.

High-Level Questions

These are questions that we ask top leadership, middle managers, marketing personnel, and even sales reps that get them thinking more about proof points and how to substantiate them. They include the following:

- Explain the real meaning of what you just stated.
- Is this new thinking or established insights?
- Are there more dynamic ways of stating this (a particular narrative pitch flow)?
- **And what if all of this happens, some of it, or none of it?**

Follow-Up Questions

In research, particularly VOC, follow-up and probing questions are standard fare in the interviewing process. With follow-up questions, rather than putting the respondents on the defensive, I like to put them at ease. Remember, this is not an inquisition; it's a process of discovery, or, as Socrates would say, an examination. Here are some examples of follow-up questions:

- If this is the case, are there other assumptions that can be made?
- What would the contrarian say; how would they respond?

- Now that your reasoning is solidified, please poke some holes in it.
- **And what if your conclusions are wrong, or some are wrong?**

Alternative Questions

When trying to determine any insights, approaches, strategies, summaries and conclusions, or findings, Socratic Questioning would all but mandate us to seek alternative arguments, possibilities, and ways forward. Typically, these would be the types of alternative questions you would ask:

- Is there a possibility that there are other alternative conclusions?
- And why are those alternatives more powerful propositions?
- What would the new proof points be for those alternatives?
- **What if those alternatives became the new narrative pitch flows?**

Consequential Questions

All actions have consequences—that we know for certain. These include strategies, assumptions, approaches, insights, alternative thinking, considerations, and the like. We will always need to examine those potential consequences and ask, *What if they actually occur?* Here's how Socratic Questioning would address the consequential:

- What if the possibilities, the opportunities, even the alternatives don't happen?
- List the consequences and the risks.
- What will be the long-term effects?
- **What if this impacts leads, revenue, incremental sales, and profits?**

Using Socratic Questioning, or questioning for examination and introspection, gaining familiarity with the principles of the unexamined life, and understanding disciplined conversations and disciplined listening are principles and philosophies that were taught by Socrates that we can all learn from. Use these Socratic insights to be a more complete sales professional and a more effective marketer. But also use them as precursors and validation techniques for *market discipline determination*, for strengthening your narrative pitch flows and proof points, and analyzing the strengths and weaknesses of your price, customer service, or technology leadership disciplines.

At this point, you will have determined if you're one of the three disciplines of market leaders we discussed in chapter three, or if you'll need to move on and look for something beyond price, service, and innovation. If you have come up empty, fear not; the single most important discipline in the *21st Century Disciplines of Market Leaders* is begging for your attention.

Also begging for your attention will always be the advice that Socrates imparted to us regardless of your desire to be a thought leader or not, or perhaps a philosopher for that matter: Whatever happens, it's probably a damn good idea to get a good wife, or a good partner, and stick with them for a very long time.

5

IT'S TIME TO SET
THE FOURTH EASEL

Although the first representation of an easel was an illustration of a structure supporting an Egyptian relief carving of the Old Kingdom, a work of art created somewhere between 2700 and 2150 BC, the easel as we know it today is a three-legged contraption that was invented in its studio variety in the 1800s.

The first flip chart that we've all used for many years was invented in the early 1900s by a gentleman named John Henry Patterson, who was the founder and owner of the National Cash Register company, known today as NCR. The company was formerly headquartered in Dayton, Ohio (it now resides in Atlanta, Georgia), and boasts annual sales of over $7 billion.[1] For quite a few years I had the distinct pleasure of working with NCR. Patterson was an interesting guy for four primary reasons. First, he's known for having fired Thomas Watson Sr., who essentially told Patterson to "shove it"—although not in those particular words—as

Watson went on his merry way and founded IBM. Second, Patterson fancied himself as the country's leading sales expert as much as he did a business owner and entrepreneur. Third, he's credited with opening one of the first known and formalized sales training centers, called Sugar Camp, which NCR occupied for many years, and a place I remember was revered, at least in historical terms, by the employees of NCR. And fourth, because of Patterson's invention of the flip chart.

But he was also known for saying, "To get your ideas across, use small words, big ideas, and short sentences." I love that; in fact, it's *pulchritudinous*.

He also stated, "Before you try to convince anyone else, be sure **you** are convinced, and if you cannot convince yourself, drop the subject." Of course, I'll never drop the subject of thought leadership because it's so *pulchritudinous*, defined as beautiful.

The whole notion of a company or individual becoming a thought leader really is extremely beautiful, the hell with all the other stuff about making tons of money in your sales career, or being a small business that makes a small fortune, or a medium-size business that makes a medium-size fortune.

Just kidding, making money can also be wonderfully beautiful, and also very romantic.

Now, I can't promise, as Socrates might have, that if you're a thought leader and a true romantic, you'll end up with a terrific life partner, but I can guarantee that you'll feel pretty excellent about yourself, perhaps even *pulchritudinous*, if you become a thought leader.

But don't go around saying you're a thought leader. That's not only bad form; it's also downright gauche, but not quite as much as a friend of mine who told me it was the most successful pickup line he ever used, to which I replied, "Give me a break, bro, the only thing you've ever picked up was COVID."

Again, let's take a look at the definition of a thought leader in the framework of sales and marketing. A thought leader is a person who focuses on three distinct areas of influence: **Wisdom and Insights**, **Trust and Honesty**, and **Ethics and Causes**. Each one of these areas of distinction is applicable to an individual or a company, and each has its own nuances and shadings that require forethought, introspection, and ongoing assessment. All of these influences work confluently to drive a company's revenue and incremental sales.

Ask yourself this, even before setting up the fourth easel: Am I, or is my company, predisposed to possessing **Wisdom and Insights**? Good golly, if you say no to this, then you're denying the fact that Socrates philosophized that because we can reason, we have every leg up on animals and beasts.

Or ask this: Am I, or is the business I own or work for, **Trustworthy and Honest**? Don't let me know the answer to this. Finally, try this on for size: Is our company **Ethical**, and do we believe in **Causes** that can further good—not just for ourselves and our employees, but also for those around us, for people who through no fault of their own might need a helping hand, and for organizations that can help us help others? I know you're all of these. And so did Aristotle who said, "Knowing yourself is the beginning of all wisdom."

Congrats. You're officially in the running to becoming a thought leader.

Even if you're a price, service, or technology and innovation leader, you can certainly add thought leadership to your list, and should. If you're none of the first three disciplines, then you've found a lifeline in the global pursuit of market leadership. Again, it doesn't matter what industry you work in, what your revenues are, your market share, or head count; you can be a thought leader and a damn good one. In fact, our friends at Marten Machining, whom we know to be innovation and technology leaders, and who are by definition a small company, could have been thought leaders, too, but one obstacle blocked their path—the time to be thought leaders. It was just too much to ask them to adopt a second leadership discipline even though it was apparent their industry wanted to hear from them, wanted to know what they were thinking, where the future was heading, what trends were nonsense and what trends were credible, and what, of course, their psychology was regarding metrology.

Any discipline of market leadership that you want to pursue and capture is going to require time; there's no way around it. Some more than others will also cost tons of dough, like technology and innovation; there's no way around that either. And you can probably add customer service to that list. Being a price leader is pricey, and that goes without saying.

But thought leadership, that's another story. There's an expense, for sure, but it's mostly time. And you might need some outside assistance helping you wade through the waters, but that'll be an investment well worth its while. First, it's an investment in you regardless of what job level you're punching at. Second, thought leadership generally impacts an entire leadership team, the total sales and marketing department, even engineering, quality assurance, customer service, public relations, and virtually every business department in your organization. And third, if you do make a monetary investment in being a thought leader, you'll be able to measure the costs and the return on investment with relative ease.

Your potential investment, which will be quite modest, is not so much a financial decision as it is the ability to manage the time it will take to become a thought leader. As Plato taught us, "Follow your dream as long as you live . . . for wasting time is an abomination of the spirit."

Invest the time it takes to be a thought leader because launching this discipline might take you only a year, perhaps even less. And that includes all the necessary steps I'll walk you through. The other three disciplines will take you far longer.

WISDOM AND INSIGHTS

Now, let's get to the easel and the flip chart. In much the same way we tackled the three other disciplines and used *market discipline determination* to assist us, we'll approach the fourth discipline in a similar manner. We'll start with an internal analysis into the first component of thought leadership, **Wisdom and Insights**. Again, jot down the company's contributions to the industry that fall squarely into the insights you provide to customers, strategic partners, friends, and employees.

So, what are the types of **Wisdom and Insights** we're looking for? To be clear, these will not be the insights you'll use for Critical Insight Selling, the money-making part of thought leadership. We're a ways away from that, and there's a strong possibility you'll need some outside assistance on the development of those types of insights. What we're looking for at the outset is anything you've written or that has been written about you. This could be your website, blog posts, white papers, emails, infographics, video scripts, case studies, customer interviews and Q&As, commissioned research, perception and attitude surveys, sell sheets, various paragraphs in your sales proposals, corporate overviews, press releases, awards, certifications and recognitions, customer testimonials, articles written about you, strategic partner endorsements, almost anything else you can think of. This is a full-scale content audit; feel free to go back at least five years in your archival search for materials.

Make notations of every item that's an insight, a trend, an expert opinion, a position, a reflection of your industry knowledge, a shout-out from someone else about your accomplishments and expertise. I would be shocked if you came up empty: That's exceedingly rare, and not in a good way. Take all of this wisdom and place it into some sort of taxonomy or hierarchy either by category type, or by what's most powerful and telling. Let the participants rank the potential effectiveness of all this knowledge. Remember this, and it's crucial: These insights and wisdom do not need to be groundbreaking, and they don't need to be new to market, patented, revolutionary, or even 100 percent original. Does it help if they are? Of course it does, but we're marketing your thought leadership, not your pricing strategy, your customer service, or your innovation disciplines. We're simply determining if you have the goods—which are ultimately your proof points—that can be repurposed into thought leadership insights.

Hopefully, you'll have a list of ten to twelve writings and accomplishments that demonstrate your influence in the industry. We want to show that you have a voice; it doesn't need to be a large voice, but it does need to represent some opinions and thoughts that have been distributed and reacted to. Now here's the kicker: If you have none of this, but you realize in this exercise that you might have a lot of information to write about and share, that you have some insights that are important to others, but you're not a writer, or you haven't had the time to note your industry insights, that's great, too. Make a list of everything that comes to mind that you could write, speak, or record a video about. You can always hire a freelance writer, just as easily as you can hire a freelance videographer to shoot and edit content, not merely from you, but also from other talented people within your organization. Either way, you simply cannot walk away from this exercise without having *some* ideas, whether they exist in a fully developed form or will exist in some form eventually.

This is why I've said, time and again, that the discipline of thought leadership is available to any company, in any industry, and of any size. And as you've learned from the thought leader's credo—*The more we know, the more we need to know*—when you begin thinking about thought leadership, it's a near certainty you'll keep thinking about it; that's just part of the human condition.

By now, your brain had better be hurting. If it's not, most likely something went haywire. It's time for a break, time to get some fresh air, but not time to grab a smoke—that's bad for the air, and for you. Since I started taking breaks in organized meetings in 1977, they made no sense to me, and still don't. What does a ten- or fifteen-minute break achieve other than a pit stop to the water closet and a quick review of your voicemails, texts, and emails? Not much, and hardly what I would call a break. You need to take more time. Now that you know your company has plenty of **Wisdom and Insights,** let's take a breather before we determine how much **Trust and Honesty** you enjoy.

It's not only important to clear your mind for thirty minutes, but it's also imperative you clear your mind like a thought leader. Clear it with positive thinking and not thoughts about your daughter's new boyfriend who possesses all the qualities of a curfew-breaker, or your meddling, ever-present neighbor who has little to do other than cast his side-eye in your direction.

Consider the things that bring a smile to your face for thirty uninterrupted minutes. Like taking your son to the zoo, which will also remind you of your place in the *reasoning chain* that puts you above the beasts you're watching in their cages. Maybe it's food, a great movie you recently watched, the latest book you're reading—just keep it pain-free.

For me, it's pretty easy. I focus on my wife because that's what Socrates told me to do, although I didn't get a good wife, I found a great wife, and therefore didn't need to become a philosopher. My wife's name is Kathy. I've always been in awe of people who were dealt a bad hand, but prevailed and didn't complain. That's what's important, no complainers; it's at the heart of Greek Stoicism and we need more of it today. She put herself through college, and through grad school, and through the ringer. She's hard on herself because others were hard on her, and that, in the *reasoning chain*, is flat-out unreasonable. Yet, she'll always look first for the good in people, even when the horrid is so obvious. What I saw in Kathy decades ago might be explained only by Plato: "To love rightly is to love what is orderly and beautiful in an educated and disciplined way." Kathy is orderly, beautiful, educated, and disciplined. Of these characteristics that apply to me, I'm probably batting 0–4.

I've never been to Cloquet, Minnesota, where my wife was raised by her grandparents, but I have been to Duluth, only twenty miles away. Duluth, in the last several years, really found its footing. It's a cool town on an even colder lake, and it grips you like the frozen winters on the North Shore of Lake Superior that hold you tight for, well, maybe seven months each year. I don't know much about Cloquet, population 12,500, but it is the home of the only Frank Lloyd Wright–designed gas station, which sits on the corner of Cloquet Avenue and Highway 33. Unlike Socrates, Wright bathed regularly, wore shoes, changed his clothing, and was diminutive. Like Socrates, Wright was one messed-up dude who treated women like shit and his staff even shittier.

In my orbit, it's always been important to clear my head so that I can make my brain hurt the next day, and the day after that. I do that by walking, and when I'm done with that, I walk some more; perhaps there's a little bit of Socrates in me in our walking habits, but certainly not in our hygiene practices. My thoughts are good because I think about Kathy. How she's always maintained a positive work/life balance while I refuse to do so. How she meditates daily and practices mindfulness. How she works out each morning before she works on work. How she climbs rocks (My Fab on a Slab, My Hunk on a Chunk, My Fox on a Rock). Paddles the Futaleufú in Patagonia (known as just the Fu), one of the gnarliest rivers in the world. Hikes the Grand Canyon, including a thirteen-mile stroll at the canyon floor in order to get some rest before the ascent. And participates in some cockamamie triathlon called the Wolfman where you whitewater paddle, then ditch your kayak for your mountain bike, and then ditch your mountain bike for a trail run.

No thank you.

She helps clear my mind because she sees wonder in what we sometimes take for granted, like the twelve-hour bloom of a bishop's hat succulent, the bountiful harvest of our fig tree, or the wonders of Arches, Monument Valley, Antelope Canyon, and the hoodoos in the Chiricahuas. And I like watching her wonder. It brings me hope; it's a personalized course correction that the world is not lost, that our youth will somehow deliver in spite of certain challenges, and in spite of themselves.

I never fully embraced the remote workplace, at least before COVID, but we were working remotely in 2001; we ditched our $30,000 office phone system in 2007, opting for newfangled ReadyTalk platforms; and we said good riddance to our server room, racks and all, in 2008, and latched on to Dropbox and other portable servers that same year, long ahead of other companies. That was Kathy, not me. If you can't clear your head on your own, have others clear it for you. It works wonders.

Break time is over. Let's reconvene.

TRUST AND HONESTY

Let's tackle the next group in the three categories of thought leadership, **Trust and Honesty**. I know for a fact that you're more than qualified in this department, but how do you prove it? You don't. You let other people prove it for you. Just like you never call yourself a thought leader, you have other people call you trustworthy and honest.

Nevertheless, we'll begin with more interactions between the participants and the flip chart. Let's start by listing the attributes that make your company (or you, personally) honest. Again, comb the archives for any content that points to these conclusions. Essentially, you're undertaking a second content audit. However, let me assist you with the types of **Trust and Honesty** content assets we're looking for.

Ask this question: What have we done as a company, or as individuals, that could be deemed trustworthy and honest? Many of my clients will quickly reflect on the obvious, which is *reverse* or *negative selling*. It's not an ineffective sales tactic, but it is a bit dated, and it's not particularly a thought leadership sales approach. Most of all, it reeks of a "hard-to-get" sales position that we ditched twenty years ago. Reverse or negative selling does not build lasting trust; it's really no different from the even more antiquated *Takeaway Close* where you literally propose a solution, retract it as not being the perfect fit, and then either present a new, more appropriate solution, or return another day with the best solution you already had tucked into your hip pocket. Don't believe for a minute that this is an act of sales honesty (a borderline oxymoron disproven in chapter nine), and consequently a representation of being trustworthy.

Reverse or negative selling is still *selling*, and the participants in this segment of determining where your company is most trustworthy and honest need to understand there's an inherent roadblock to any trust-building if it's labeled as blatant selling. So, that's not what we're searching for when we pursue pitch flows and proof points supporting honesty and trust. Any way you cut it, if you're selling, you're telling, and that's not going to further your thought leadership position. Remember, if thought leadership is in your sights, you'll be listening far more often than you'll be telling.

But let's start with Socrates who said, "The way to gain a good reputation is to endeavor to be what you desire to appear." And since your desire is to appear to be a thought leader, let's start there. Very few companies are talking and writing about the importance of **Trust and Honesty**. Don't minimize its significance, not even for a second. There are so many organizations and consultancies that have hopped on the trust train and continue to do so year after year. From Edelman and McKinsey to PwC and Gallup, there wouldn't be such an enormous emphasis on **Trust and Honesty** if we didn't have a problem with **Trust and Honesty**. In fact, for many years, I've thought long and hard about adding a fifth discipline to my *21st Century Disciplines of Market Leaders*, but I never believed it was completely necessary, opting instead to integrate trust into the thought leadership discipline.

To more than appear to be honest, you'll need to actually share your thinking about honesty with your customers and prospects. And that means starting at the top. Tell the narrative why you can be trusted, not by saying you're trustworthy, but by providing anecdotes about it. Here are three different stories I tell clients and prospects about the value of trust, but your team will have their own thoughts.

First, the average tenure of a client in marketing and advertising agencies is less than three years. Our first four clients in 1983 were still clients of ours in 2012. Those are relationships that have lasted almost thirty years, which is unheard of. I do not mention trust or honesty; it's not necessary.

Second, a leadership member of a real estate company named Avante Properties, which has been a client of our firm for more than twelve years, once told me when I asked her why the owners selected us—after searching for more than a year for a marketing partner—"Because they trusted you." That was pretty much the end of the conversation and we turned our attention back to the matters at hand. But not before I asked, "But you talked to ten or more companies?" Her response was even more brief: "Yes we did."

That's pretty much all anyone needs to hear.

Third, in almost all cases, our firm took the time to meet with sales representatives regardless of what wares and services they were hawking. It didn't matter if it was media, travel, IT support, phone systems, production and craft services, research bureaus, and so on. We took the time when most others wouldn't consider it. Sales is a tough occupation, and rejection is many times more the norm than the exception, and even though our employees might not have had an immediate interest in what was being sold, we were always interested in listening to a sales pitch because it's a great learning experience, particularly if it's a solid sales presentation. Plus, there were plenty of times when some of us changed our minds and went from skeptical to being on board during the process.

After a short period of time, we were known as the agency who met with reps and listened; again, when hundreds of others wouldn't. And whether a purchase was made or not, it was always said that we took the time for others, that we listened and asked questions, that we cared and could be trusted as straight shooters. In the end, if someone in the rep's orbit wanted to know whom to call for some marketing advice, it was our firm. Years later, we literally had dozens of non-active people selling for us perhaps only because we carved out a few minutes every week to meet with people who, most often, had been rudely sent out to pasture.

Tell these stories about **Trust and Honesty** in your tone, but always in an unassuming and humble manner. After you review some of the anecdotes that might be your internal honesty and trust proof points, search for the external proof points. These will be all the wonderful mentions about you from customers and partners. Perhaps they'll be testimonials and quotations, case studies, videos, or business transactions where others had failed, but you succeeded because of your honesty and trustworthy disposition. If these don't already exist, go out and produce them.

There will be nothing more impactful and forceful than a message of **Trust and Honesty**. Further, when it's time to start talking to your prospects about thought leadership in general, and **Trust and Honesty** in particular, you'll begin to see traction in engagement, interest, and ultimately closure. It happens all the time when your sales process includes thought leadership and Critical Insight Selling.

When you have perfected your position of **Trust and Honesty**, surprising and weird things will happen. To our amazement, somewhere around 2010, we hired a marketing consulting firm for marketing consulting firms. Mirren is the name of the company we hired, and they're still around today because they understand that even a good shrink needs a psychiatrist to level-set every once in a while. Our homework before our sessions was to determine where our new business came from over the last five years. We listed every client on our conference room whiteboard, and in spite of some failing memory, we tried to pinpoint how we won each account. The exercise was telling and somewhat excruciating as we wanted to be precise. Actually, I highly recommend doing this not just because we're discussing the importance of trust, and how best to sustain it, but also because it's downright enlightening . . . and surprising.

When it all shook out, we learned we won about 85 percent of our new clients over that five-year period as a result of a referral from an existing client or former client (although some could have been referred to us from the sales reps we took the time to meet with). It was amazing, in a good way, that of the six new clients we gained each year, about five of them came our way because our clients trusted us. The other 15 percent? We welcomed them aboard through indirect referrals, basically either from the thought leadership content we created and syndicated, or from my speaking engagements. Case in point: WEA Trust, which I referenced previously, was a direct result of thought leadership articles.

You'll always need strong relationships to succeed in sales and marketing and those will most frequently be based on honesty, which is followed by trust. There's nothing new or innovative about that. But thought leadership takes it to an unrecognizable level. When you become so trusted and your relationships so strong, you'll add unparalleled success to your business development department without adding to its cost because your clients are part of the team. Also, those strong relationships, combined with your wisdom, insights, honesty, and trust will aggravate your competitors to epic proportions, one of the few times that aggravation is a good thing.

Although what I'm explaining might seem complicated and intricate, it is not; in fact, it's quite simple. Don't feel overly pressured to prove too much. It's like saffron: A little goes a long way. The recipe calls for only a few pitch flows, only a few proof points, and only a few examples with each discipline within thought leadership. I can't remember why we developed seven different narrative pitch flows for WEA Trust. Perhaps the times called for it, but you won't need that many for any of the three categories of thought leadership; three or four will suffice.

At times, explaining the **Trust and Honesty** story can be deeply personal. For me, and this is the weird part of the impact it can have, it was never clearer than during a divorce proceeding our firm was a part of. This isn't necessarily a thought leadership anecdote, but it is a narrative about being loyal and devoted to clients and vice versa. Which, of course, is deeply rooted in both the characteristics of thought leaders (**Trust and Honesty**) and the results that thought leadership can have on the longevity of relationships. Although, I must say, when I tell this story, whether it is to prospective clients or in casual conversations, it's met with the fairly uniform response of, "Dude, you've got to be kidding," but it's the truth. The fact is, we were literally part of a divorce proceeding between two clients, obviously married, who owned an enormously successful law firm with multiple offices. Have you ever heard of co-owners making a consulting firm part of their divorce? If you have, that's news to me. Like child custody hearings, that's how we were involved. Who got us was literally part of the legal entanglements. That's the power of long-term relationships fueled by **Trust and Honesty**, with the scales of justice tossed in for good measure.

You'll have your own stories, pitch flows, and proof points that highlight your honesty and trustworthiness. In all likelihood, those proof points will alleviate the constant pressures of business development where you're selling, and when you're done selling, you'll need to sell some more. Perhaps, you'll demonstrate preference and loyalty through long-term relationships guided by trust. It works wonders; I've seen the results time and again for four decades.

Let's not forget what Plato reminded us of: "Success is determined not by the completion of some action, but by how one engages in all action with wisdom and intelligence." This is your road map: that all your actions about **Wisdom and Insights**, **Trust and Honesty**, and **Ethics and Causes** will drive your success because you took the necessary and intelligent steps to become a thought leader.

ETHICS AND CAUSES

When I was on the professional speaking circuit where I spoke about thought leadership and the original Greek thought leaders, scholars, and philosophers, people would want to know some of the key highlights of my remarks. Depending on the type of audience, I might tell them that day's topic was corporate ethics, and nearly every time they'd respond, "It must be a short speech." That's very funny, but also extremely sad.

Just as thought leaders are always knowledgeable and insightful, and honest and true, they are also ethical and understand the importance of causes and cause marketing. In the case of **Ethics and Causes**, this is the time when you should write and speak directly to the causes and ethical practices that rule your corporate philosophy, how you serve and support your employees, customers, providers, and communities. Still, you're not calling your company or an individual a thought leader, but you can certainly chest thump about your ethical inner workings. Of course, it needs to be true, and if not, you'll be outed quickly.

The fact remains that **Ethics and Causes** are the icing on top of the thought leadership cake, or, if you're healthier than that, the sesame-toasted tofu on top of the kale/arugula salad. As you work through your proof points about corporate ethics, begin to list all the examples of what makes your company ethical. Segment this between internal and external samples. Internally, this might include the treatment of employees, the paid time off you provide for volunteerism, workplace recognition and awards, employee community service achievements, and the like.

Then, do the same for external examples, but spend even more time assessing your ethics in this regard because, quite frankly, the high-quality manner in which you treat employees is rapidly becoming table stakes. Employment reviews through Glassdoor, Indeed, and countless other social platforms, including Net Promoter Scores, will validate or discredit your claims in seconds, and that means the emphasis really needs to focus on why you're an ethical corporation. Aside from benefit corporation (B Corp) status that will add validity to your ethics proposition, you'll need to do some heavy lifting here. But it's valuable heavy lifting that should be highly emotional and extremely marketable.

You'll want to tell these stories in the most high-touch and high-feel manner possible. If you don't have a writer on your team, hire a freelancer. Ultimately, stories about your pursuit of ethical behavior, and your disciplined approach to it, should write themselves. You will want to discuss the measures you take to do the right thing; how you've resisted the temptation of a quick sale in order to build long-lasting preference and loyalty; how you've solved customer problems and concerns in a forthright manner where others weren't able to deliver; how you despise shortcuts and workarounds in product development, quality assurance, and sales support, preferring a more balanced and ethical approach to innovation and solutions; and how the treatment of your employees is a reflection of how you treat your customers, or vice versa, with compassion, understanding, decency, and respect. And you should do this every month through messaging that resonates by way of articles, videos, position and opinion papers, infographics, and whatever other means are customary and suitable to your industry. And, better yet, find a customer or two who will help you prove it.

In several respects, this encompasses many of the aspects of content marketing, at least in the delivery of ways to position, promote, and syndicate your thought leadership discipline. However, in other respects, it goes far beyond the parameters of content marketing that has almost universally dissolved into just another glorified sales-focused communication channel.

I've considered myself a content marketer for nearly five decades. So was Ben Franklin, who published *Poor Richard's Almanack* in 1732, or the people behind *The Locomotive*, a company magazine first produced by Hartford Steam Boiler in 1867, or the communications department at John Deere with their newsletter, *The Furrow*, in 1895, and the list continues to this day. The point is, as discussed earlier, marketers are very fond of coining words and terms for strategies and approaches that have existed for years, sometimes centuries, as it makes sense to ultimately slap a label on things. In this case, it's purported that content marketing was given its name in 1996 by a fellow named John Oppedahl at an American Society of Newspaper Editors' conference.

Whatever content you choose to deliver, whether it be on price, service, technology/innovation, or thought leadership, it will assuredly be beneficial to your company and your brand. Certainly feel free to call it what you may. But content regarding thought leadership needs to be tempered of overtly blatant promotion, with a limited sales and marketing component and tone. It must show wisdom without bluster, demonstrate knowledge without bravado, and provide insights without insolence. Because *bluster, bravado,* and *braggadocio* are now the three Bs of content marketing, many view content marketing as nothing more than an ongoing sales and marketing tactic. All of that is fine, and purposeful, but outright and outsize selling is not part of thought leadership. We share, we listen, we advise, and when the timing is right, we close a deal. It's a done deal because we elected to build a relationship based on wisdom and knowledge, on **Trust and Honesty**, and on ethical behaviors. We don't sell "hard."

We don't need to.

This is not particularly difficult if all you need is one piece of content each month to talk about ethics. And even at that, you might want to consider providing that subject matter only six times per year, reserving the other six content assets about the causes you consider near, dear, and crystal clear to your heart for a later date. That's because the moment you latch on to a cause or causes, you not only support your thought leadership persona, but you also become a more effective marketer. So take the time, right about now, to list the causes that you're active with, followed by the causes you intend to participate in.

Cause marketing is essential to thought leadership, but it's also essential to becoming an effective marketer. I can push, cajole, strongly recommend, and even pound my fists on the kitchen table, to make certain any-size business in any industry adopts and promotes some sort of cause marketing strategy, but in the end, you need to believe in it, not just take what I say as gospel.

There are unavoidable facts, statistics, and reasons why cause marketing is unavoidable for astute sales reps and marketers.

But before we dive in, here's some cause marketing context to think about. The actual term *cause marketing* or *cause-related marketing* is believed to have been first coined by American Express (Amex) around 1983 when they became active in various non-profits, including the Statue of Liberty restoration campaign. In this instance, Amex would contribute a small amount of money to a specific charity for every purchase on their credit card, and most often, merchants would contribute, too. Ultimately, the results of these efforts spiked increased spending on the Amex card, but also added a bevy of new customers, which strengthened the relationships between Amex and their merchants. When the promotion ended, it was a win-win-win campaign for all.

More than likely, the first publicized cause marketing campaign was introduced in 1979 between Famous Amos cookies and the Literacy Volunteers of America when Wally Amos became their national spokesperson (although, it wasn't labeled cause marketing at the time). This hugely successful effort ultimately expanded literacy programs throughout the country, and it benefitted the chocolate chip cookie company as well. At the time, Famous Amos was a regional brand without a media budget and what they lacked in advertising dollars, Wally Amos more than covered with his outsize personality. The partnership between Wally and the Literacy Volunteers of America became a PR bonanza for the cookie company, and the final result was that Famous Amos was valued at $200 million when they sold to Keebler in 1998.[2]

Just as we slap labels on the newest marketing trends, although I'd hardly say that the formalization of a marketing trend established in 1983 is anywhere remotely revolutionary, the fact remains that cause-related marketing is hardly new. In Andrew Carnegie's article, "The Gospel of Wealth," published in 1889, Carnegie wrote about the responsibilities of wealthy individuals to fund non-profits and other organizations. This sentiment was echoed by Phoebe Apperson Hearst who had similar beliefs, although her emphasis was on education and public schools. The fact of the matter is that corporations have embraced causes since the early 1900s, starting with the YMCA, USO, and the

American Red Cross. But again, we tend to forget or dismiss the historical roots of where these trends generally got their start.

For modern-day cause marketing, the benefits are enormous and so too are the results. And driving this success are demographics and sentiments that are absolutely unavoidable. Let's start at the beginning. According to a research study conducted by Cone Communications, 92 percent of consumers have a more positive image of a business that supports a cause or an environmental issue.[3] In the inimitable words of John McEnroe, "You cannot be serious." But serious this is. What's striking about this is that we're talking about ninetieth percentile findings, and as any researcher knows, that's sky-high stuff. This isn't a solid 70 percent or even 80 percent. This is inarguable, as in the reasons to not participate are beyond argumentation. So here you have the double whammy: Cause marketing is an essential component of sales and marketing thought leadership and an absolute must-do, but it's also a must-have for marketing departments. It's a home run plain and simple. Or put another way, back-to-back home runs.

If your business happens to be a price leader, take note of this. According to an article in Marketing Week, a 2022 study from Salsify[4] found that 46 percent of consumers will pay more for a brand they trust and find ethical than a brand they're uncertain of. And most likely, those percentages will continue to climb as all indications show year-over-year percentage growth. But this isn't just for price leaders, hardly. This is as pertinent to the thought leadership position as it could possibly be. As a thought leader, you are already trusted and ethical, so more proof of your efforts, through cause marketing, will continue to enhance your position.

When businesses of all shapes and sizes fret over price increases, as they should, consider this: If you had only become more trusted and more ethical to your buyer segment, perhaps fretting over price increases would be less fretful and a whole lot less agonizing than the roll of the dice that accompanies any price increase strategy.

And when you think about making public all your thoughts about **Wisdom and Insights**, **Trust and Honesty**, and **Ethics and Causes**, or, better yet, having your customers do it for you, remember that in the same study by Salsify, 71 percent of consumers indicated they are more likely to trust a brand that is transparent about its values and ethics through its communication. Frankly, it's amazing that everything circles back to **Trust and Honesty** in some sort of manner, which only strengthens any and all arguments to pursue the fourth discipline of market leaders, thought leadership. Ultimately, you just won't be able to avoid it.

But there's more, a lot more.

In a research report from Gitnux,[5] it was stated that 66 percent of women are willing to pay more for a product from a company they deem as socially responsible. This, of course, is highly subjective and in need of a bit more meat for us to chew on, including what social causes are more influential than others. But it's interesting to note, although without definitive evidence from this information, that perhaps women are amenable to paying more for socially responsible products than men are, but the unavoidable fact remains that if you want more value and a higher price for your wares, put more effort into the values that go beyond price with honesty and ethics.

What's intriguing to me is analyzing research that precedes this. Although I've never been an advocate of fact-finding that's more than a few years old, it can be valuable to analyze what might be foundations and catalysts for some of these findings. After all, remember, "History never really says goodbye. History says, 'See you later.'" Plus, an extremely important distinction to all of this, and almost always overlooked by sales and marketing executives, is the difference between trends and trendy. In fact, the former can lead you down a path of success while the latter can motor you down the roadkill highway of Pet Rocks, Google Glass, Myspace, and Nehru jackets.

Here are some research trends to think about that are real eye-openers from only a short time ago. In a 2023 study by Havas, titled "Meaningful Brands,"[6] it was determined that 72 percent of consumers stated it was important for brands to be good for the planet and society. Additionally, 71 percent of consumers believed that brands should be improving their personal health and well-being or, in homage to our Greek scholars, contributing to a life of quality. Now that sounds more than borderline ethics and cause marketing; it sounds like consumer expectations are reaching life-changing status for your products and services. And speaking of **Ethics and Causes**, in a 2022 study conducted by Cone/Porter Novelli and referenced in a 2023 article by Linchpin SEO,[7] 89 percent of consumers were likely to switch to brands they believed were associated with a good cause. Of course, this should get us thinking about how to best allocate our resources in trying to gain a leg up on our competitors. Should we be combative to them, or berate them through the sales process, or discredit our competitors through social media, and disparage them by way of invasive digital stalking? It seems like the most solid competitive advantage is to just be ethical and forthright, which shouldn't require a huge cash outlay unless something has gone horribly wrong. We are no longer our worst enemy. Because of thought leadership, we are now our strongest proponent.

But these non-trendy trends are even more significant upon closer examination. In a 2020 study conducted by Zeno Group,[8] 82 percent of consumers indicated they supported companies when they believed in that company's purpose—with aspects of purpose being defined as ethical business practices, a strong set of values, and support for important social causes—and in that same report, 76 percent of consumers said they would refuse to purchase from a company whose cause they disagreed with. That right there is a balancing act that's fraught with peril, which is why for decades I've told my clients that their brand should remain politically neutral, unless their company is part of the political landscape. It's far safer to help organizations like the Boys & Girls Clubs of America, Junior Achievement, the American Red Cross, Gilda's Club, the local animal shelter, and any number of the thousands of organizations that also contribute to a life of quality. And without the divisiveness.

As Aristotle taught us, "Every community is an association of some kind, and every community is established with a view to some good; for everyone always acts in order to obtain that which they think good." And that leads us to **Ethics and Causes** that are always part of the most ubiquitous community of all: the social media and online community. And in that community, there is also peril around every corner that further endorses your need for corporate ethics, truthful behavior, and transparent communication. While much of it can be good, as Aristotle suggested, the fact remains that it is an individual's *view to some good* that is never going to be the same from one person to the next, which has never been more evident than in online reviews.

In statistics researched by Qualtrics^{XM}, we learned that consumers are willing to spend 31 percent more for products and services from companies with excellent reviews.[9] That's good. And 92 percent of business buyers are more likely to purchase after reading a trusted review. Even better. Similarly, in a survey conducted by FinancesOnline, 74 percent of consumers stated that positive reviews influenced their trust in a business and 73 percent indicated that they'll trust a local business even more if there are positive reviews.[10] And if it's revenue you're after (and who isn't?), 49 percent of buyers need at least a four-star review before they'll purchase from a business.[11]

That all sounds good until it isn't. The research can get dark pretty quickly. In a *Go Fish* research study,[12] a three-star review resulted in a 70 percent decrease in trust (oh boy); only 13 percent of all customers will even consider a purchase from a company with one or two rating stars (very troublesome);[13] sales can decrease 70 percent for a product with as few as four negative reviews (very negative);[14] and each time an unfavorable Google review is published, a business can expect to see as much as an 86 percent reluctancy from consumers to make a purchase (ouch).[15]

Navigating any social platform that includes reviews and ratings is fraught with more terror than Jason with a hockey mask and machete in *Friday the 13th*, which sounds about right since your revenues and reputation can be slashed faster than a Zamboni can clear a square foot of ice. And that begs the question, why not insure your company with the best policy you can protect it with? That's the discipline of thought leadership; it's the armor to prevent people who have a definition of good that's not quite . . . well, that good.

But this isn't merely an outside-in type of attribute. It's also an inside-out strategy that can strengthen against the rating and reviews naysayers. In other words, what occurs inside your business is just as important as what happens outside, at least in regard to helping you be more bulletproof to online judgments. Take for instance the statistic that reveals that 90 percent of employees who work for corporations that are committed to social and environmental causes feel a stronger sense of loyalty, inspiration, and motivation to their company than employees who work for businesses with little or no commitment to cause marketing.[16] This is more than the obvious commitment to building a dedicated and loyal workforce. Think how valuable it can be to have that team of personnel be your spokespeople for your employment goodness and reputation. They'll certainly legitimize reviews about your company for greater accuracy on employment review sites, as well as traditional social platforms, and they will be the most forthright ambassadors for your company if negative reviews lack credence.

Further, 86 percent of consumers expect corporate chief executives to speak out and support social issues.[17] Again, this isn't just an external advantage, but also an advantage that leads to a more loyal workforce. It all operates together to create a stronger company internally and externally and strengthens your thought leadership discipline inside and out. Think of it as the truth behind the truth of you being a thought leader.

So, speaking of truth, now is the moment of it. Do you believe you are ethical, support causes, are truthful and honest, possess **Wisdom and Insights**, have or will have the stories, narrative pitch flows, proof points, and customers to help tell and support those proof points? If you can answer yes to most of these, you're in like Flynn. I wouldn't exactly say it's downhill from here, or you have your hall pass to thought leadership, but at least it's game on and the pursuit becomes more mechanical from this point forward. From here, it's back to the Via Egnatia where riches abound, where the starting line is far behind us, and the finish line is in sight. Now, we need to map our path to the greenest pastures that have a variety of waypoints, historical markers, and tollbooths along the way. All that remains is a little more acknowledgment and some further verification in order to achieve true and honest thought leadership achievement and success.

Those waypoints include learning the ins and outs of VOC research and what questions to ask, how to ask them, what it takes to read between the lines—understanding that sometimes what's not said can be as informational as what is said—how to tabulate and group like-minded answers together, and how to draft a meaningful summary and conclusions document. It also includes a complete understanding that no thought leadership discipline can begin its launch without a successfully completed VOC assignment.

But first, we need to tackle the ethics of thought leadership, and for that we return to our Greek scholars Socrates, Plato, Aristotle, and Aspasia who taught us that some of their philosophies really do make perfect sense when we analyze an examined life, community, storytelling, quality of life, and the common threads that can make corporations—and the individuals who work for them—better in nearly every regard. Here's to ethics and ethical behavior by corporations of all shapes and sizes.

6

THE ETHICS OF
THOUGHT LEADERSHIP

I hate it when money gets in the way of ethics. Which is almost always. In fact, quite a few years ago, a CEO once asked me what the difference was between a B-plus consultant and an A-plus consultant. I told him, "The A-plus consultant doesn't need the money." Several years later he mentioned he never forgot our brief conversation, but it was extraordinary, nevertheless. He hadn't stopped thinking about it, and for him, it was the truth behind the truth about consultants. He went on to tell me that it forever impacted how he hired consultants, or if he hired them at all. We never discussed the meaning of my response. He knew it all too well.

And plenty of others know it, too, including Aristotle who said, "Each man speaks, and acts, and lives according to his character. Falsehood is mean and culpable, and truth is noble and worthy of praise. The man who is truthful where nothing is at stake will be still more truthful where something is at stake."

The fact is, telling a CEO of a multibillion-dollar company that they're traveling down the wrong path, that there are better alternatives, or that costly mistakes are on the horizon might be asking for a pink slip before you even slip out the back door. There's no question that this type of advice is far easier to deliver when you don't particularly need the cabbage than if you're supporting a family, or if you own a consulting business where many families are counting on you. Yeah, the truth hurts, in more ways than Carter's has little pills.

The stakes for speaking the truth are always high whether your life or others' lives are hanging precariously on your opinion, and on your truth telling.

I won't elaborate on what the lifetime award for honesty is, but it's significant. But I can tell you that thought leadership is the place you want your company to be, and the place where you want to be consulting from. And that goes back 2,500 years to our Greek scholars who were ethicists just like you are, and just like every CEO should be. We already know that honesty and wisdom are the framework of thought leadership, but let's pursue the ethical part of this framework and what we can learn from Socrates, Plato, Aristotle, and Aspasia.

But first, more truth.

I am not a philosopher, or a Greek scholar. Aside from having taken a few philosophy and Greek mythology classes, I'm just a person who is fascinated by and curious about a lot of things, including the Greeks, Romans, music, movies, art, art history, AI, business, the business of AI, travel, pop culture, theater, sports, world history, politics, technology, plants, gardening, food, interior design, architecture, and plenty of other stuff. My curiosity keeps me awake at night, but my fascination keeps me going throughout the day.

I've found that CEOs in general have a difficult time understanding the concepts of ethics, but not so much the importance of corporate ethics. I've also found that CEOs appreciate history and the lessons we can learn from it. In that regard, leaders have an easier time understanding the rationale behind corporate ethics if it's reviewed within the context of Socrates, Plato, Aristotle, and Aspasia. Does it make it more fun to learn this way? Maybe a little. But it sure as hell beats sitting in a classroom, or in front of a screen watching someone lecture us about metaphysics, axiology, epistemology, or transcendental synthesis.

I typically start at the beginning. And it begins this way: You cannot practice thought leadership without practicing corporate ethics. Period. They are hopelessly intertwined without any way of untangling them. As we learned in the Havas "Meaningful Brands" study,[1] 75 percent of consumers want brands to contribute to a life of quality, and many Greek philosophers believed that ethical behavior should not be merely a personal belief, but also a collective belief if we truly desire some sort of quality of life. We must, together as a society, all believe that our ethical behavior will contribute to a life of quality.

I very much like talking to CEOs and their leadership teams about the Greek notion of soul. "And what, Socrates," Plato asks rhetorically in *Protagoras*, "is the food of the soul? Surely, knowledge is the food of the soul." In Plato's works, including his most famous teachings, which can be found in *The Republic*, he writes about various dialogues he has had with other philosophers, and it's in these dialogues that we can learn about certain ethical beliefs—how they might apply in today's business climate, and also how they are fundamental to thought leadership.

There is little dispute that knowledge is the food of the soul just as there is little dispute that Socrates was considered the smartest man in Athens, or perhaps the world, after he proclaimed, "True knowledge exists in knowing you know nothing," which pretty much defines the role of any leader in recognizing that curiosity and fascination should never have an ending point, no matter your age, upbringing, education, or corporate position. Socrates continued, "Awareness of ignorance is the beginning of wisdom."

As a thought leader in sales and marketing, you will ultimately rely on selling your wisdom and knowledge, not features, benefits, or reverse selling techniques. So, the groundwork of these beliefs and philosophies is not just the knowledge you possess, but also understanding that the search for wisdom, even in the industry you represent, begins by wanting and needing more wisdom to remain relevant.

Again, we define a sales and marketing thought leader as a person's or a company's discipline that focuses on three distinct areas of importance: **Wisdom and Insights**, **Trust and Honesty**, and **Ethics and Causes**. Realistically, you need to possess a healthy dose of each one of these disciplines within the discipline of thought leadership, and you need to be able to prove it consistently and without much doubt. **Wisdom and Insights** are the fuel that drives you, the food for your soul. **Trust and Honesty** are noble and worthy, and serve as not only what you appear to be, but also who you are and what your stake in the ground stands for. And **Ethics and Causes** drive a life of quality, a belief that together we can live in a better society.

Wisdom (what Plato called knowledge), the truth, and your ethical behavior, both as a corporation and as an individual thought leader, can bring you so much more gratification in your business life than chopping your price. Customer service and innovation are certainly disciplines that are rewarding, although we know they can be fleeting and difficult to sustain when viewed in the context of competitive differentiation, not to mention being open to diminishing returns. But thought leadership . . . now that's a discipline for the ages that's not necessarily subject to diminishing returns. You control the narrative; no one else does. Again, as Plato reminded us, "Human behavior flows from three main sources: desire, emotion, and knowledge." It's important to consider Plato's wisdom because you, as a CEO, will always have the desire, the emotional privilege, and the knowledge to educate, inspire, achieve, and create benefits—financially and ethically—for a better life, and a life of quality. It's the ethics that guided the masters, and those are the same ethics that can guide a business to unparalleled successes.

THE DIFFERENCE BETWEEN DEONTOLOGICAL ETHICS AND TELEOLOGICAL ETHICS

I always think the difference between deontological and teleological ethics is like the difference between a cactus and a succulent. To the botanist, the difference is as wide as the Mississippi River, but to the casual observer, the difference is as subtle and minuscule as an amoeba swimming in the river's basin.

There is much we can learn from deontological and teleological ethics, the two primary schools of philosophy during the Greek heyday of thought leadership. The differences are subtle, but in many ways both can teach us key attributes of thought leadership and why these philosophies and theories are critical for leaders to understand and to live by.

In general terms, deontology is derived from the Greek word meaning "duty" where teleology is derived from the word meaning "goal" or even "outcome." I think, even at this early juncture, you might be able to see where this is heading. For me, when thinking about the distinction between the two schools of thought, I remind myself in today's context that deontological is real time where teleological is future focused, although this is probably an oversimplification of two complex theories.

Deontology deals more with the attributes and motives of right and wrong rather than if the outcomes are right or wrong. Its theory is to act responsibly (ethically) toward all living things and the environment. Teleology, on the other hand, is more attuned to the consequences and outcomes of good and bad actions. Deontology subscribes to the dictum that the end does not justify the means, while teleology finds its footing in the end always justifying the means.

Although these two philosophies are often debated, in a more modern-day business context—particularly within the framework of the discipline of thought leadership—there is probably room for both competing beliefs. I have always viewed this as the best of both worlds if you can balance the two. As a leader, you want to be driven by outcomes and goals, but you also need to be sensitive to the means you employ to achieve those goals. At the same time, you would need to analyze the means by which your goals will be achieved to make certain they don't leave a trail of ill will and mistrust in their wake. It's a subtle difference, but an important distinction.

In its most basic business scenario, take the phrase *there's no such thing as a bad question*. Well, the truth is there are loads of bad questions, just as there are bad ideas, misguided strategies, incriminating ad headlines, marketing concepts that are so fraught with half-truths and preposterous claims that it would make Linda Blair's head spin (which it did in *The Exorcist*). And we could say, "That's a really bad question," because that's the truthful outcome of that particular inquiry. Or we could say, "I'm not sure if that will fly or not. Can you think about this more? Are there other alternatives? Maybe you could tell me what potential consequences there might be?" If you're thinking about Socratic Questioning as an alternative to, say, teleology, then that lightbulb just turned itself on to the tune of about 1,500 lumens.

You can see how all of this is co-mingled and intertwined, how with close examination it can work marvelously to describe corporate ethics within your position as a thought leader, and how the ethics of yesteryear can guide you regarding the behaviors of this current year. And honestly (of course) this is historical talk that makes you sound really smart—which you are—when you are speaking about philosophical theories and how there's an interplay between them and business.

Much of what we know about deontological and teleological ethics comes from Plato as he spent considerable amounts of his time studying the thinking of Socrates. As far as we know, Socrates wrote either nothing or very little, and consequently the meanings and translations are mostly by either Plato or Xenophon. However, most scholars tend to favor Plato's writings. One reason for that is because Plato had a front row seat at the trial of Socrates in 399 BC, where Socrates spoke about many of his most treasured beliefs in his own defense. Plato, who was forty years younger than Socrates, was the prize student, which also afforded him nearly unlimited access to Socrates's thoughts, insights, and wisdom. Much of Plato's writing did not occur until after the death of Socrates, which, as you remember, resulted from his drinking a hemlock cocktail prescribed by the jurors who found him guilty of impiety and corruption of the young, although the jury pool was actually taking orders from the ruling oligarchs.

Excuse the intentional digression about Plato, but his findings and beliefs are of critical importance to understanding not just Socrates, but also modern thought leadership. Plato's writings were divided into three distinct stages: They were known as the "Socratic" dialogues, the "Middle" dialogues, and the "Later" dialogues. Most of what we have learned about Socrates can be found in the "Socratic" dialogues where Plato imagined a somewhat fictional conversation between Socrates and Euthyphro.

This is the point in time at which Socrates analyzes the charges brought against him. In the *Apology* section of the "Socratic" dialogues, Plato reviews the famous speech Socrates gave in his own defense at the trial where, as we know, he said, "The unexamined life is not worth living." Again, this is imperative for future thought leaders to under-stand. As we discussed previously, human life lacks a certain amount of meaning and purpose if we don't examine ourselves, or attempt some sort of introspection. The final section of the "Socratic" dialogues is called the *Crito*, and in this section Plato tells us of the acceptance by Socrates of his punishment in spite of its unfairness.

I like to think about this in terms of a CEO's role in education, transition, and the final succession. All of these are, of course, the nature of passing the torch from one thought leader to the next, and then to the next, in much the same way Socrates did to Plato, and Plato did to Aristotle. This makes perfect sense because hogging thought leader-ship for yourself is the antithesis of the actualities of thought leadership. As I've mentioned, once you own this discipline, the odds are pretty high that your company can own it for decades just as IBM, Patagonia, Salesforce, and Adobe have.

When we combine deontological and teleological ethics with the history and stories of the great Greek philosophers, along with Plato's dialogues, Socratic Questioning, the unexamined life, the trial of Socrates and his untimely fate, and the disciplines of thought leadership within the *21st Century Disciplines of Market Leaders*, we see an emerging pat-tern that extends far beyond the little-known fact that Socrates, Plato, Aristotle, and Aspasia were the original sales and marketing thought leaders. What we have right in front of us are lessons that can make us better leaders, more effective consultants, superior educators and men-tors, exceptional sales professionals and marketers, and, essentially, far more interesting humans than had we not been aware of these lessons.

The study of Greek philosophies, and for that matter many philo-sophical theories that have spanned centuries, are never simple exercises to examine, but they are worthwhile to think about. At the very least they teach us lessons in behavior, both good and bad, what should be part of our daily diet (knowledge), and whether we should be more concerned about moral actions regardless of the consequences, or the final consequences of those actions whether they were particularly moral or not.

Yes, I know, it's probably time to take a walk; I think I'll make it a long one.

WELCOME TO A WORLD OF *NICOMACHEAN ETHICS*

And enter Aristotle who had his own opinions about ethics. Rest assured, Aristotle's beliefs as presented in his *Nicomachean Ethics* will absolutely astound you, and that's an intentional spoiler alert. As previously discussed, there's a tendency for marketers to apply our own labels on "things" because it's a notch in our belts, and a self-applied ego stroke. But Aristotle brought it to a new level when naming his famous ethical theory after his not so famous son, Nicomachus, probably best known to his bros as Nic.

In very general terms, the *Nicomachean Ethics* establishes that there are two types of virtues. There is the virtue of thought further defined as wisdom, and the virtue of character that Aristotle defined as generosity, justice, and courage. For purposes of adding a small notch in my belt, I'm going to add honesty to the "character" part of Aristotle's belief because without honesty, you are basically pointless. In chronological terms, a human would first develop character and then develop wisdom all in pursuit of what Aristotle called virtue. Overall, at the heart of Aristotle's *Nicomachean Ethics* is a single word, which doesn't translate very well today, called *eudaimonia*, or, loosely, "happiness." But "happiness" as a feeling of pleasure comes and goes and that's not what Aristotle was angling for. More appropriately, *eudaimonia* was the highest form of euphoria we can feel, something that we can relate to as being the *total human good*. To reach the ultimate in *total human good*, we need wisdom and character that will result in *eudaimonia*. Knowing that part of the components of *eudaimonia* are generosity, justice, and courage, we now understand that part of the ethics of thought leadership would include your generosity (excuse me, cause marketing), justice (excuse me once more, being fair so that everyone can enjoy a life of quality), and courage (yes, it takes courage to be a thought leader, to tell the truth, but also knowing that by today's standards, telling the truth should not result in drinking a death cocktail or losing your head).

All of our ancient philosophers were so deeply committed to self-examination and knowing yourself before knowing anything else, or, as Plato suggested, "The first and greatest victory is to conquer yourself; to be conquered by yourself is of all things most shameful and vile." What Plato was saying is that everything is inconsequential, all the battles, all the victories, even the business wins you notch are meaningless until your first victory is completely understanding yourself, what makes you tick, and why you behave the way you do.

I fully understand the need for and the accomplishments of business coaches, but there's more to modern business advice than meets the eye. Understanding history is the foundation that opens our minds to so much more; understanding Greek philosophy makes us wiser and packed with more wisdom, and, ultimately, understanding examination and the ability to know ourselves opens the door to being able to gain *eudaimonia*, which makes us better leaders (and better humans). That's tough duty for any business coach to learn, but it really is the groundwork for understanding how ethics play a critical role in thought leadership and why we need the historical footing to be really virtuous.

I'm not kidding. CEOs dig this stuff, not just because it's fascinating, which it is, but because it's sticky as well. Frequently, after I've worked closely with CEOs and their leadership teams, I'm told that they think about ethics on a regular basis particularly after they learn more about it, that they research these philosophies deeper because it makes so much sense and because it's transferable to others, which makes it sticky in all directions.

In total, all of this works in favor of a life of quality, supported today by your company's **Ethics and Causes**, which, in turn, support your thought leadership discipline. You can sit around your boardroom table, continue to flip your flip chart, or gaslight your whiteboard searching for a market-leading discipline that might or might not be honest and true, but ultimately you will need to decide if you are really a price leader, a customer service leader, or a technology and innovation leader. You'll know soon enough, but to prove that you are is almost always tough sledding; at least that's been my experience of being in this business since 1977. And perhaps more importantly, can you sustain one of those disciplines without worrying about a competitor doing it better than you?

My money is on thought leadership because it's available to all of us, it's affordable, it's relevantly different, and no one is going to throw more money at it than you are because it doesn't require more money. It requires more knowledge, wisdom, insights, honesty, truth, self-examination, and ethical behavior, all of which you already possess because we all want *eudaimonia*, and that, my friends, is *pulchritudinous*.

When I began researching this concept of the original thought leaders being the standard-bearers for what thought leadership is today—and this research never ends—I spent more than two years in discovery and analysis. And when I decided it would be my newest and primary subject matter on the professional speaking circuit, I knew that I would need to find my voice, that it would require another year of organization, rehearsal, memorization, video analysis of my sixty-minute speech, and confronting all the technical witchcraft that is tossed your way during a presentation, including every AV hiccup you can think of, even delivery without slides, microphones, and a working laptop.

You'll find your voice as part of finding your way to thought leadership, and I guarantee you it will be contagious, and sticky. Just as Aspasia helped Socrates find his voice.

ASPASIA LENDS A HAND, AND A VOICE

Regrettably, female Greek philosophers were pretty much muzzled during the times when Socrates, Plato, and Aristotle were writing, speaking, or practicing their beliefs. No writings exist from the leading female philosophers such as Arete of Cyrene (her father had been a student of Socrates); Themistoclea (the teacher of the mathematician and philosopher Pythagoras, who influenced theories developed by Plato and Aristotle); Hipparchia the Cynic (who married an Athenian philosopher named Crates, who was the teacher of Zeno of Citium, who is believed to be the founder of stoicism, which makes a great deal of sense since Crates himself lived an impoverished life on the streets of Athens, refusing money even from his fellow philosophers); Leontion the Epicurean (a student of Epicurus and who was one of the few women, if not the only woman, to attend his school); or Hypatia of Alexandria (who was the headmistress of the Platonist school in Alexandria where she also taught mathematics and the philosophies of Plato and Aristotle). There is much to praise about these female thought leaders and their struggles to have a voice in the philosophies of the day.

Somehow, Aspasia of Miletus, as she was formally known, was able to navigate the treacherous waters of second-class citizenship that women were relegated into, at birth, I might add. It is believed that because she was from the town of Miletus, an area part of Ionia, which today is in Turkey, Aspasia was probably able to work around the severe restrictions of Athenian law that prevented women from having any rights, from going to school, and from entering most forms of public life. In spite of these awful restrictions, Aspasia managed to be a renowned intellectual, philosopher, and orator. In fact, her influence was so significant that many of the great thinkers, including Plato, Aristotle, and Pericles, were in awe of her.

After Aspasia arrived in Athens, she established an elite school for women where the exchange of beliefs, ideals, philosophies, and writings was free flowing and open to discussions. To some extent, the discussions were probably lively and noteworthy as Aspasia herself was one of the greatest rhetoricians of her time. It is said that her lectures were not-to-be-missed events and drew the most prominent thinkers, philosophers, mathematicians, and thought leaders of the day. She was charismatic, intellectual, and witty; again, much like Dorothy Parker, and was a muse to many.

Although Aspasia was best known as the mistress of Pericles, who at the time was one of Athens's primary leaders, she was a contentious figure, in part because she was deemed as the agitator behind Pericles's divorce, but also because, I suspect, she was a feminist and an equal to many of the leading male Greek scholars. This is why I frequently refer to Aspasia as our first known feminist, and she should be honored accordingly.

It really wasn't until Judy Chicago, in her groundbreaking work *The Dinner Party*, created between 1974 and 1979, that Aspasia began to receive the recognition she deserved. In Aspasia's individual place setting within Judy Chicago's work that featured thirty-nine of the most impressive and historically significant women of all time, Aspasia's plate and runner are described by the Brooklyn Museum of Art in the following manner:[2]

> *In her place setting, Aspasia is represented through elements commonly found in the art of ancient Greece. Her plate shows a blooming floral pattern, suggestive of her femininity, and done in earth tones used in the art and architecture of 5th century B.C.E. The runner references*

the types of clothing and jewelry that both men and women wore during Aspasia's time. One of the most familiar elements of ancient Greek attire, the Greek chiton (similar to a Roman toga) is suggested in the draped fabric on the front and back of the runner. Two embroidered leaf-shaped pins hold the draped fabric to the runner, similar to the jeweled clasps the Greeks would have used to fasten their robes. On the back of the runner are six black palmettes, embroidered as a stylized version of a honeysuckle or palm tree frond, a dominant motif in Ancient Greek paintings, pottery, and architectural detail. The floral vine pattern, stitched in gold, silver, and black on the runner's edges, mimics motifs found on many Greek vases and urns. This pattern is also repeated in the illuminated letter "A" on the front of the runner.

In spite of society's objections surrounding Aspasia, she was renowned as a gifted orator, or more commonly described as a master instructor of rhetoric. In fact, it was Socrates who credited Aspasia as his teacher of oratory skills, and most likely, she was the reason why Socrates's moving defense speech at his trial, hallmarked by the words "and if again I say that to talk every day about virtue and the other things about which you hear me talking and examining myself and others is the greatest good to man, and that the unexamined life is not worth living, you will believe me still less," is so highly respected, at least according to Plato who attended the trial. Interestingly, there is a belief that the most accomplished Greek orators were probably no match for Aspasia. Even Aristotle, who is credited with being the founder of the study of rhetoric, was influenced to a great degree by Aspasia.

In chapter ten, we will analyze the premise that all thought leaders are great storytellers, and maybe even great orators, or at least masters of the school of rhetoric. We'll also discuss why the telling of stories is so important in the syndication of your thought leadership content.

THE CHIEF GOOD IS CHIEF AMONG US

Corporate ethics are shaped so much by the notion that *the more we know, the more we need to know*. Not that we ever stop learning, but when we understand the basics of ethical behavior and ethical beliefs, we have a better handle on why it matters to be honest, to be reflective, to strive for a life of quality—not just because your customers want you to help them have a life of quality, but also because as thought leaders, you can deliver quality of life through your understanding of **Wisdom and Insights**, **Trust and Honesty**, and **Ethics and Causes**. Eventually, this brings longer-lasting relationships, better sales results, and more well-rounded forms of success and achievement.

Importantly, those successes and achievements are available to everyone. This isn't just for the big players, the behemoths, the publicly traded, and the private equity funded. Certainly, they need this as much as anyone, as many of these companies have lost their way, but this is every person's discipline regardless of financial size, market share, manufacturer, service provider, or individual sales representative.

"The Chief Good we feel instinctively must be something which is our own, and not easily to be taken from us," exclaimed Aristotle in one of his lectures.

The chief good is yours for the taking, not anyone else's. You will own thought leadership, and damn it, no one is going to take it from you. Now, let's get after it.

7

YOU CAN'T BE A THOUGHT LEADER WITHOUT VOICE-OF-CUSTOMER RESEARCH

nd here's more about the "spoiler alert" you read in the introduction. In the days of yore, I was known as the VOC King, not because of any breakthrough innovations, but because all the other VOC Kings had transitioned to retirement and were sitting by the pool. There were only a handful of traditionalist holdovers still ticking, and I was the only person using VOC to develop critical insights for the purpose of selling wisdom. So, what follows is the first-ever published, step-by-step guide on how to conduct VOC from start to finish. In the past, no one wanted to reveal their secrets, and that's understandable, but secrets be damned. I've figured that if I'm going to break the seal, it's going to be the real deal.

But here's the alert. This is detailed. It's thirty-three pages of not the second-best but the very-best primer on how to conduct VOC to add revenue to a company and to an individual's wallet. Now that the VOC cat is out of the bag, it's my sincere wish you tackle this with two things in mind—first, bagging new customers because in your pursuit of thought leadership, you're going to need to pursue VOC in order to develop new business, and second, new business will come from your **Wisdom and Insights** and much of that knowledge is discovered through the process of VOC.

VOC research, as legend would have it, was developed in the 1990s as a feedback loop for product development specialists. It was popularized by ad agencies and marketing consultants shortly thereafter. However, in recent years, as the founders of the VOC movement have passed or retired, the traditional protocols of VOC have given way to a more cumbersome yet highly profitable variation of the original intent of the research methodology.

In truth, VOC, in its original context—which was benignly called one-on-one interviews—has long been a mainstay of qualitative research. Regrettably, its newfangled format plays squarely into the hands of any ad agency's not-so-newfound purpose: profits. What was once a one-person show has now become a three-ring circus, and at times a shit-show, where questions are developed by one team, interviews are conducted by another, recommendations and insights are drafted by a separate group, and the creative, if called for, falls into the hands of another team.

This approach, which is many times more costly than the original method (more hands are in the kitchen), loses the valuable consistency of what VOC was intended to be—that is, a start-to-finish exercise that analyzes the perceptions and attitudes of individuals by grouping answers together in an effort to unearth reoccurring themes. Like the childhood game of telephone, there's such a significant loss of insights, and perhaps even the truth—as results are handed from one group to another—that today's VOC is almost a roll of the dice rather than an honor roll of certainty and precision.

As one of the founders of the VOC movement, I always conduct the research in its original format. I write the questions (although VOC is not scripted, it's a conversation), conduct the interviews, explore reoccurring themes, develop the insights, draft the recommendations, and, when necessary, formulate the creative.

In this manner, VOC is as close to bulletproof research as a company can get. It's a record of what people say, how they say it (oftentimes the meat of the research is between the lines; in other words, what people don't say can be as valuable as what people do say), and how they feel. There's no second-guessing: You can discount the voice of the respondents if you don't care for the outcomes, but turning a blind eye to people's beliefs is rarely an advisable research strategy.

You cannot be a thought leader without VOC because the development of the insights that are required to be a thought leader is directly dependent on the findings of your VOC. I know of no other way to formulate the insights you'll need without VOC.

And for the record, I have been involved in more than 4,000 interviews and I've never seen this type of qualitative research conducted with *any*, and I repeat, *any* effectiveness when it's conducted by an internal department or employee. It's a total and complete waste of time that will result in bad findings, misjudgments, and extraordinarily damaging recommendations that will lead you down a path of ill-advised strategies and half-witted tactics.

"But, Tom, it doesn't cost anything if we do it," says the skinflint.

"Except your business and a life of quality." Which apparently is insignificant.

VOC is the front door to thought leadership. You must enter, engage, and pass through it, hopefully unscathed, and no worse for wear, upon its completion. And the only way to be free from scathing is to have someone else do it for you, a VOC pro who fits snuggly into a ten-gallon hat because VOC specialists are made up of one gallon of each of these ten characters: journalists, professional interviewers, branding experts, top-notch listeners, conversationalists, purveyors of trust and confidentiality, arbiters of impartiality, Socratic Questioning practitioners, artful dodgers (carefully crafting their introductions as not being employed by the company you're being employed by), and connectors of dots where there are no dots to connect. And let me add that only a few times a year will I say to my partners, "What's the big deal about people chest thumping on their LinkedIn profiles that they are connectors of dots? Wasn't that a puzzle we did as infants?"

No one will ever talk in confidence to or completely confide in a company official who thinks they can get to the bottom of a customer's sensibilities, their true beliefs, and what inherently pisses them off about the company, their employees, the CEO, and the like; it's just never going to happen. And believe me, even the best companies who honestly believe there's not much wrong with their products, business practices, customer service, price, product road maps, quality assurance, engineering, sales department, help desk, ethics, and other departments should probably pound a little sand. Or, better yet, hire a VOC expert who can shed some light on the darkness and spare yourself a pounding.

VOC to develop or enhance a brand is one commonplace research practice, but using it to develop insights is a whole different animal. For purposes of distinction, and as an added bonus, I'll provide my questions and techniques for branding VOC, as well as for insight development. Ultimately, whatever discipline you or your company chooses for market leadership, and most assuredly you must choose one of these to be a market leader—**Price and Value, Customer Service and Customer Intimacy, Technology and Innovation**, and **Thought Leadership**—you're going to do it to profit from it. Of course, there are other reasons, but profit is a corporate requirement, and in order to fulfill that requirement, you need to sell something in the form of a profitable transaction. The best way to do that is through Critical Insight Selling, which can't be done without VOC.

But don't give short shrift to other important aspects of market leadership beyond profits. First, it's good to be a leader. Second, it's really good to be a highly respected leader. Third, leadership of a discipline increases the value of a company, and an individual, regardless of company size or shape. Fourth, you'll have a stronger brand, which means stronger messaging, which means more proficient selling, which most likely means more profits. Fifth, you'll have the pick of the litter when recruiting employees. Sixth, you'll increase employee retention rates because, well, who the hell would want to leave? Seventh, from those record-breaking sales you'll be able to reinvest in your company and employees more than ever. Eighth, adding to a life of quality for yourself, your company, and others is your *eudaimonia*, and being virtuous is probably all that it's cracked up to be. And ninth, being a recognized thought leader is actually pretty damn rewarding.

One of the most significant problems with ad agencies and consultancies, and there are many, is they promote headstrong creative strategies ahead of sales, rather than headstrong selling strategies ahead of anything else, and I'm being hospitable. The truth of the matter is that these organizations are so hooked on the *shiny new toy at Christmas syndrome* that they can't get out of their own way. In most regards, that's the syndrome where we bedazzle them with the creative, which results in closing the door on any long-term thinking . . . and then what? Not only should there be an act two and an act three to any creative, but there also needs to be deep considerations about how and when the creative will generate sales, increase market share, and broaden TAM (again, total available market). To some extent this is an understandable approach by agencies and consultancies. They are not sales organizations, and generally don't profess to be any such thing. Sure, they might hire business development personnel, but that's to line their own coffers, which is also understandable. But they're novices when it comes to understanding the sales motion, how to boost incremental sales, how to expand a company's TAM, how to structure a sales department for efficiency and purpose, and, of course, how to sell wisdom. Don't believe me? Just ask them.

In any meeting I suffered through, and there were thousands, I found myself either wondering or saying aloud, "When are we actually going to sell something?" That's because the *dance of a thousand jesters*, as I call it, has this uncanny knack of avoiding the obvious and embracing the ridiculous. Essentially, let's talk our way around everything that matters most, which is obviously sales, incremental sales, and sales messaging. It's not surprising because we avoid what makes us most uncomfortable, and what we know the least about. It baffled me in 1983 when I founded my agency, and it continues to baffle me today. I'm troubled by why agencies don't hire sales professionals—usually in favor of inexperienced account managers who wouldn't last eight seconds in a sales meeting—knowing full well that sales pros could really affect change for a client.

The beginning of this is, of course, VOC research. It's not only the beginning of the sales component of being a thought leader, but it's also the beginning of developing the insights that you'll need to demonstrate your wisdom, honesty and trust, and high standards of ethics. The step-by-step process of VOC is important to follow, and it will be equally important to hire an outside resource to walk you through this. There aren't many out there—probably a lot more B-plussers than A-plussers—but you'll know soon enough who's the right fit, and by following the VOC steps that I outline, you'll know the right questions to ask your prospective consultant.

WHAT YOU SHOULD LOOK FOR IN A VOC PARTNER

When using VOC to develop critical insights, here's the start-to-finish process I've used for decades. If you're new to starting your VOC career as a consultant, or potential thought leader, this is the surefire way to do it. And if you're a client embarking on a VOC project to either become a thought leader, or strengthen your thought leadership position, this will assist you in better understanding the processes and the protocols for engaging a consultant, while at the same time better understanding why you can't possibly do this if you're an employee of a company.

In either case, you might want to add your own wrinkles to this; after all, no two VOC assignments are ever the same, and adjusting by industry, by scope, and for time constraints is essential. Also, it's important to remember that traditional VOC protocols are not what might be customary if you hire an ad agency or marketing consultancy. As I mentioned previously, traditional VOC—which is the most beneficial, cost-effective, and reliable VOC there is—has taken a turn for the worse, but hardly an unexpected turn as the process needed to become far more profitable for advertising and marketing firms. Properly conducted, VOC should always be handled start to finish by one person so nothing is lost in the translation.

Before you hire anyone to assist you on this project, make certain to ask them the number of people who will be involved. The more the merrier is not what you're looking for; in fact, the more there are, the more costly it will be, and the quality may suffer as the baton is passed from one department to the next. You'll also want to see samples of the work your strategic partner has accumulated over the years, and not just a single sample; ask for several samples across different industries with ranges in scope from twenty interviewees to hundreds or more. For our client Foot Locker, we interviewed more than 1,000 "boarders"—that's skateboarders and other board sport enthusiasts of which most were teens. You'll want to explore the consultant's processes, examine samples of their VOC questions and answers, look at the write-ups of their interview findings (which are a quick snapshot or synopsis of their immediate, top-level conclusions), and then you'll want to review the final decks they prepared, which might include creative elements, strategic and tactical recommendations, and, of course, any truly original, groundbreaking insights they develop.

As you zero in on your partner, you'll want to ask about timelines. Be suspicious of a turnaround time of eight to nine weeks, and even more suspicious if it moves into a time frame of four months. Assuming the scope of interviews is around thirty to fifty, a VOC project should take about twelve to fourteen weeks. If it runs longer, it will certainly run over budget. If the turnaround is short, you won't be receiving the information and findings you need. Once the timeline is established, you can structure your payments accordingly. Typically, VOC payments are invoiced in three equal parts: 33 percent to begin the research, the next third upon completion of the interviews and the interview overview draft, and the last third just prior to the presentation of the final deck. Your strategic research partner should not have to wait on any of these three agreed-upon payments, and I certainly would never schedule the final presentation without the last payment already in hand.

There is a step-by-step process that will provide you with the cadence of how this works. You can use these steps and their tempo as a guide to hiring and working with a VOC partner, comparing my protocols with theirs. They won't completely align, but they should be damn close.

THE STEP-BY-STEP PROCESS—SETTING THE EXPECTATIONS

I always begin each VOC project by managing the expectations, which in the world of consultants is probably the one thing you should always do, regardless of the project. In fact, if you don't, you're asking for trouble with a capital T and that rhymes with C and that stands for *catastrophe*, and that's in deference to Robert Preston who played Harold Hill in the Tony Award–winning, Grammy Award–winning, Academy Award–winning musical *The Music Man*.

Here is how I've managed expectations over the last nearly five decades: Stick to the timelines, but always tell your client that "I can only move as fast as you can. If there are delays, the delivery dates will change and so, too, the costs." This draws a fairly clear line in the sand because no client ever wants to hear it might be their fault the project could run over budget. That's scope creep, two of the most dreaded words in the accounting department's lexicon. Right off the bat, you'll have their attention.

Next, set tentative target dates that, without saying it directly, are also some of the payment due dates. You'll want to be clear that the following milestones need to be adhered to, or else:

- List of interviewees, whom we also call respondents
- Introductory letter from the company to the respondents about the project
- VOC script and questions approval
- Interview time frame
- Scheduling of interviews
- Interview summary draft document
- Final presentation deck that includes all elements in the original estimate and the statement of work (SOW)

The next expectation you'll want to establish is the distinct possibility that you'll need to conduct more interviews than what was in the original scope agreement, or the SOW. This might impact the overall price of the project. You simply cannot know at the outset how many respondents will be no-shows, how many will cancel at the last minute, and how many will cut short the interview because of a pressing issue.

Moving on, the next expectation, and perhaps the most important, particularly from the consultant's side of this, is making certain that after the final presentation is completed, the project is over. Clients will always ask for more, and they should, but not without a cost estimate for the additional work. This should not be open to interpretation. When it's over, it's over, and clients should understand that, too.

Implementation of the recommendations includes check-ins, workshops and training for employees, writing, content marketing, additional research, strategy meetings, and anything else that comes to a client's mind. Yes, strategy meetings on selling, not just meetings for reasons of drivel, or, as Peter Drucker said, "Meetings are by definition a concession to a deficient organization. For one either meets or one works. One cannot do both at the same time."[1] Of course, by today's standards, Drucker might have actually been wrong because all I see in meetings are people doing other things: looking at their laptops, hiding their phones under the table as if no one knows what's going on, or, worst of all, the resident gadfly who rises abruptly from their chair and blurts out, "I need to take this call," as if it's so important they're *taking* it for the team. Whatever it might be, further implementation needs to be estimated separately; do not try to predict what might be required and build that into a VOC estimate. And the same holds true for the client. If you believe that further work might be required, wait until you learn the full results of the VOC.

The next to last expectation I set is about results. I tell all my clients that they might dislike what is discovered, but I'm just the purveyor of truth. VOC is the opinions of others, and therefore they can't be wrong. I remind them that shooting the messenger does little good since the insights I have developed will only be actionable insights if I'm still alive.

As you might guess, I always add in a little history and tell them when Sophocles wrote the play *Antigone* in about 440 BC, the more precise translation was "no one loves the messenger who brings bad news" as opposed to actually shooting the messenger. This is a refreshingly more benign translation than the modern-day interpretation.

For me, the last expectation I always establish is the expectation of continuity. VOC should not be a one-shot drill, although most often it is. I suggest that every eighteen months they re-ante and do a follow-up with different respondents. I recommend different respondents because far too often people come and go in an eighteen-month period and tracking them down is just too difficult a scheduling exercise.

THE STEP-BY-STEP PROCESS—INTERVIEWING

Now that you've set some expectations, or heard the expectations from your research partner, it's time to take a look at how the VOC process unfolds. It always begins with the selection of the interviewees. Here's how I work with my clients in the selection process. You want to be able to assist in determining the correct number of participants. Most often, this would be between thirty and fifty, and while that's a big spread, the wild card is almost always how many external interviews you want to conduct (customers or former customers) and how many internal interviews are required (current employees). Herein lies the first of a few debates. Remember, our ultimate goal is to develop original critical insights into your industry that no one has ever formulated, written about, or syndicated. Along the way there will be plenty of other discoveries, but the ultimate payday is the one that brings the thought leadership insights you want to walk away with. So, the determination of how many people to interview—and what the external and internal mix should be—is probably best placed in the hands of your VOC expert.

The mix for me is generally 75 percent external and 25 percent internal. It's important to have 20 percent more external names than the target number of completed interviews. That's about the number of prospective interviewees who will not respond to a request for a phone conversation. From there, it's important to understand why we conduct internal interviews. That explanation goes like this: You need the internal perceptions and answers from your employees (including leadership) to determine how "off target" or "on target" your company is with their perceptions of their customers' opinions. This is the bonus of VOC: to learn just how significant the gap is between what a company believes the answers to the questions will be, and what the true sentiments are of the customers. At times, the gap between the two is as wide as the Capertee Valley canyon in Australia, the widest in the world, and sometimes quite a bit narrower, but there's always a gap, and it's usually considerable.

This is always an eye-opener for company executives, although it shouldn't be. Usually, we think we're better than we are, or stronger in certain disciplines than what is truly reality, or, even worse, believe we're something that in actuality we are not. To say that *perception is reality*, a notion first expressed by the political consultant Lee Atwater, is a bit juvenile and simplistic; for the record, there are far too many market disparities, too many possible segmentation variables, and continued systematic irregularities for something to be that conclusive, but Atwater's quote is noted. There will always be a distinction between what we think our company is and what others believe the company to be. Understanding those differences is essential to leadership, particularly thought leadership because, as Plato taught us, "The first and greatest victory is to conquer yourself . . ."

I also believe that conducting external and internal interviews is a sorely needed balance in VOC, and that goes for VOC conducted as part of brand research or for the development of critical insights. Many insights can be identified from conducting interviews on both sides of the desk, and almost always there's some sort of sweet spot in the middle of the external and internal interviews that yield a critical insight or two. It's a valuable exercise and should not be scrapped for cost or timeliness.

It is the client's responsibility to provide the respondent's information to the VOC strategist. For instance, if your company is a consumer-facing business, then your interviewee mix must be diverse by geography, gender, age, income, and other important segmentation. If the company is trade-based, then segmentation by position and title, company size, geographic propensities, length of relationship, and other factors will play a role in whom is selected to participate in the project. Whatever the industry, I always tell my clients that there are two overriding factors in the selection process. First, there's no value to stacking the deck with brownnosers and bootlickers who are going to respond with favorable prejudice. Second, the respondent's availability for an interview is a pre-requisite. Chasing down people who will not respond, or are unlikely to respond, is an exercise in futility and a waste of time for all.

The client must provide the consultant with a spreadsheet of all the respondent's critical information, including full name, city, email address, phone number, title, company name, and other information as required. After this information is agreed upon, the activities of VOC begin to take shape.

For this, the first step is to contact all of the respondents, typically by email notification. The email should be sent from the client (the company) directly to the interviewee with a member of the organization's leadership team copied into the email to signify the importance of this project. The email should also include the consultant, their email address, and phone number. Here is the sample email I provide my clients to begin the VOC recruitment process:

Dear _____,

(Company/Client Name) is undertaking a significant research project that will assess industry trends, pinpoint critical present and future challenges, and look for clarity in the wants and needs of our customers over the course of the next decade. These efforts are going to make us a better company on every level, a more valuable influencer in the industry, and as strong a partner to our customers as we can possibly be.

Helping us with these efforts is our consultant, Tom Marks, from the company TMA+Peritus. Because you are a valued partner of (Company/Client Name), and have critical points of view about (Company), we have asked Tom to reach out to you in hopes that he can spend as few as 20 minutes on the phone with you to get a better feel for your perceptions about us and the industry. Not only do we appreciate a few minutes of your time in this important initiative, but we further appreciate your candor and your insights as we move forward with this project.

I usually let the email rest for a few days and then start the follow-up process with each individual respondent. I make no mention of VOC as most people are unfamiliar with the acronym, and it only adds confusion to the request for an interview. I will email each respondent a total of two times, which is actually a total of three contact requests, and then I remove them from the list. Also, I never allow the client to schedule interviews; it's fatal in every regard. Between cancellations, rescheduling, no-shows, time zone changes, and the like, the communication at the beginning of the relationship must always be in the hands of your VOC partner and the customer. And never, ever allow the client to sit in on an interview; if they demand it, walk away from the project. That's an outright invasion of confidentiality, and will almost always result in worthless interviews because the key to successful VOC is honesty and truth from the respondent.

Now it's time to begin the interviews. Depending on the goal, it's always my intent to complete the interviewing process in three weeks. I'm pretty steadfast about that. Even if the interviewees ultimately respond to my email request after the three-week window, I don't oblige; the train has left the station and the schedule needs to remain intact. There are, of course, exceptions to this three-week period particularly when the scope of the project surpasses more than 100 interviews, but by and large, I'm usually comfortable scheduling as many as four or even five interviews each day.

I'm often asked why I will conduct my interviews only by phone. First, I don't want a video chat to be a distraction for me or for the respondent. Second, because of time zone differentials, it is not unusual that I might be conducting interviews on Pacific time, which could be four or five in the morning on my end, and likely a firsthand horror show for those I'm interviewing. Last, having someone watching me pecking away at a keyboard is counterproductive to all parties.

I schedule and conduct my interviews in sixty- to seventy-minute segments. Although I ask for only twenty minutes (this strategy increases the number of scheduled interviews as opposed to asking for thirty minutes or more), I average about forty minutes per interview. Approximately 10 percent of the time the interview will last the requested twenty minutes, 25 percent of the time it'll last thirty minutes, 45 percent of the time about forty minutes, and 20 percent more than forty-five minutes. You need to be a conversationalist—without talking too much—to effectively conduct a VOC interview. The balance is delicate, but the results are not; they're almost always telling, surprisingly revealing, on target, and frequently astounding.

The allocation of an hour or more for an interview is derived from doing this for nearly forty years. Although I mostly learned on my own, it was back in about 1965 that I was first exposed to the importance of one-on-one interviews. I recall very little of the specifics other than my father, Melvin L. Marks, who was a consultant primarily in the food and drug industry and found some notoriety as one of the creators of Orville Redenbacher's Gourmet Popping Corn; yes, my dad was hired by Orville, an agriculture extension agent in Indiana at the time, who was spending the vast majority of his waking hours experimenting with different corn varieties and seedlings. My father and his partner, Irv Gerson, had a small ad agency in Chicago, not too far from where Redenbacher was living in the Valparaiso area. Redenbacher hired them to create and market a popcorn that he was selling to local taverns, reportedly in plastic baggies, under the name of Red-Bow Popcorn. After some back-and-forth and a little horse-trading, the two Chicagoans recommended that it be called the brand we know today, with further recommendations that the label should be an illustration of Orville's mug on a glass bottle—another recommendation that was innovative for its time—and to call it Gourmet Popping Corn, doubling down on the gourmand status while doubling the price over the leading in-home popcorn, which at the time was Jiffy Pop.

Long after Redenbacher sold the company to Hunt-Wesson for millions, I was told by my father that he ran into Redenbacher at the Food Marketing Institute trade show that was annually staged at McCormick Place in Chicago. Flanked by two suits from Hunt-Wesson, Orville introduced my dad to the two executives as the asshole who charged him $20,000 to "tell me to put my name on the label of a glass jar."

Decades later, my father told me Redenbacher stiffed him and Irv for half the money.

I vaguely remember driving through the Iowa cornfields and stopping at grocery warehouses and offices, waiting in the lobby as my dad would talk to "guys" for about an hour or so. And then I recall we would pile back into the car, driving only a few blocks, and parking on a quiet street while my old man scribbled notes about the interview he just conducted. I also remember him telling me that you must talk to people one-on-one to really understand the market, the products, and their thinking. I've forgotten most of it, but obviously not all of it.

That's why I schedule an hour or more for each interview, because I need to make notes on much of what we discussed in the VOC. Although I'm furiously typing the responses, I'm still a slow mover on the keyboard, and listening intently is my number one priority. Again, that's why I conduct only telephone interviews for my VOC: no Zoom, no Skype, and no Teams. I don't want to be distracted by anyone's appearance or mannerisms, and they certainly don't want to be distracted by my hunting and pecking on the keyboard.

In my VOC questions and answers, I always begin with some conversation that's probably completely irrelevant, but necessary as a harmless starting point. It might be something about the city the respondent lives in, a local event, a restaurant, even something in the state that I'm familiar with. The point is, you need to get the respondent talking, and talking almost immediately. After that, do not, under any circumstances, dive right into hard-charging questions; toss them a few softballs about their tenure, different jobs they've had within the company, current rank (you'll already know that from the spreadsheet), and anything else that's fairly lightweight that comes to mind.

After that, it's time to begin the questioning and the probing. Remember, the questions I ask are not in script form; this is a measured conversation with a lot of back-and-forth. Generally, for a VOC project where I'm trying to unearth insights that have never seen the light of day—while at the same time trying to learn more about the company and its nuances—I'll ask the following questions. This was for a company called SunGard K-12 (a tech firm specializing in school information systems), which was a division of FIS Global, a business headquartered in Jacksonville, Florida, with nearly 70,000 employees and assets of $85 billion, but don't be fooled by their size; this VOC script works for any-size company.

- How long has your school district been a SunGard K-12 customer? (Icebreaker)

- How long have you served in your current position? (Icebreaker)

- Were you part of the committee that selected SunGard K-12, or was that decision made by others? *Probe for who was the decision-maker and what was their rationale.*

- What was the primary deciding factor for you in selecting a student information system or district financial software?

- What were the secondary and tertiary factors?

- What are some other factors that might not have been as relevant but proved to be somewhat important?

- In the selection process for technology partners, what type of information proves to be valuable, and what information would you like to have but few, if any, provide? *Probe for specific examples and ask what types of information competitors might be providing that are actually really useful.*

- Conversely, is there information that is provided that you find to be ineffective? *Probe for what's most annoying.*

- What do you value most in a sales rep, not just someone selling technology, but any sales representative? *Probe to make certain the rep is identified with a particular industry like sporting equipment, school furniture, library science, and so on.*

- What is the one greatest strength that SunGard K-12 possesses? *Probe to keep this conversation going with further types of Socratic*

Questioning like, Why do you say that?, Might it have been something else a few years earlier?, and so on.

- What is your next greatest strength?

- And what is your one greatest weakness?

- And your next greatest weakness?

- In one word, please describe SunGard K-12.

- Okay, one other word.

- How would you describe the SunGard K-12 brand?

- If you could choose three distinct topics that SunGard K-12 could research and write about that would keep you better informed, what three topics would be of interest to you? *Probe to get many more; this is the beginning of how you formulate your critical insights for Critical Insight Selling.*

- On a scale of one to ten with ten being very valuable, just how much value would you place on this research?

- If it would be valuable, in what types of ways would you use this research; for instance, would you share it with others both inside and outside your school district?

- In what format would you like to receive that information: Would you be interested in longer format white papers that were very in-depth, shorter articles about your topics of interest, blog posts, videos, e-books, or some other type of format?

- And how often would you like to receive that information? *Probe to find out if there are others in the district who would find this information valuable.*

- If I asked you to define the K-12 educational ecosystem, how would you define it? *Probe if there's confusion about the definition of the K-12 ecosystem, although many administrators are quite familiar with the concept.*

- If a parent approached you in a hallway and asked, "What drives student success?" what would your response be? *Probe beyond class-room grades.*

- If a school board member asked you the same question, would your response be any different?

- If the district superintendent asked you the same question, what would your answer be?

- If there was one thing you could change today in the entire K-12 education process, what would that be? *Probe because this does not need to be related to software. This is leaning into the development of critical insights.*

- Let's say that magically that change occurred. After that change, what would be the next thing you would change?

- And finally, one more change.

- Now, if money was no object, and I know full well that it's an obsession in education, verbally create for me the most perfect, the most idyllic school district. Paint this picture for me. *Probe for more detail on all of these.*

- Similarly, paint me a picture, a persona if you will, of the perfect high school principal.

- And now a perfect persona of a district superintendent.

- And now the perfect school board.

- What is it about your job that you really like?

- And one other thing.

- Now tell me what you dislike about your job and some ways that it could change for the better. *Probe further because this can frequently provide insights that might become critical.*

- And one last question. Is there anything you'd like to "get off your chest?" Remember, all answers are completely confidential, and all I do is group the answers together; no names are attached.

I try to limit my VOC length to thirty-five questions or less, but you'll find that most often a client will ask, "As long as you're speaking with people, do you mind if you also ask these other questions?"

Yes, I do mind.

THE STEP-BY-STEP PROCESS—TABULATION

After all the interviews have been conducted, I begin the tabulation process, which for VOC, with under 100 interviews, is always manual. This is not quantitative research, at least for the most part, so the tabulation is slow and deliberate. Depending on the scope of the project, I usually allocate a one-week period for tabulation, sometimes shorter, but most often at least that length. By this point in time, between the setting of expectations, selection of the respondents, initial email recruitment, follow-up for scheduling, final approval of the questions, actual interviewing, post-interview notations, and tabulation, you're probably seven to eight weeks into the project. That's why you need to be fearful of any consultant who offers an eight-week turnaround time; it's just not possible.

During the tabulation process, you'll be making some significant judgment calls. In some cases, these judgments might impact the overall results, particularly on how you rank all of the responses. What makes this process particularly tricky is how much note-taking you do after the interviews. I do a lot. Your post-interview notes will play an important role in the tabulation process because you're recording feedback that's not particularly open to traditional tabulation protocols.

In your annotations, you'll want to call attention to pauses and hesitations regarding a respondent's inability to answer a particular question or questions. This is noteworthy if others are having similar problems. It means you've hit a potential nerve that might become an insight, although at this point it's too early to tell. Frequently, interviewees will want to circle back to questions they're having trouble answering. Try not to allow this to happen; it's a momentum killer. Help them without helping them too much. Suggest what others might have said, but only generally: "Well some people talk about the brick-and-mortar aspects of schools." Also make notes if someone doesn't provide an answer that many others did provide. Oftentimes what isn't said can be as fruitful to you as what is said.

As you tabulate the responses to your questions, you will group like-minded answers together into categories. You might receive a total of sixty or seventy different answers to one question as respondents can give you multiple answers to a single question. You want that; again, this is not quantitative research, so nothing needs to add up to 100 percent. The judgment part of this is how you ultimately group and categorize the responses. For instance, if someone says the strength of an organization is its ability to develop products for the future, and another says the company has a strength in producing future product road maps, you'll need to group those together. If you don't, you will end up with VOC that's all over the map and tries to prove too much. Eventually, the VOC becomes useless because it can't be digested. Keep in mind that when you group and tabulate VOC, regardless of it being used for branding or insight development, it's all about recognizing, and then interpreting, reoccurring themes. That's the name of the game, and nothing else is singularly more important.

There are two characteristics of VOC that can throw you off your game and result in numerous misfortunes. The first is what I not so fondly call the *kiss of death*: That's when thirty different people give thirty different answers to thirty different questions. Obviously, that's a rarity, but some semblance of that can happen. If it does, you're toast, actually dry and burnt toast. That's because you won't have any reoccurring themes to work from, you won't have a foundation for your recommendations, and you can pretty much kiss your critical insight development good riddance. It happened to me only once, and it was many years ago, but essentially my client recruited, unbeknownst to me, interviewees who had almost no familiarity with the company even though company officials thought they did. It was a complete waste of time and I bailed from the project before the cauldron reached a boiling point.

The second problem, also a mortal blow, is when the VOC becomes nothing more than a bitch session, a beef box if you will, because the company is so despised, the leadership is full of such nincompoops, the products are crap, and the warranties aren't worth the paper they're printed on. Like the first example, that's happened to me only once before, but truth be told, it's a great opportunity to reboot, explain to your sponsors what the problem is, reassess the scope of the project, and start anew by pivoting to perception and attitude research, which might be far more relevant. When all is said and done, you cannot possibly conclude a successful VOC project without spotting the reoccurring themes. In 99.5 percent of the instances, those themes will be there, and they should be prevalent.

THE STEP-BY-STEP PROCESS—REOCCURRING THEMES

The reoccurring themes will be responses that are repeated to your thirty different questions. Depending on the mission—particularly in the case of open-ended, thought-provoking questions like determining what sort of research topics a customer might want a company to invest in, or what a respondent might want to change in an industry if they could change only one thing—you won't typically see reoccurring themes, although you might see some duplicate thoughts and ideas, and this is a very good result. For more traditional branding types of VOC, you will want to see very conclusive themes that are a result of your questions, such as a company's greatest strengths or weaknesses, or describe a company in one word.

In the case of Mister Car Wash, where external and internal VOC was used to assist in a modest rebranding of the company, the external reoccurring themes throughout the entire VOC were (1) hospitality, (2) clean cars, (3) convenience, (4) superior facilities, and (5) professionalism. When these were cross-referenced with the reoccurring themes in the internal VOC, the order varied, but the themes did not: (1) clean cars, (2) hospitality, (3) professionalism, (4) superior facilities, and (5) convenience. Here's where you are ultimately making judgment calls regarding the rankings in your tabulations and then your final recommendations. Of course, the internal employees are going to place a higher rank on the themes that are closer to them and more identifiable to their orbit. The way they clean cars and the manner in which they act are far more important to them than convenience, but they do understand from their interactions with customers that convenience is critical. Also, because many car wash visitors referred to customer service, or the way they were treated, in addition to hospitality, it would be imperative that you group those responses into a single category.

When the responses are more open-ended and require some soul-searching, a few duplicate answers, or answers that are similar, are just as critical. For SunGard K-12, for instance, if a respondent laments about the money required to build a high school, on average perhaps $50 million, and another reflects on the budgets for secondary education being cockeyed, it is your role as the VOC practitioner and strategist to add clarity and possible groupings to these two responses. In your probing, you would certainly want to know what was off-kilter in the budgeting, and you would likely discover the concern that teacher compensation and retention was placed much further down the education ladder than, say, school construction and maintenance costs. Because of this, test scores in students would continue to decline, which is evidence the entire allocation of educational funding is completely out of whack. Obviously, with further research, that could become a critical insight with some more questioning, investigation, and follow-up.

THE STEP-BY-STEP PROCESS—AFTER THE TABULATION

After my tabulation is complete, I clearly denote the reoccurring themes as they will become part of my VOC respondent recap that I review with my clients. As far as determining critical insights, we're not at that point yet, and that's never part of my review of the interviews. To give you a barometer of how extensive my summary and conclusions are regarding the interviews, I put this into draft form, not a deck, and generally summarize the results in five or six pages. It is here that I might also allude to a problem interview or two, not mentioning names, unless the problem was so strident that it needed corporate attention. In these instances, I'm speaking about complaints surrounding an employee, or a product failure, or a customer so royally pissed off that they need to be contacted. This is the only instance when I break from my hard-and-fast rule about interview confidentiality.

There are two different ways to conduct VOC when comparing external and internal questions and answers. Sometimes, the internal VOC questions are not identical to the external questions and this can present tabulation discrepancies that can be difficult to deal with, but not impossible. Further, this can make exact comparisons extremely challenging. I try to seek a balance in the questioning, and to that end, I have experimented for years with two methods, both yielding fascinating results.

The first method is to ask the identical questions between both VOC groups, and that is the traditional and most sound approach. But there are times when I've tried the second method, which I formulated after years of trial and error and that I not so clinically call *let's play the game*. This can be conducted only with internal VOC. In it, I ask the employees to guess how the external respondents answered the questions. I use this approach only when several factors have come to light. First, when I have the sense that a company truly doesn't know their customers as well as they might think. Second, when there are so many customer segments, and consequently so many internal employees serving those customers, that it's literally impossible to conduct the interviews any other way. And third, when there is potential overlap in segmentation, roles and responsibilities, product applications, and customer service segments and I can't possibly separate one revenue stream from another. Although this exercise is immensely fun, it is not my usual VOC path forward.

A terrific example of this is a Salt Lake City, Utah–based company named ArbiterSports that was formerly owned by the NCAA. Arbiter is a technology company that has developed software that pretty much dominates the scheduling of high school and middle school sports and events in much the same way a student information system would do for a school district. Without getting overly technical, Arbiter's software schedules not only millions of sporting events each year, but it also schedules and digitally pays referees and umpires, of which there are hundreds of thousands; offers online referee training and certification; digitally registers students for sports and other event participation; interacts with a variety of software platforms that stream high school sports; and uses data collection to offer important services to students and their parents. The VOC problem in this case wasn't merely that ArbiterSports had many different products, and consequently many different employees to sell, service, and manage those products, but it also served an incredibly diverse audience, including students in general, student-athletes, parents, student friends and families, school adminis-trators, coaches, teachers, referees, and anyone considered to be a sports enthusiast. In fact, I recall that the software developed by ArbiterSports impacted one out of every four Americans. Now that's a large and diverse buyer segment.

In any event, I had no other choice than to invoke the *let's play the game* method in Arbiter's VOC. Ultimately, it will always be imperative to take the time to implement VOC in the correct manner, which is a balance between external and internal respondents.

THE STEP-BY-STEP PROCESS—PREPARATION OF YOUR FINAL VOC REVIEW DECK

Now the time has come. I typically allow four to five weeks for the final part of the process. One week is allocated to our art directors or graphic designers to prepare the deck since my design skills are clumsy on the best of days. At this point, I'm comfortable scheduling two meetings, the first by phone or video chat, and the second in person regardless of the location. I never, absolutely never, present the final deck, the results, and the critical insights in any manner other than in person. And for that meeting, I insist on a minimum of four hours, not including a break of, you guessed it, at least thirty minutes. The first meeting is always a "pre-read" of the deck that is sent two or three days in advance to the project sponsor. Although there are rarely any surprises, people on the leadership team want a first glance in case they think I might have fallen off my rocker. But I still need to build in time to make a change or two to the deck, which I'm generally not capable of doing, and my design team doesn't want me messing with their artistry.

To give you an idea of the construct of my deck—which by the way is not a PowerPoint and never was because those presentations require dimmed lights in a conference room, which is not practical for note-taking, follow-up questions, or being able to read people's faces—my graphic designers always politely told me that PowerPoint and Keynote presentations do not allow for much design flexibility, and for that general reason, I've avoided them. In any event, my deck for a final VOC presentation is a PDF of around sixty or seventy pages for a project with about forty interviews.

I always begin my decks with an overview of VOC—reiterating the expectations that I purposefully discussed up front, followed by a little bit of VOC history, and then a detailed explanation of what we absolutely DO NOT want to happen, which as I mentioned previously is of the bitch-session and not-knowing-your-customer variety. I do this intentionally to put my audience on edge, to make them think they're about to be an infinitesimal mathematical exception to the VOC rule, and that their organization is about to be flagged as the next Enron, or, even worse, Johns Manville. Again, it's expectation setting, but I'm doing it in real time during the unveiling of the tarot cards. It always works. From that point on, the presentations always go beautifully because everyone knows at the outset that the results are encouraging, if not extraordinarily rewarding.

If my final VOC presentation deck has some weight to it, I'll probably begin with a table of contents (TOC). This will typically include the following (but in no particular order):

VOC: What It Is and How It Works

Methodology

VOC Research Findings and Conclusions

Critical Insight Selling and Recommendations

Content Marketing and Recommendations

Brand Restructuring

Corporate Messaging Composite

Of course, the scope of the project will dictate your TOC. Regardless, in your Methodology write-up, you will discuss the number of interviews but not list anyone's name, how long the average interview lasted with reference from the shortest to the longest, the date range during which the interviews were conducted, the questions asked, any segmentation and filters used in the selection process of the respondents, any deviations that occurred, and, if you choose, the entire cadence of the project with specific timelines and milestones.

In your VOC Research Findings and Conclusions, you will present the questions in the order you asked them and then the results (answers) to those questions by way of the groupings you decided upon. I always begin with the external results for two reasons. First, they're generally more applicable to the matter at hand, but also because I prefer to set the stage for the gap that almost always surfaces between the external findings and the internal ones. Second, because the external reoccurring themes carry the most significance, and if those same reoccurring themes are not as prevalent in the internal findings, it illustrates how the company might not know itself as it should, which will likely be the basis for some of the forthcoming recommendations.

I present Findings and Conclusions in various graphical manners depending upon the client. Some like it stripped down with very few graphics, no photos, with only their PowerPoint brand guidelines as a border and a logo at the lower left or right. Others prefer the full pizzazz and believe that the more it's designed, the more professional it might appear, which, of course, is total bullshit. In many cases, after the presentation, I am asked to prepare a board of directors deck that is generally no more than ten slides. My estimates almost always include this iteration.

Depending on the client and the project's scope, I will use either pie charts or bar graphs to illustrate the hierarchy of the answers, but I prefer the stripped-down method where all I really present is a list of the responses in order of their popularity with the number of those answers in parentheses. Invariably, a rookie will always point out very proudly that the total responses do not add up to 100 percent. Of course, I point out very proudly that this is qualitative research, not quantitative, and that multiple respondents will provide multiple answers to one question. From that point forward, I rarely hear from the rookie again.

In this same section, I frequently provide annotations as a sidebar to the findings. I can't begin to tell you how appreciative my clients are for this strategic maneuver, and truthfully, it's a reminder to me to discuss some of the deeper meanings of the results while reducing the amount of interruptions in my presentation, which are frequent, but also welcomed. These annotations, or running insights, take a quick look at some of the more hidden, or not so obvious, conclusions we can surmise from the results on that particular page. Here are some fairly typical annotation examples:

- This probably tells us we need to talk to our customers more often and in different ways from how we're communicating presently.

- These are very definitive information requests for an industry we previously thought we couldn't sell directly into.

- Our internal focus seems to be less product-centric; perhaps we're more fearful of the inner workings of our products than our customers are.

- Internally, we think in terms of what the product is and does; externally, they think in terms of what the product achieves. This is a significant differentiator between what our messaging needs to be versus our competitor's messaging, and how we think about messaging internally today, and how it needs to change tomorrow.

- Here it is again. It's always the product's fault; that's our standard default excuse, but customers don't see it that way.

- This shows the lack of alignment more than any other question. We're not aligned internally with what the customer thinks, or with one another (ten different answers and only one was repeated).

I strongly suggest you capitalize on this method as it adds enormous value to the VOC project and I have never seen this technique used in projects from other consultants. After you have completed the Findings and Conclusions section, you can go in many different directions, but the path you select will be determined by the scope of the project and your SOW. You might choose to stick only with branding scenarios if that's the overall intent of the VOC, or if your SOW includes sales and marketing recommendations, initial messaging taxonomy, or creative concepts, this is the time to include your thoughts and examples in your deck. In the case of VOC that is exclusively focused on thought leadership, you have some decisions to make, but again, these decisions will be based on the scope of work and how inclusive the estimate was for your services.

If your efforts include the whole ball of wax, you will need to present the critical insights you developed—which will be discussed in the next chapter—and you will also be required to explain how the new thought leadership messaging will read. This will also include your level 1, level 2, and level 3 narrative pitch flows, but I do not include the full scope of the statistical and factual proof points, or the emotional proof points, as I'm never quite sure there's been a complete verification of the proof points at this stage in the project.

There are instances when I prepare the messaging and the critical insights as a separate document since these are more applicable to sales and marketing than the other top leadership positions. Whatever the case, those become separate meetings, usually workshops and training sessions, including further role-playing, when I teach Critical Insight Selling with a deeper analysis into the insights themselves.

After the presentation of the deck, I'll have a postmortem conference with the one sponsor of the project to assess the attitudes, acceptance, and sentiments of the last four hours. In this meeting, we will always address next steps, if there are any, and what those next steps might look like. If I'm relatively psyched about the company, there might be some recommendations I'd be interested in implementing. If I'm a bit cool toward the business, the industry, the people, and I'm not sensing a good fit, I'll mention that to the client. There's no harm or foul in this; it's an honest assessment and it's always appreciated. Again, you know the honesty drill by now.

Of course there is always one last step. Upon my return, I write thank-you cards to everyone who attended the four-hour session. Not an email, a text, or an IM. And each card I handwrite, although virtually indecipherable, is completely different from the next, even if there were ten people in the meeting. I don't feel like I've successfully completed the VOC project until my fingers hurt and the side of my left hand is covered in ink, one of the curses of being left-handed.

This is how you conduct VOC in its most traditional and effective manner. The critical insights you develop will become the centerpiece of the sales component of your thought leadership discipline. There's no other way to approach this. As an added bonus to this type of VOC process, you will discover what your customers want you to research and write about, not what the company wants to send their customers, which is one of the biggest and most common mistakes in content marketing. You will also know how to deliver content to your customers, in what formats, the frequency, and what's pissing them off about the content they're inundated with from your competitors. Not too shabby.

Not only are you officially a thought leader, but you also have the green light to start chilling with other thought leaders as you increase your circle of influence by working together across multiple industries and sharing insights and content that are helpful to all. Always remember, *nothing moves people like people,* and the greater your sphere of influence, the more influential you'll become both as a thought leader and as a company promoting its thought leadership discipline. As Peter Drucker once confided in a manager, "I'm more interested in people than I am in how businesses work."[2] That's because businesses don't work without people and won't work nearly as well without thought leaders.

8

HOW TO DEVELOP CRITICAL INSIGHTS

There were, and still are, many benefits to attending the Claremont Colleges in Claremont, California. That is, if you can even get into the place. Back in the seventies when I attended, the admission standards were obviously far less restrictive. The campus is California beautiful, and if you want, you can ski in the morning on Mt. Baldy and swim or play golf in the afternoon.

You can also attend classes, if you want.

It's much like the famed University of Oxford in England. At Claremont, the colleges are independent and self-governing, they share a delightful campus, and the facilities and classrooms are relatively co-mingled. You can take classes at all of the colleges; in fact, it's encouraged. The Claremont Colleges are comprised of Pomona College, where the alumni broil at the distinction of being the "Harvard of the West" and prefer their own not so nuanced distinction that "Harvard is the Pomona of the East"; Scripps College, which is a distinguished liberal arts school for women and a top producer of Fulbright Scholars; Pitzer College, known for an unwavering commitment to the instruction of social justice, and for one of its graduates, Matt Nathanson, who is a contemporary singer/songwriter of enormous talent; Claremont McKenna College, which boasts as alumni George Roberts *and* Henry Kravis of Kohlberg Kravis Roberts & Co. private equity fame; Harvey Mudd, one of the top engineering and science-focused schools in the country; and Claremont Graduate University, home to, you guessed it, the (Peter) Drucker School of Management.

After my dad, Drucker remains one of my business heroes, and like many students on campus, I had the pleasure of attending some of his lectures. Actually, they were more like events, as everyone wanted a piece of the master (not the guru, since Drucker hated that word and famously remarked, "I have been saying for many years that we have been using the word 'guru' only because 'charlatan' was too long to fit into a headline"). In my estimation, there is no single person who has had a greater influence on business, and the management of it, worldwide than Peter Drucker. In fact, his timeless book *Management: Tasks, Responsibilities, Practices*, first published in 1974, remains today one of the best business books ever written. Drucker's principles and astounding intellect have withstood the test of time more than any other business book. "Management is doing things right," Drucker said, "leadership is doing the right things." That's my man, pinpointing the exact attributes of thought leadership— "doing the right things," which can happen only through honesty, wisdom, and ethics. One aspect of "doing the right things" when you're a thought leader is having a handful of critical insights in your hip pocket that you can effortlessly recite as a validation of your thought leadership without boasting about it, of course. Having the ability to recite those insights at will is something we'll discuss shortly, and you'll need that capability when you find yourself at a trade show, seminar, in an interview, or when you're called to a podium when you least expect it, which happens when you're a thought leader.

We'll get back to Drucker in short order, but doing it right includes learning how to develop critical insights the right way. There aren't many of us around who do this, but that's mostly because there aren't many of us around who do VOC the traditional way, which is the most effective way. And since you can't develop critical insights without VOC, it places companies in a bit of a pickle, unless you read this chapter, the previous chapter, and avoid retreating into the darkness. That won't be necessary as my intention is to shed some light on the entire critical insight development process.

I define critical insights as an expertise you have in educating your industry about trends, challenges, new opinions and viewpoints, embryonic thoughts, new and original discoveries, critical thinking that hasn't yet been critical, and entirely out-of-the-box reasoning that causes people to stop in their tracks and wonder. They don't need to be 100 percent original in every aspect of their structure and texture, but they better be damn close. To do that you'll need to conduct a comprehensive search to make certain you're on to something unique; the last headache you'll need is to be headstrong on your insistence that a particular thought is original when it might not be. As my mother frequently said, "Let's search the Google."

Critical insights will be the wisdom you create that sells and proves your thought leadership position. Approximately every fourteen months, you'll need to add new critical insights to your repertoire. This should give you plenty of time to produce the subsequent batches of insights needed for the next phases (you should be able to develop the first five insights, start to finish, including VOC, in about six to seven months). Considering that it will take about four months to produce five new insights, the second round of development will commence around the ten- to eleven-month mark in your thought leadership campaign. Because the majority of critical insights are developed through VOC, you'll need to schedule a new VOC research project for the next inventory of critical insights, but I've found that round two can be as simple as focusing only on insight development and content wishes from your customers; you will not need to participate in a complete research reset that analyzes company strengths, weaknesses, brand authenticity, and the like. So, an insight development schedule might look like this:

- **First Set of Critical Insights:** This includes all the up-front work of hiring a consultant, assessing your chosen discipline of market leadership, conducting VOC, developing critical insights, implementing a thought leadership campaign into your organization, and writing the introductory content assets for launch: **This will take six to seven months**.

- **Second Set of Critical Insights:** Begin phase two of your VOC for development of new insights approximately ten months after the first set was developed. You should then have your second set of insights available for Critical Insight Selling four months later: **This will then be year two of your campaign**.

- **Third Set of Critical Insights:** Follow the same timetable to transition to year three. Begin developing the third set of insights ten months after the second set: **This will require four months of work and you'll be ready for year three**.

Continue with this protocol for as long as you wish, but remember, it's okay to recirculate your first-year insights, assuming they're still applicable in subsequent years. This can extend the life of your insights and double their tenure. Do not directly copy the repeated insights, but update and refine them to keep them fresh.

I have also found that you might be able to develop one or two new critical insights from your first round of VOC that did not make the final cut. My guess is some of the initial insights that were not used may have morphed into something more relevant during the last year or two. Also never discount the notion that you'll stumble upon insights during a trade show conversation, a road show, some one-on-one interviews, a discussion with a thought leader or industry influencer, or when you're least expecting it, perhaps even from a colleague in the field.

The point is, rounds two, three, and beyond always seem a lot easier in the development of insights than round one. If you pass through round two, for instance, you'll have your feet firmly planted on the thought leadership pedestal as you'll be going on three years deep into the beauty, splendor, and achievement of thought leadership.

PROBING FOR YOUR CRITICAL INSIGHTS

My suggestion is to always create five critical insights. You do not need to wait until all five insights are developed before you can launch your thought leadership campaign. You should have three critical insights developed and a solid idea of what the other two might be. You'll probably choose to distribute and syndicate the insights to your industry audience one insight every sixty days, but this will occur only after the insights are privately shared with your prospects during the sales phase of Critical Insight Selling. In other words, work the room first with your sales efforts before making any of the insights public. The sales aspect of this will be covered in the next chapter, but let's continue to focus on developing the insights.

If you take a closer look at the VOC questions in the last chapter, particularly those relating to critical insight development, you will see a total of more than twenty different questions that will help you develop the insights. You might have more, or even less, and, of course, you'll need to craft these questions to be more specific about a particular industry, but here are mine that should get you started:

- In the selection process for technology partners, what type of information proves to be valuable, and what information would you like to have, but few, if any, provide? *Probe for specific examples and ask what types of information competitors might be providing that are actually really useful.*

- Conversely, is there information that is provided that you find to be ineffective? *Probe for what's most annoying.*

- If you could choose three distinct topics that we should research and write about that would keep you better informed, what three topics would be of interest to you? *Probe to get many more; this is the beginning of how you formulate your critical insights for Critical Insight Selling.*

- On a scale of one to ten with ten being very valuable, just how much value would you place on this research?

- If it would be valuable, in what types of ways would you use this research? For instance, would you share it with others both inside and outside your company and industry?

- In what format would you like to receive that information? Would you be interested in longer format white papers that are very in-depth, shorter articles about your topics of interest, blog posts, videos, e-books, or some other type of format?

- And how often would you like to receive that information? *Probe to find out if there are others in the company or industry that would find this information valuable and who they might be along with their job functions.*

- If I asked you to define the following (insert some aspect of the industry that is known to everyone, like an ecosystem, a trend, or a characteristic that might be waning or emerging), how would you explain it? *Probe; if there's confusion about defining this aspect or characteristic, this has the makings of a critical insight.*

- If someone approached you and asked what the three most significant problems in the industry are, what would your response be? *Probe each answer thoroughly; there might be an insight hiding there.*

- If a financial analyst who was incredibly prominent in the industry asked you the same question, what would your response be?

- If a CEO of a Fortune 500 company who was taking a leadership position in the industry and was considering you for a top-level job asked you the same question, but you knew she was a stickler for telling the truth, how would you answer the same question?

- If she came back and asked you again, sensing that your answer might be fairly benign and not "deep" enough, what would your next answer be?

- If there was one thing you could change today in the entire (name the industry), what would that be? *Probe because this can be just about anything as long as it's industry-centric. This is leaning into the development of critical insights.*

- Let's say magically that change occurred. After that, what would be the next thing you would change?

- And finally, one more change.

- Now, if money were no object, and I know full well that it always is, verbally create for me the most perfect, the most idyllic industry company that you could ever imagine. Paint this picture for me. *Probe for more detail on all of these.*

- Similarly, paint me a picture, a persona if you will, of the perfect CEO.

- And now a persona of the perfect customer.

- And now the perfect CMO. *You can keep probing by position type depending on the industry.*

- What is it about your job that you really like?

- And one other thing.

- Now tell me what you dislike about your job and some ways that it could change for the better. *Probe further because this can frequently provide insights that might become critical.*

- And one last question. Is there anything you'd like to "get off your chest?" Remember, all answers are completely confidential and all I do is group the answers together; no names are attached.

DEVELOPING YOUR CRITICAL INSIGHTS

Previously, I bemoaned the LinkedIn profiles that state that an individual is a *connector of dots*. It was tongue in cheek, until now. This is the point in time when you'll be connecting the dots when there are no dots to connect. This is borderline thought leader heroics, where the wheat is separated from the chaff, the corn from the stalk, and the peas from the pods. I can assure you that once your first set of five critical insights are developed, you're home free, it's clear sailing, and the tough stuff is in the rearview mirror. But during the insight development stage, you'll really need to make your brain hurt, and you will need to tap into your incredible research skills.

Remember, we are looking for insights into your industry, not necessarily insights into your products, services, or even your company. To some extent, that might come later when we'll align the insights with your company brand, or your personal brand, in the next development stage.

There will be two primary uses for these insights. The first is internal and the second will be external. The internal usage is strictly for business development, to schedule appointments, nurture leads, and close the deal. Approximately six or seven months later, or when your sales and marketing departments believe they have exhausted some or most of the insights as the catalyst for profitable sales transactions, the second external use kicks in. But be advised: If you're in an industry where the sales cycle is long, or relationship building takes more time than usual, you'll probably want to use the first batch of insights for up to a year until you make them public. Fair warning, the moment you inform the world about these insights, their use as a sales development resource is over, they're toasted and roasted like a campfire marshmallow, and there's no going back. Do not act too early to implement the external part of this campaign.

The second use of critical insights is to demonstrate your thought leadership discipline to the public, or, more befittingly, to your industry's buyer segments. This is the content marketing component of your campaign, although this differs substantially from what content marketing is today. Before we begin to explore the processes of developing critical insights, let me shed a bit more light on this.

Content marketing, which we know in its original context is almost 200 years old, was created to inform, educate, and keep the lines of communication transparent between a business and a customer. It was intended to be a subtle bridge between awareness and influence. For me, since practicing content marketing for the last several decades, it has been the bedrock of my theory that *the more people interact, the more they'll transact.* It was never intended to be *the more people are told to transact, the more a company can extract.* But that's what content marketing became, just another arrow in the quiver of Genghis Khan, or perhaps it should be *con.* That's where we are today in our endless pursuit of financial gain at the cost of long-term customer relationships. Like most everything else, content marketing has become a blatant money grab thinly veiled as an educational resource. That's not how the external part of thought leadership works when syndicating and distributing your content. Anyone with a keen eye for this stuff will stuff this down your bullhorn and "out" you for not being a thought leader. You must resist the temptation to outwardly sell. You should always refrain from pushing the goods before you've even pushed your wisdom. And you must certainly keep in check any tendency—particularly in your thought leadership writings and discussions—to talk too much about yourself, your company, your product's features and benefits, and all your wonderful solutions that will solve the problems of the universe and bring world peace to humankind.

Playing it straight in content marketing is the right thing to do. This is, in effect, "doing the right things." Don't promote your precious critical insights as if they were a BOGO coupon. Share them as an instruction manual to steer the trust train, contribute them to show you know the ins and outs of the industry without asking for anything in return, and treat them as a gift without strings attached. It's the opposite of *if you scratch my back, I'll scratch yours.* Leave the scratching for your next mosquito bite. Just be honest and truthful. And, yes, be ethical and cause-centric, and don't let money get in the way. Your payday will come with patience, and when it's time to collect the dividends, they'll be larger, more meaningful, and longer lasting than a quick sales fix that might not even deliver. Think of it as *an annuity with a helluva lot of gratuity.* Perhaps in the turf of private equity, speed is all that matters, and that flipping companies should have a private equity motto all its own; mine is "Like sands through the hourglass, so are the days of our flipping lives." We know this to be true and it's part of the game, a game where the rules are streamlined to sink our teeth more quickly into the bottom line. It's understandable and I appreciate it—hell, I've worked in private equity for years. But thought leadership and private equity are like fire and ice, and rarely do the two dance well together. The only result, of course, would be liquid, and not the type of liquid that your balance sheet can brag about.

I can't tell you what your critical insights will be. They are too depen-dent on your industry, the current environment, your VOC method and results, and the trends that are occurring, or are about to occur. But I can provide you with examples of some insights I've developed for a few clients along the way. Rest assured, these insights have long been in the public domain, they've seen the light of day, internally and externally, and they've been used to schedule appointments, develop business, and replace content marketing with content that builds long-lasting relationships and fosters trust and solid corporate ethics.

SunGard K-12: Critical Insights That Educated Educators

SunGard K-12 was a company headquartered in Allentown, Pennsylvania, formerly owned by FIS Global, a multibillion-dollar conglomerate that reaches most parts of the world. When I think of Allentown, it's impossible for me to not think about the Billy Joel song. It's not so much about the city, or its largest employer, Bethlehem Steel, as it is about a state of mind, a fierce fight to not give up, and not letting someone stand in the way as times change in just about every direction you can imagine. I particularly like how the song begins with a steam whistle; it's symbolic of hard work, of a tough-as-nails attitude, and, in a metaphysical way, it is a reminder of how we begin our day. SunGard was acquired by PowerSchool, which is owned by the private equity firm Vista Equity Partners. PowerSchool is headquartered in Folsom, California, which, strangely enough, is the home to another famous song, Johnny Cash's "Folsom Prison Blues" in which Cash imagined that one day he'd be far from prison listening to a train whistle carrying his blues away.

Two towns, two whistles, and a lifetime of sales and marketing lessons to learn.

SunGard was not a thought leader. They became a thought leader because they needed a competitive edge in the noisy world of student information systems, referred to in the trade as SIS. There were statewide and endorsed SIS companies, regional players, and national players, all wanting a piece of a pie that was getting harder to slice by the year. Being a thought leader was SunGard's only valid market leadership discipline to embrace. Price-chopping wasn't going to fund the research and development investments to keep a software provider afloat. Customer service wasn't a differentiator, and technology and innovation were table stakes in the endless pursuit of who had the most toys to hawk each year. We went after thought leadership and went after it hard.

It was a smooth move.

The critical insights we developed were bold, spirited, and flashy. Here's a higher level overview of a few of these insights with a bit of explanation about them. But not too much explanation as that would distract from the particular power of each insight, and what might run through your mind when you read each of them at first blush. Here are three critical insights that we developed for SunGard over the course of several years of research:

Critical Insight One: How technology can increase superintendent tenure. At the time, this was revolutionary and still is many years later. To provide insights and research that show school boards, administrators, and various other decision-makers how a software solution can increase the tenure of a school district superintendent is like telling a restaurant owner that enterprise resource planning will run your organization more efficiently, and oh, by the way, it will make all your food taste better. It's a compellingly disparate proposition that they've never heard before—or ever imagined could even exist. In the trade, we call it a "door slider," a proposal so powerful you can slide it under their office door and walk away. *As you can see, this is what it means to connect the dots when there are no dots to connect.*

With school district superintendents bouncing around like Slinkys on a staircase, and the exorbitant fees for professional searchers to find their replacements, not to mention the costs of ramping up, training, and public discussions, and the risk of bad hires, this insight grabbed the attention of the most influential stakeholders faster than a World War II veteran returning home to the arms of his bride. It was emotional, differentiating, forceful, and 100 percent original.

Critical Insight Two: When you think about it, K-12 education is run by a clock, not necessarily by any particular student need. This is actually true and was a predominant conviction expressed by VOC respondents in the questions about being able to change one thing in education, and one thing only. On the surface, this doesn't sound like a salable insight—how this might benefit a software company, or why this would be part of a pitch that ultimately includes an ask for a multimillion-dollar, long-term commitment and investment by an entire community. If you're thinking about this insight in that manner, you are absolutely correct. However, if you suspect that there's more at play here, you're also on the money.

In the first instance of this insight, the fact that the dots aren't initially connecting is fine. The worst-case scenario is SunGard is not selling here, the company is listening, and that's what SunGard as a thought leader does extremely well—listening intently before actively selling. *We're sharing our insights that we've developed from our own research investments, insights that we'll continue to share with you in our relationship going forward.* It shows the SunGard commitment to thought leadership, to putting wisdom ahead of wealth (although only temporarily), and it illustrates how the company approaches solutions, not just by tackling the matters at hand like managing meal plans, the reporting of grades, and teacher recruitment, but also how SunGard thinks about other more complex challenges the industry is beginning to encounter that will grow worse over time.

Is this relatively benign and a tad bit ethereal for some? I think it is, but not when layered on top of other matters at play.

The true value of this insight, and the second part of it, is that it aligns perfectly with what we were trying to sell and how the software suite of solutions can actually alter the outlook of most decision-makers on what will be important in the future. If K-12 education is run by a timepiece, that is to say by periods and classes in certain incremental cycles, over various days and weeks, governed by semesters with start and end dates, then how do we address an alternative, even if it's years beyond our grasp? This is not selling by product road maps, it's selling by road maps of wisdom that generally elicit responses like, "We're really fortunate someone is looking at solving problems beyond the immediate, and even the foreseeable future, while at the same time looking out for our best interests five and even ten years from now. We're recognizing that middle and grade school students will have needs entirely different from our current high school students." At the time, and this was a decade ago, it was revolutionary stuff, and it was a winning insight that became a winning sales strategy. It was an understanding that while others were selling solutions that addressed immediate problems, SunGard was selling solutions that addressed all possible problems, even those in education's crystal ball, which included adding flexibility to scheduling and time periods that might become relevant in the distant future.

The key to these insights was that the pitch wasn't trying to deliver on a promise that could have been overdelivered. It didn't need to be. Layered on top of our long-term insight-sharing was our thought leadership approach to sales that showed how insights can create a revenue pop and still be steadfast in creating trust, honesty, ethics, and a heavy dose of shared knowledge and wisdom. This should be a reminder that you don't need to mortgage tomorrow's future on a quick sale today, and there's no guarantee that the quick sale will even materialize. Let the insights do the selling. Again, you're hawking wisdom, nothing else, and your swag is knowledge, and that gives you thought leadership swagger. When you try it, there's no feeling like it.

The third insight I'd like to share with you that we developed for SunGard K-12 was a real doozy, as if the two previous insights weren't. You'll be able to tell that this particular critical insight was one of my all-time favorites, and it spread like wildfire across many school districts, and across the country. Not surprisingly, when it was time to syndicate this particular content, the trade magazines went apeshit in an effort to win the story.

Critical Insight Three: School districts can learn a lot about managing their vast amounts of moving parts by taking the time to study how to manage those moving parts as analyzed, measured, and chronicled by Peter Drucker. That's right, we hit them square in the noggin with "doing the right things," managing change, getting down to the basics of effective communication, and changing the thinking of administrators who believed they knew a lot more than they did. As Drucker humbly said, "My greatest strength as a consultant is to be ignorant and ask a few questions."[1] Does this sound vaguely familiar? Remember, it was Socrates who said, "True knowledge exists in knowing you know nothing."

Here is an excerpt from that insight:

In 1959, Peter Drucker forecasted the rise of what he called the "knowledge worker" and the "knowledge economy." Later he wrote, "Education will become the center of the knowledge society, and the school its key institution." Drucker died in 2005, after a long and influential career as an author, professor, and consultant for major corporations and nonprofit organizations. A great many of his ideas about management should resonate with K-12 leaders, such as how important it is to continually examine whether your district's daily operations are actually tied to its top priorities. As Drucker put it,

"There is surely nothing quite so useless as doing with great efficiency what should not be done at all."[2]

If you think this isn't a hard-hitting sales proposition, please read the last Drucker quote one more time: "There is surely nothing quite so useless as doing with great efficiency what should not be done at all." In a nutshell, this was exactly what the SIS solutions were doing for school districts, at least at the time. Piling on more features on top of more features—some as useless as the next—just like a deep-dish pan of lasagna, which doesn't necessarily make it better, but it does make it robust; this is a favorite descriptor in the software trade. That was the perfect sales notion to put in motion. You're not a better whistler with more bells and whistles; you just have a greater load to carry. Be smarter, leaner, more visionary, and more thoughtful.

And I know right now you're thinking about introspection and self-examination. My guess is you saw that before I did; that's because you're a thought leader and have a full understanding that the unexamined life, introduced to us by Socrates, needs to be applied to any organization and to all leaders within those organizations. As you can see, the dots are connecting, but in ways that will drive revenue, incremental sales, and long-lasting relationships. As we discovered, no one in this technology sector had ever connected K-12 education with Peter Drucker, even though it was right in front of us all along. But when the connection was made, and then turned into an insight for selling, it was a bonanza of unfathomable results.

ArbiterSports: Critical Insights Hit the Playing Field

Let's return to the technology company ArbiterSports in Salt Lake City. Using the same series of approximately twenty VOC questions previously listed, plus additional research, here are three of the five critical insights we developed for Arbiter:

Critical Insight One: With Arbiter products, student-athletes can become better students and better athletes. We give you back as much as two hours every day to spend how you need to.

Athletic directors on a school and district level tell us the administrative demands of the job prevent them from spending more time with students, more time with coaches, and more time on the field. If they could just have an extra hour or two away from their computer and be closer to students, they could make a difference in the lives of student-athletes. Arbiter products can give them that extra two hours, and with that time they can—

- Be the teachers and leaders they've spent their lives training to be

- Work with coaches to be transformational rather than just transactional

- Implement more professional development programs and resources for coaches, which will impact their students

- Have more time to focus on sportsmanship at every level, a lack of which is a root cause of many high school sports problems today

As you can see, the "hook" is being able to give back time to the people who need it the most so they can solve problems that need the most attention. Even with this first example, it's easy to tell how the insight aligns with the brand, how there is a very real sales component, and how we're avoiding, at all costs, any reference to particular product features and benefits. Now, on to the next insight:

Critical Insight Two: A concern throughout the country is the mounting shortages of quality officials and referees. Arbiter is the best technology solution to alleviate this ongoing and growing challenge.

Alleviating just the official problem results in peace of mind for athletic directors and administrators.

A common refrain among athletic directors and administrators is the growing concern of finding referees. In fact, in some parts of the country, it's getting so fraught that there's a common narrative: no referees, no sports; no sports, no athletics; no athletics, no athletic directors. Arbiter can reverse that narrative.

More than 210,000 officials are currently using Arbiter; this illustrates that there's such a high demand for loyalty that many referees won't even officiate games unless they are scheduled through Arbiter. Where Arbiter goes, officials will follow. And that will both alleviate the referee shortage and provide more time for making student-athletes better students and better athletes.

In this insight, we are speaking to an enormous problem that school officials need to change—the shortage of referees in high school sports. Arbiter contends that they can solve that problem. Their proposition isn't to use a particular software set, but to highlight what's bothering people, what they feel needs to change, and how the problem can be resolved. Here's another insight that was very telling for many administrators:

Critical Insight Three: Sportsmanship and bad behavior directly correlate to the lack of officials, with many saying it's just not worth it anymore. For athletic directors, district athletic directors, and administrators who can resolve this issue, it will be career-changing and lead to greater opportunities, increased recognition, and longer tenure, if desired. By using Arbiter, career paths accelerate, greater recognition can be forthcoming, and more opportunities present themselves.

The sportsmanship and parent behavior problem is not exclusive; it's problematic in every state, school district, and school. Resolving it takes time and patience. But it can be done. And when it is, most concur that it will be a career-changing event. Arbiter will free up the time needed to tackle this challenge. Arbiter can also provide thought leadership and insights into this issue through research and expert advice from professionals.

By having a resource that offers as close to an end-to-end technology solution as possible, all in one place for high school sports and event management, along with thought leadership research and content that is free to you, Arbiter is the only company that can provide the ability to technologically problem-solve the challenges of sportsmanship, which in turn can be career-changing.

It's important to remember that developing your insights is not exclusively a result of your VOC efforts, although a good part of it will be. You'll need to conduct further research to make certain your insights are original and to see how they might need to be segmented and revised depending on your buyer personas. In these three cases for ArbiterSports, we have introduced our first insight that can enable students and student-athletes to be more proficient while at the same time giving administrators more time in a day to make that aspiration actually happen. In that particular industry, no one had ever spoken about freeing up more time for administrators to dig themselves out of a hole that had buried them in bureaucratic phooey. The pitch isn't "buy this software," but it's "buy yourself some time."

Layered on top of that is the second insight that offers peace of mind. Now, not only are we offering more time in the day, but we're also offering a better day. There's no babble about technical requirements, implementation, ease of use, and the usual technology rigmarole. And as personal as this sounds, and it's certainly meant to be personal, the third insight gnaws at what is most compelling to athletic directors—and it's not just the problems that bad sportsmanship have created, but it's also the ability to resolve the issues of bad sportsmanship, which can lead to more career opportunities. As you can see, you don't need a blatant sales pitch within your critical insights, but it's certainly present.

M3 Insurance: Risk-Free Critical Insights That Sell

Our corporate headquarters is in Madison, Wisconsin, a town that's a perennial squatter on just about every best-place-to-live list in the United States. It's not a pay-for-the-listing type of thing; Madison is the real deal, and I can't imagine a better place to call home if you can handle the cold weather that blankets the area for about five months a year. The older I got, the more difficult it became, but I endured a helluva long time because it is, quite simply, a smorgasbord of everything anyone could ask for. Great food and music, wonderful people, a topflight university, a healthcare and tech center, a capital city, low unemployment, recreation options galore, a platinum-designated American biking city, more walkability than a fifty-kilometer Olympic race walk, and the best farmer's market in North America. It's also a city that sits on an isthmus, sandwiched on a spit of land between Lake Monona and Lake Mendota with the Yahara River connecting the two. Not too far from our offices, with a breathtaking view of Lake Monona, sits a terrific insurance company that I've had the pleasure of working with for many years. They call it M3 Insurance, and thankfully they condensed their name from its original birth handle of Mortenson, Matzelle & Meldrum. I'm sky-high on these guys because they're sky-high on their customers. I think they're customer service leaders, probably technology and innovation leaders, but, most importantly, thought leaders.

M3 is one of the largest privately held and independent insurance companies in the country. They're pretty big, but they don't feel big. They feel caring, understanding of the life of quality that Socrates, Plato, and

Aristotle taught us to pursue, and they are committed to "doing the right things" as Drucker mentioned. Quite a few years ago, they embarked on finding the right disciplines of market leadership. Without knowing it, I moved them in the direction of thought leadership because it was obvious they were a torchbearer. It was even more obvious after they reviewed the results of a large-scale VOC project.

Many of these insights will seem almost commonplace today, but sixteen and seventeen years ago, long before personalization and customization became the hallmarks of effective sales and marketing, these critical insights paved the way for a company restructuring, not to mention an effective business development strategy. Here are three insights that illustrate the forward-thinking culture of M3:

Critical Insight One: The entire *knowledge is power* axiom is getting corny, overused, and overworked. We are changing that because you really don't possess knowledge unless you know your client's industry and their business principles. Most insurance companies wear whatever hat is necessary to win the business. We're going to divide our business into practice groups so we can know an industry and therefore know a client. Our hats won't be interchangeable.

After that, quite a few professional service corporations began implementing practice group structures, but M3 was a pioneer. For many years, even those companies that restructured to practice groups were cosmetic in nature. They weren't really experts in specific industries and tried to serve up their expertise by joining trade associations and displaying at local and regional industry-specific shows that doubled in brass as networking events. At M3, they positioned themselves as thought leaders within thought leadership segments by hiring experts in each industry, by developing research and sharing it, and by being very transparent—long before many other companies—that their initial knowledge was in construction and real estate, education and government, manufacturing and distribution, transportation, and senior living and social services. And for each one of those practice groups, there were level 1, level 2, and level 3 narrative pitch flows with factual and emotional proof points all along the way. So, there were a minimum of fifteen pitch flows working concurrently within the company and dozens of proof points to support the practice group structure all within this single critical insight.

Insight One was aligned with a Critical Insight Selling sales proposition that addressed three primary needs that were revealed in the VOC. The first was the need for a structure that supported thought leadership and industry-specific knowledge, which was a proposition, and ultimately a discipline, that customers (and assumably prospects) were clamoring for. The second was to highlight the relevant differentiation between M3 and their competitors who either wore many hats across dozens of industries and pulled their industry expertise hat from the costume box when it was the appropriate time to don it, or to have subtly exposed insurance companies who claimed to have a practice group structure only to discover that it was in name only. And third, the actual practice group structure allowed M3, and companies like them, to implement other disciplines more easily, if they chose to do so, within a particular practice group rather than, say, an entire organization, which would be incredibly cumbersome.

Critical Insight Two: Our research is conclusive that customers of insurance companies want insights, and this is what they're saying: "If you're not delivering meaningful, industry-specific insights to us all the time, well, you're just not delivering." In other words, what our customers are telling us is that we better become a thought leader, and deliver on that discipline, or else.

As I mentioned previously, it did not seem to me that M3 was necessarily looking for a thought leadership position as much as they were searching for the best discipline to match their culture, their examined life (they had quite a bit of previous customer perception and satisfaction research), and their sales requirements. But like the consultant who borrows your watch to tell the time, the correct discipline to embrace was right in front of them, wrapped around their wrist like the most beautiful bracelet imaginable. It just needed a VOC element for validation, and a write-up on how to proceed. From a sales perspective, their second insight was money. It was astoundingly simple to demonstrate their leadership proof points with exceptional content that ran the gamut from narratives and e-books to webinars and videos. And because they were structured into practice groups, they weren't wasting their customers' time with content assets that were important to a transportation company, but useless to the owner of a senior living facility.

Critical Insight Three: It is clear from our research that nothing is more relevant than the relevancy of risk. Our customers believe that insurance brokers who are sitting in an office all day long are riskier risk advisors than those who are working in the industry, and spending time in the field. That's because risk is so relevant and all-consuming that the best way to manage it is to be in the center of where the risk might be.

If we look closely enough, we can see these critical insights work together in layers to be formidable statements and Critical Insight Selling approaches. A practice group insight is the catalyst for being able to offer industry-specific knowledge in much the same way WEA Trust was able to offer insights exclusively to municipalities. It's also the entryway to a thought leadership campaign that makes it easier for a company to provide a discipline, and its supporting messages, to an audience segment that's most interested in learning and buying.

The second insight builds on that structure by proving the thought leadership discipline is supported by research that verifies that the buyer segments want the insights, and consequently will be open to sustaining the relationship as long as the insights are regularly delivered. And the third insight solidifies the thought leadership discipline by claiming that M3 employees aren't whiling away the hours in their office pretending to be risk experts, but they're actually placing themselves in the epicenter of risk. The metaphor is, of course, that you won't be a thought leader unless you're getting your hands dirty in the industry you claim to actually be a thought leader in.

NOT ALL CRITICAL INSIGHTS SHOULD BE SIMILAR IN THEIR COMPOSITION AND STRUCTURE

You've probably noticed that the composition of the critical insights that were developed for SunGard K-12, ArbiterSports, and M3 Insurance lack similarities in their formats, narratives, sales potency, and even the manner in which they are integrated with other insights. That's purposeful, at least from the consultant's perspective, particularly if you're developing critical insights for various companies across a wide swath of industries.

Don't get hung up on formats. It really doesn't matter. If you're going to get stalled on anything, make certain your critical insights are as original as possible, that they ultimately have a sales component, and that they will lead to curiosity, wonder, and more engagement when presented to your buyer segments. If you're a consultant, one company to the next won't know, or even care, how your critical insights look or are structured, so you shouldn't care either. Be flexible and amenable to the formats that work best for a particular organization. In fact, you might need to rewrite an insight to better align it with a company's mission, or a financial objective, or even a new brand launch. Aristotle said, "Even when laws have been written down, they ought not always remain unaltered." If a law might need to change, then it's entirely possible an insight might need to change, too. Wisdom is not a concept permanently carved into a stone tablet. It's meant to be debated, challenged, and, at times, pushed to the boundaries of Socratic Questioning.

And Aristotle would know. Not just because he learned his craft and refined his philosophies from the teachings of Socrates and Plato, but also because he encouraged a lot of soul-searching in one of the most revered places in Greece, Aristotle's own school known as the Lyceum. The school was named after Apollo the Wolf-God whose images look like a cross between a half-man and a half-beast that you wouldn't want to show an adolescent before bedtime. The site of the Lyceum wasn't discovered until 1996 when excavation began for a new modern art museum in Athens, but it has been reported that Aristotle's school and library were situated in lush gardens and walkways that were conducive to both the pursuit of knowledge and the study of nature and the world around Aristotle's students and disciples.

Aristotle opened the school in 334 BC after returning from a tutoring gig of King Philip II of Macedonia's kid who was probably falling behind in his studies. Later in life, the slacker son would become Alexander the Great, so apparently Aristotle's tutoring skills had some effect on the young man who later became the ruler of one of the largest empires in the history of the world, stretching from Greece to India.

In any event, the Lyceum was an educational refuge for the most promising minds in Greece and is where the Peripatetic school of philosophy took root. There, among nature's most beautiful surroundings, philosophers studied the mysteries of the universe in a collaborative environment that fostered intense discussions, lively debate, and a pursuit of wisdom in much the same way we are discussing your pursuit of thought leadership.

The Lyceum remained in existence long after the death of Aristotle, and was ultimately destroyed by General Sulla of the Roman military in 86 BC, when he waged his assault on Athens. Like the long-term existence of the Lyceum, your thought leadership position can also last a long time, but in your case, there will be no assaults, only the wisdom you have developed that places you far ahead of your competitors.

Now, let's sell that wisdom.

9

EMBRACING THE SALES PROCESS OF CRITICAL INSIGHT SELLING

Your patience is about to be rewarded. Any great sales rep can't wait to start selling regardless if they're equipped to do so or not. So, just a little bit longer and your doorway to a much larger payday is only a few minutes away. There's an adage in life and I subscribe to it: *Sometimes our greatest strength can also be our greatest weakness.* It applies to all of us, but most specifically, it applies to salespeople more than any other professionals I know. That's because good sales reps were born to sell. They want and need the action. It's why, if they're superb, they favor 100 percent commissions above any other form of compensation, and it's also the reason some may fail at the outset, waste a little bit of time, and reflect on the notion—particularly later in their careers—that they should never have abandoned the necessary sales training in favor of hitting the ground running well before they should have.

The best and most efficient types of sales training should never be overlooked, and sales leaders, as well as hard-driving CEOs who don't understand this and seek immediate results, obviously haven't worked with the very best. I have. The very best don't just know how to sell; they also know how to teach. The very best understand that there's a process, that it can take months, if not an entire year, for a sales department to hit their stride and find their groove, and they all realize there will be failures. But they also know that those failures will be limited if the process and the cadence are followed. Like the disciples of Aristotle at the Lyceum, it's important to follow the process of the pursuit of wisdom and learn the art of Critical Insight Selling. After all, Aristotle told us, "Those that know, do. Those that understand, teach."

Critical Insight Selling doesn't necessarily replace other sales strategies and philosophies, but it does provide an overwhelming and compelling sales arc that sets the tone for selling your wisdom before selling much of anything else. You will still need to follow up, and that's a tempo that's set by your sales director. You will still need to work with your marketing team as they schedule trade show dates, road shows, webinars, e-blasts, and whatever tactical flavors of the day are top of mind with them. And you will always need to achieve the goals you sign off on that keep you employed and in the money. But the process and the training of Critical Insight Selling is a learned specialty that requires practice and perfection.

SALES AND MARKETING—WHAT'S THE DIFFERENCE?

I was cut from a different cloth, or, in ancient Greek fashion circles, a different toga. I've never been of the opinion that sales and marketing are anything other than interdisciplinary disciplines. They are joined at the hip and will forever be co-mingled and intersecting. If they are not, and they usually are not, the effectiveness of each is diminished. If you don't sell something, there won't be the money to fund marketing. If you don't understand how to message a product or service, in effect how to market it, there won't be sales reps to move the product. It's the circle of life for business and there's no reason to cut short anyone's life.

Sales should support marketing by doing a better job at listening to the drumbeat in the field—who's doing what, where the competitors are hovering, the places other sales reps are migrating to, what leads are solid and what leads are spoiled—and that drumbeat is never silent. This is fieldwork; it's ears to the ground and nose to the grindstone. This is not a marketing-only function as sales departments believe. Marketing can't know where the transaction action is in a state or a region anywhere near to the extent a salesperson would know this information. It's understandable that there can be finger-pointing; after all, salespeople want to sell, and the up-front legwork is grunt work and it doesn't pay immediate dividends.

Likewise, marketing teams need to better understand the sales process. Generally, they do not. We'd have more efficient marketers if they rode shotgun with a sales rep for a few weeks a year. The cadence of the sales motion has many milestones and flashpoints along the way. Defaulting to the standard marketing fare is not always the answer. Marketers should be required to have an inside view of sales cycles and then design tactics that push those cycles along faster, with more immediate calls to action, and with more clearly defined expectations that are occurring in real time in the market.

The same holds true for ad agencies and marketing consultancies. I said this before, and I'll keep saying it: Ad agencies need to stock their rosters with sales professionals who, like Aristotle said, know how to *do* and understand how to *teach* it. Does it really make sense for an ad agency to advise clients on how to best sell a particular product or service when the account executive or chief strategist doesn't know the basics of selling? Similarly, how can a marketing consultant write a brief without knowing the challenges a sales rep encounters in the field, if competitors are "wedge selling," or if the sales cycles are suddenly turning upside down? You need to understand sales to become a better marketer. And you need to understand marketing to know how to sell better.

That's one aspect of Critical Insight Selling: It forces the two professions to work together. Marketing departments are developing the critical insights and sales departments are selling the insights that were developed. If that doesn't happen, it's like eggs Benedict without hollandaise, a gyro sandwich without tzatziki sauce, or Thanksgiving turkey without your grandmother's gravy. It's just not going to be as tasty as it could be. And maybe a bit dry. So work together, not disparately, and you'll achieve your predetermined goals.

THE CRITICAL INSIGHT SELLING PROCESS

And we're off. I'm going to take you through the Critical Insight Selling process step-by-step, one detail at a time, so you can begin to fulfill your sales objectives—no, wait, not just fulfill, but also surpass your sales objectives so you can capitalize on your new thought leadership discipline. But we need to be disciplined in our efforts and our training. Here's how we sell your wisdom in order to achieve the wealth you desire.

Step One: At this time, we're assuming all five critical insights have been developed. I view step one as the training portion of your familiarity with Critical Insight Selling. If your insights have not been fully developed by your sales or marketing departments, or your consultant managing this project, or a thought leader whom you have employed, you're not ready for the first step. This simply cannot occur until the insights are finalized.

You will need to know, inside and out, each critical insight within the framework of five different parameters. First, you must understand how each was developed. What was the research trail? Did the consultant conduct the VOC, another resource, a combination of several, or was it an approach that differs from the processes I explained in chapter eight? If all five insights were developed using different techniques, then you'll need to know the development process for each one of them. I've found that there's a fifty-fifty chance you'll be asked how your company discovered a particular insight. Rarely is that a question of disbelief or even contempt. It's almost always legitimate curiosity and discovery, and you should treat the question with pride and enthusiasm. I can tell you at the outset that this is a positive buying sign, so know the development procedures top to bottom.

Second, and you'll smirk at this, memorize each insight so you can recite them in your sleep, while you're wide awake, or even during a commercial break when you're watching one of your screens. Every sentence, every word, every insight, and without notes, needs to be committed to memory. When I was on the speaking circuit, I would memorize my sixty-minute speech over and over again for six straight months. I did it with slides and without slides, with a clicker and a stick mic in my hands and hands-free, and I did it with ambient noise and silence. So, five insights should be a breeze for you. Believe me, when you least expect it, you'll need to refer to an insight in your own animated style, and when you do, it'll be a jaw-dropping moment for the person, or people, listening to your wisdom.

Third, if your business is like most others, you'll be talking to vastly different buyer segments, and your marketing department will have already developed the personas within each segment that you've already become more than familiar with. I remember during the course of our ten-year engagement with Foot Locker, there were twenty-three different personas we needed to keep top of mind, and they changed faster than the Tucson weather during monsoon season. So, depending upon who you're talking or pitching to, you might have an alternative version with an added wrinkle or two that helps you further personalize the insight. You will need to have those versions memorized, too. But make certain you've worked through the versioning process, noting all the different variations you have developed for each persona.

Fourth, I want you to record audio and video of the recitation of your five insights, including any nuances for segmentation you've decided to include in your repertoire. When I rehearsed my speeches, I frequently recorded them; in fact, I remember asking a friend in Rockford, Illinois, if he could assemble some people from the local American Advertising Federation chapter, as well as a videographer, to tape my effort. I hated it—from not liking the sound of my voice or my appearance, or my mannerisms that continually reminded me of my father's—and even the way I seemed a bit robotic. However, the value of doing this is immeasurable. I understand that in these practice sessions you're not delivering the insights to an audience of a single person that might occur in a sales presentation, and you might not even be doing it face-to-face anymore, but you'll need to listen to your delivery, make changes to your cadence if a sentence falls flatter than another, and know that the last sentence of your insight must be delivered with the forceful wisdom that it's intended to convey. Do not forgo recording yourself under any circumstances. It's my belief that it can be more difficult to talk to someone one-to-one, or even a few people, than it is to 1,000 people; after all, when you give a speech to a packed audience, you always focus on several unsuspecting individuals in the center of the room, about two-thirds of the way back.

And fifth, this is optional. When you have nothing to do, no soccer games to take the kids to, no work that needs to be completed, a garden that doesn't need tending to, and a movie that doesn't need to be watched, spend a little time on your Socratic Questioning that you learned in chapter four. Punch a few imaginary holes in the insights. I know, they're bulletproof already, but sometimes it's fun to work through the questioning when you're talking to yourself. Do it when you're taking your lunchtime stroll, or your afterwork power walk. If you're old enough, it's like Brylcreem, *a little dab'll do ya.*

Step Two: Now is the time your sales director will ask you to perform the dreaded role-playing booby trap. But it's not dreaded to you because unbeknownst to anyone else, you've already succumbed to the self-inflicted torture of recording yourself by delivering every nuance known to humankind of the five critical insights. I can tell you this: The criticisms I've seen in role-playing exercises in front of your sales peers is as benign as a game of Candy Land with your daughter compared to the critiques I've heard in creative writing classes. Since you're more prepared than a Boy Scout, you'll want to volunteer to go first, and that's the secret to acing these exercises. I repeat, always go first.

Many years ago, after we won the California Avocado Commission account, one of the reasons for our success was our ability to name the position we wanted to pitch in. It started with a request for proposal (RFP) that was sent to sixty-four agencies all with food and agriculture experience. It was winnowed down to thirty-two, but I honestly can't remember how the beheading happened. From there, another sixteen agencies were whacked and then we all convened on a bidder's call for some Q&A. I instructed our team to not say a word on the call, that there would always be more talkers than listeners, and most assuredly, the talkers would more than embarrass themselves. Although my chronology is somewhat off, we were given an assignment to write a one-page overview of why we were uniquely qualified to handle the account. I reminded everyone that this was a test regarding how well we followed instructions. It was as much about limiting our unique narrative to one page as it was about our expertise in general.

I knew that most people would go well beyond a one-page write-up. They just can't help themselves, and every one of those agencies would be trashed because of it. Over time, the agency search consultant narrowed the survivors down to three, set the pitch date for an unreasonable two weeks out, and then the shit hit the fan. Two of the three agencies, both from California, balked at the deadline even though they were only miles away from the Irvine location. The date was changed, but we were ready and had booked our flights and hotel reservations. I asked the team doing the pitching, which did not include me, to wage a formal complaint with the search consultant and the commission. After discussions and an affirmation that we had been screwed, they asked how they could make it right with us. I instructed the team to respond with the request that we pitch first, with plenty of extra time to spare.

Our team went in with avocados blazing, and because they went first, there was no place for the other two agencies to go but down. Our team pitched thought leadership, VOC, critical insights, content marketing that was educational and not a money grab, and they did it with their Wisconsin-nice presence. Imagine awarding an account of that significance to a Wisconsin agency ahead of a California firm. Unimaginable. Part of the reason is we pitched first. And another part of the reason is because I sold 86 percent of the agency to my wife, Kathy, who was the head of our digital division, one of the best in the country.

At that time, women-owned businesses were considered minority-owned businesses. Also at the time, RFPs of that overall weight awarded extra points if the business was woman-owned and I felt we'd probably need the extra points if we were to compete against California-based agencies. And to this day, I still believe if there were more women-owned businesses in the United States, businesses would be better run—less anchored to guff and more attached to goodness—and more balanced in the pursuit of a life of quality. In any event, between the extra RFP points and the lead-off position in the pitch, we used our insights to become knee-deep in the wonderful tastes and aromas of our new superfood, California avocados.

If you're going to suffer through role-playing, go first; it's a winning strategy every time. And if you're a woman, go whenever you wish because you'll show those bros how it's supposed to be done.

Step Three: This is the phase when you start to use your critical insights to sell, but, more specifically, to begin scheduling appointments. This can be done in three different communiqués. One type is not necessarily better than the other, although I have my favorites, so it will be your choice in tandem with the overtones and protocols of your industry. You can use email, leave a voicemail, and wait until you can speak directly to your prospect. Essentially, here's your pitch:

Good afternoon, this is Tom Marks from SunGard K-12, one of the leading cloud-based SIS technology companies serving the needs of school districts across the country. We have just completed our annual research study and I wanted to share two of our five critical insights with you. These are insights that have never been seen, heard, or discovered in the industry. They were developed from a year's worth of research and an untold dollar investment. Please let me know when you can carve out a few minutes for me to share these insights with you. Obviously, I can't share all five, that would be overly generous, but I am willing to share a few. And by the way, the first insight is incredibly revealing; it's how our technology can increase the tenure of administrators, and it's groundbreaking!

What you are doing is teasing your expertise and thought leadership. You may choose to offer one insight, two at the most, but absolutely never three. You'll need to keep these in your hip pocket for a follow-up, lead nurturing, and building trust in the sales process (more on this shortly). Now, I've chosen to write this as a voicemail message, and that's my second preference. I always prefer to speak to a person directly, but that's difficult the first time around. My least favorite way to introduce the selling of critical insights is through an email; that's a better alternative as a follow-up.

In the previous instance, although this is 100 percent hypothetical, I'm imagining this voicemail as a message to the school district's superintendent, a finance VP of a large school district, the technology VP, or the chief people officer. If I had a connection to a school board member, I might leave a message for them, too.

It's difficult to estimate, but my sense is that our clients received a call back about 75 percent of the time using this Critical Insight Selling technique. That's far more effective than cold-calling, or some other selling approach. Certainly, my estimate for return calls is industry specific, and relates definitively to the significance of the critical insights, but by and large, you need to be a bit of a kook if you have no desire to learn more. And assuming your company is well known in the industry, as was the case here, the odds of a call back might even be higher. In the rare instance you don't receive a follow-up call, send an email recap of the message forty-eight hours later.

Assuming you have 100, 200, or even 300 school districts on your prospect list (at last count there were over 13,000 in the United States), you're going to be damn busy for quite a while, in addition to other appointments on your docket, so schedule accordingly.

Step Four: You will continue with this same process using your remaining critical insights as you slowly begin to build the relationship with your prospect. Do not throw in the towel on those who don't respond. Keep leaving a voicemail and send an email follow-up. Because you're a superb sales rep, you'll know when it's time to move on. I never had much patience to begin with, and a lot less the older I became, but if I had 200 or more prospects in my folio, I wouldn't waste too much time with the non-responders. In all likelihood, they might not be a good fit anyway.

Under no circumstances should you ever reveal an additional critical insight to anyone who hasn't responded; it's not deserved and you need to draw a line in the sand. It's time to think like a business owner. If you want to play, you need to pay, and the payment is a meeting. In my playbook, a total of two critical insights is all they should initially receive, but each prospect will be different. For instance, you might need to feed the whale two tunas to grease the barnacles where a smaller prospect might need only one insight to gnaw at the lure. This is your decision, but you'll need to keep track of who is getting what either in Salesforce or another method.

Step Five: In actuality, there isn't really a step five; you keep on keeping on until you're out of gas. The last step is the act of turning all the critical insights back to the marketing team so they can begin to syndicate the insights, talk to the trade press to pitch some exclusive content for their coffers, and start the content marketing machine to show the industry your smarts. And as you advance this knowledge, you *will* pick up some stragglers along the way. Don't be surprised if a few of the non-responders bubble to the surface and appear to have a newfound interest. That's human nature. In the vernacular they don't want to be left at the trough, but clinically, the fact remains, and my clients hear me say ad nauseum, *nothing moves people like people*, and that's an irrefutable marketing fact. And that is what we mean in thought leadership when it's said *the more we know, the more we need to know*. In other words, the taste of the critical insight fruit will only drive your prospects to want more insights and more knowledge from you. And that's another buying sign you can take to the bank.

CEOS DON'T TRUST SALES REPS—THE RESEARCH PROVES IT

Many years ago, I produced a video series for our website titled *Front Lobby Confessionals*, which, not surprisingly, I shot in our front lobby, generally on Sunday mornings when it was quiet and not a distraction. Typically, I would shoot three or four at a time, changing my shirt for each new video, and that way, in one session, I could knock out about two months of content.

Three of my *Front Lobby Confessionals* come to mind when writing about trust, distrust, the sales process, and what the C-suite thinks about salespeople in general. It's not good. Unless you're a thought leader or work for a company that is a thought leader.

The entire dynamic of the research changes in an instant if you're a practitioner of Critical Insight Selling because the findings are that conclusive. There were three research studies I referred to in my video series. None of them are particularly fresh meat, and to some extent that would typically bother me because I don't put much stock in research that's more than a few years old. At the time of this writing, the three research studies I'm going to reference are about five years old, but they're so compelling, the takeaways so striking, and my sense is that the results are locked in a time warp and that it's akin to saying, "Research findings conclude that negative company reviews can impact sales." Yes, that's true, and has been for a long time, and probably not much has changed regarding negative reviews over the last several years. The three research studies I'm going to discuss are from *Harvard Business Review* (*HBR*), not exactly a slouch in business reporting, and their research initiatives;

Edelman, one of the most prestigious global public relations and communications firms you could ever come across; and the RAIN Group, a sales research company, and a great content marketer, with offices across the globe.

Let's begin with the *HBR* and Edelman studies. I prefer to look at these two reports in tandem rather than separately. In that manner, we're better able to take a more global view of how sales personnel are viewed by leadership executives. In the first report, *HBR* researchers determined that only 18 percent of all salespeople are trusted by C-suite executives. These same executives believed that 70 percent of all sales reps were actually *unable* to have a meaningful conversation or dialogue with them about the industry they were representing.[1] Of course, nothing about these two discoveries is particularly encouraging, but at first I wondered what types of reps the study was researching. Upon further examination, the research included only reps in B2B industries, thus eliminating some of the least trusted consumer salespeople we know—car salespeople, used car dealers, "tin men," telemarketers, and other professions. Consequently, the *HBR* findings eliminated all of these types of reps that generally get a bad rap, making the study even more damaging.

So, if you're a sales manager, or sales administrator of some sort with eight sales reps on your team, only one of them would be trusted by a C-suite executive, and two or three members of your team, at the very most, would be able to engage in a meaningful dialogue with an executive. This is terrible news. The odds of your sales professionals being effective are worse than any Vegas odds of any game they try to hook you on, including slot machines (the worst), Wheel of Fortune (almost as bad), and keno (a definite loser).

When viewed in conjunction with the Edelman research,[2] which, by the way, was a massive study of 1,300 C-suite executives, the findings are somewhat more encouraging, but only if you are a thought leader, work for a company that has harnessed the thought leadership position, or have perfected my Critical Insight Selling technique. In the Edelman research, it was determined that company leaders believed that the purchasing funnel—which includes the five milestones of awareness, opinion, consideration, preference, and purchase—was dominated by thought leaders, or thought leadership companies. In addition to this, Edelman's findings called close attention to the fact that 90 percent of the surveyed executives believed that thought leadership in the sales process was either very important or somewhat important, and 81 percent of the executives expressed the opinion that thought leaders were the only type of sales reps who could be trusted. Ouch. According to Edelman, if you have five sales representatives working for you, executives believe that only one of them is trustworthy.

What I think is sort of odd, yet extraordinarily encouraging, is that the same survey's findings indicated that 51 percent of the interviewed executives freely surrendered all of their contact information to someone they deemed a thought leader on the very first meeting. Now that's trusting trust.

So let's do a quick recap of these two studies while at the same time asking a few probing questions. If only 18 percent of all sales reps can be trusted, and only 30 percent can have a meaningful conversation about their industry with an executive, and if the majority of the milestones within a purchasing funnel are dominated by thought leaders, and 90 percent of executives trust only thought leaders, why on this green earth would you want to be anything other than a thought leader, or a company that adhered to the thought leadership discipline within the *21st Century Disciplines of Market Leaders*? You would not. And further, why wouldn't you want to learn, and then put to practice, Critical Insight

Selling strategies that you know C-suite executives are responding to? Of course you would.

If you want to capture revenue, if you want to demonstrate your wisdom, your industry knowledge, and your intellect, then you want to begin by pitching your insights, not your product's features and benefits. But there's more research that not only encourages you to be a sales thought leader, but also warns you against feature/benefit selling.

Now, on to our third research study. This survey was conducted by the RAIN Group,[3] a formidable sales training, research, and content marketing firm with a far-reaching global impact. For this study, they interviewed more than 700 buyers over an extended period of time who purchased more than $3.1 billion of goods and services. The RAIN Group analyzed forty-two different factors and characteristics of the salespeople who sold to the 700-plus buyers in an effort to best determine what were the most effective and least effective approaches in the sales process.

For the reps who won the business of the 700 purchasers, there were three distinct categories the winners excelled in. At the top of the list and ranking number one were salespeople who "educated me with new ideas, new insights, and fresh perspectives." Weighing in at number two were the salespeople who "educated me as to the pitfalls I should be aware of before I make my purchasing decision." And third were the reps who were "so knowledgeable about the industry that they were able to tell me the real requirements we needed, not necessarily the requirements our internal staff claimed we needed." Hmm, do I even need to say anything? Well, of course I do: The fact remains that if 700 purchasers ranked the sharing of insights as the winning formula to gaining new business, is there any reason to not share your knowledge through Critical Insight Selling?

What fascinates me most is when we begin to review some bottom-up findings of this research. For instance, when looking at the salespeople who *did not* win the business, of all the forty-two factors that played a role in winning and losing, the losers ranked forty-second in sharing insights. In other words, almost none of the losing reps shared a single insight. When they failed to do that, they finished dead last with the 700 buyers. We know that it's good to win. We also know that in sales it's impossible to win every time, but to finish at the bottom every time is cause for a sales director or sales vice president to reformulate his or her hiring practices.

Further, of the top ten reasons cited for winning an order from these 700 buyers, there wasn't a single reference to features and benefits. Not one single response to that type of selling. As I stated previously, feature/benefit selling does not differentiate you from any other salespeople; in fact, it probably hurts you as you're relegated to the unenviable pack of players who rely exclusively on product sales at the exclusion of many other more important considerations and attributes.

If these three research studies don't conclusively convince you that thought leadership is the most powerful and desired discipline to embrace, I'm not certain what will. Similarly, if these three studies don't illustrate how important it is to executives and buyers for the sales process to include either a thought leader, or a company that subscribes to thought leadership, trust, and industry knowledge, you've got me completely stumped. And finally, if these three reports don't persuade you to learn, adopt, and integrate Critical Insight Selling into your sales motion, I doubt that there's anything more I can do to assure you that the way to wealth is through developing critical insights via VOC, all in your pursuit of thought leadership.

DISTRIBUTING YOUR INSIGHTS TO THE PUBLIC BY USING THE TRADE MEDIA

Obviously, we've learned how Critical Insight Selling can lead to appointment setting, lead generation, lead nurturing, building long-term relationships, and closing deals, but distributing and syndicating your insights is also of significant importance. When you have used your five insights as part of the selling process, it's time to make your insights public. It's also time you have the next five insights in hand to begin the second round of your selling efforts.

Always begin the distribution of your insights with the trade press before anything else. Most assuredly, that will provide you with the largest audience for recognition of your thought leadership discipline. I prefer to pitch articles regarding critical insights on an exclusive basis starting with the most formidable trade magazine in the industry and then working my way down the list. Others want to pitch their articles to everyone and see if there are any takers. Over the years, my best results for "pickups" have been the promise to an editor, at the very outset, that this is exclusive content, that I won't present it to another journal and it's theirs for the taking, but I need to know the depth of their interest in the next day or two.

It's best to understand the composition of today's newsrooms. They're evaporating faster than rubbing alcohol on a bug bite. Trade magazines, and their online equivalents, need good content, which means well-written articles that aren't promotional, aren't self-aggrandizing, and don't blatantly state how great thou art.

They need help and they know it. And you know it, too. Their online versions chew up so much daily content they can't possibly keep pace, and you can play right into their needs. In fact, don't even bother pitching a single article if you have a series you're tinkering with. That might even be more appealing, particularly a series of, say, five articles, *as in five critical insights.* But there's an art to pitching concepts to magazines, and like any art form, there are all sorts of techniques, brushstrokes, and glazings. My best advice is to show an editor you know your stuff, that you can write like no one's business, that you're not in it to stuff your article with references to your company and its products, and that you are writing to inform and educate, not to promote and sell. Of course, this is obvious to you because you're a thought leader. And soon, it will be obvious to everyone else.

I want to hit you with a few examples of what these articles look like, and I'm going to continue using SunGard K-12. Please notice the use of the words *Hed* (headline), *Dek* (sub-headline), and *Lede* (the opening sentences or paragraphs of an article that summarize the important features of the story). You'll need to be using these prominently.

Hed
From Silos to Ecosystems

Dek
In data technology for schools, nobody wins unless everybody wins.

Lede
School districts face a series of challenges when they look to invest in leading data-management technology. Surprisingly, most superintendents will say that the biggest task isn't finding the money for a new or upgraded system—although that is always tough. Instead, securing buy-in from teachers, parents, board and community members, students, elected officials, and others is often the most daunting challenge.

After all, every constituency in a school district has its own expertise, needs, and concerns. Who will track achievement and use the data? What protections will safeguard student privacy? How will parent–school communication be improved? Can a system be customized by school or classroom or student? Will taxpayers and community members see the ease of use and transparency they want?

Again, make certain you use the Hed, Dek, and Lede protocols in your articles. In that regard, the magazine's editors will understand in seconds that you know the ropes. It adds instant credibility.

Here's another example:

Hed

Business and K-12 Education: Different Animals that Face Many of the Same Challenges

Dek

Let's get this out of the way right up front: K-12 superintendents and school boards don't need business experts to step in and show them how to work together.

Lede

However, from SunGard K-12's perspective as a business that partners with K-12 school administrators, educators, and boards—as well as with a variety of commercial entities—we've seen how the two realms can teach one another valuable lessons.

For our part, we've certainly enhanced our business structure and management by working with some of the best educators in the world. In return, we're sharing some business practices we've seen help school district leaders collaborate effectively with their boards of directors. We've focused this report on three areas:

Part 1. Enduring leadership ideas from Peter Drucker

In 1959, Peter Drucker forecasted the rise of what he called the "knowledge worker" and the "knowledge economy." Later he wrote,

"Education will become the center of the knowledge society, and the school its key institution." Drucker died in 2005, after a long and influential career as an author, professor, and consultant for major corporations and nonprofit organizations. A great many of his ideas about management should resonate with K-12 leaders, such as how important it is to continually examine whether your district's daily operations are actually tied to its top priorities. As Drucker put it, "There is surely nothing quite so useless as doing with great efficiency what should not be done at all."

Part 2. Build a network of teams

A top worldwide business trend is redesigning organizational structures to get leaders and employees more engaged. Building flexible teams is on the rise. We examine a research report from Deloitte that delves into this trend and offers some best practices for team building. K-12 districts can use dynamic teams to get more buy-in—and more hands-on engagement—from board members, administrators, and others from throughout the school community.

Part 3. The real ROI: "return on interactions"

There's an axiom in the marketing field that creating one thousand markets of one is more effective than creating one market of one thousand. In other words, people are more loyal to a brand that treats them as individuals. In the realm of school boards and administrations, one-on-one interactions can yield an enormous return on the time and effort spent. We break down the art of dialogue with Dr. Sylvia Lafair, and return to Peter Drucker for his take on creating an effective relationship between an executive and a board of directors.

And finally, here's one last example of how the beginning of these articles might appear:

Hed

The Hidden Financial and Workflow Snags to Eliminate in Your School District

Dek

Automation—with accountability—is the answer. K-12 school systems have made great strides in automating key financial/HR functions— few districts still operate solely by pushing paper and/or sending email attachments. Even if your district has an integrated software solution for finance/HR, you may be losing productivity by getting caught in these four common workflow snags:

1. Dancing the procurement two-step

Do your district's purchasers have to double-enter requisitioned items? That is, do they have to look up an item's purchasing data from a vendor's online catalogue, enter it in a purchase order, and then enter it again to make the actual purchase?

These days, that extra step shouldn't be necessary, especially with vendors from which you routinely purchase standard supplies. Many vendors will have the capability to integrate their online catalogue into your purchasing software, so the purchaser enters the order only once and a purchase order is generated automatically.

Check with your key vendors and your purchasing software provider to see if this capability—commonly referred to as a PunchOut—is available. Make sure the PunchOut automatically updates the catalogue in real time.

2. Chasing documentation for professional development requirements

If your staff is required to enter their professional development course completions into a spreadsheet within your HR system, congratulations: You're at least one step above a file folder full of paper documents that employees dropped on an admin's desk.

Now, take a few more steps up so it's easier for staff members to find, complete, and document the courses they need to keep your district in compliance.

If your HR management software allows you to post available courses, do so, and be sure to include all the relevant details, including when and where the class meets. Course entries should link to sign-up pages.

You should be able to see at a glance which staff members are taking which courses, and when the course requirements have been met. Build in email alerts, if possible, to keep course participants on track in completing the courses and reporting results.

This type of system does require more up-front work. But ultimately it will save a great deal of time when you don't have to chase after documentation of course completion, or scramble to get people signed up for courses in time to fulfill requirements.

3. Finding the phantom approver

An automated approval process, if it's set up correctly, can usually shave a significant amount of time from a manual approval process. However, one good thing about the manual process was that if somebody in the approval chain was out of the office—on leave, on vacation, at a conference, etc.—someone else in the approval chain probably knew about it.

But in an automated approval process, absent approvers won't always be on your radar screen.

Build into your automated approval process a trigger that notifies the initiator when someone in the approval chain isn't available. The trigger should also automatically route the request to a backup approver, if possible.

Without the notification and re-routing built into your system, a purchase order, change order, job posting, etc., can be stopped cold. Maybe that won't create a huge problem. Or maybe . . . it will.

4. Riding the payroller coaster

Most folks who handle payroll for school districts will tell you their phone and email traffic always spikes on payday. Questions. Concerns. Crises.

The more information your employees can find online themselves, the fewer workflow snags your payroll and other HR employees will hit. So, in addition to the basic pay stub information, consider adding these options for employee online access:

- *Expense reimbursement status*

- *Accrued vacation, sick leave, family leave, etc.*

- *Absences*

- *Downloadable or electronic forms to request changes in tax status*

- *A calculator that shows employees the effect of a change in tax status, retirement account contribution, etc., on their future paychecks*

Not only do these features allow employees to see basic, up-to-date payroll information, they encourage employees to take more control over their paychecks. Fewer payday surprises equals fewer interruptions for your payroll staff.

Watch for hidden workflow snags like these, and schedule a review with your finance/HR management software provider.

When pitching a series of articles, particularly your critical insights, you might want to provide an editor with a quick overview of what you're proposing for your series. For instance, it might be as simple as the following:

- How K-12 education is provided makes no sense anymore. There's a need for a lot more flexibility. We no longer require huge investments in brick and mortar.

- We're run by a clock. One size, one system. Where's the individuality in that? How does that promote student success? It doesn't.

- The grading structure is centuries old. A student's pace shouldn't be tied to an archaic system that's literally hundreds of years old. There are better methods, and technology can assist with that.

- The entire funding process is unfair in every aspect of K-12 education. Aren't there better ways to spend between $50 million and $65 million than on a new school? How about putting that money into recruiting better teachers, developing more comprehensive lesson plans, and bolstering more complete communication protocols between all parties within a school district?

- Are we really teaching the right subject matter for the real world? Some kids never get past K-12, but they're still valuable members of society, and still have enormous potential to contribute to a better world.

The introductions to these SunGard K-12 stories, and how to appropriately draft the highlights of these five critical insight articles, represent the way I handle the distribution of content to the trade press. Your marketing, public relations, and thought leadership consultants will have their own processes and approaches, as they should. My method of promising exclusivity is only an ideology I developed over time; it's based on the idea that I'd rather have a piece of the pie than no pie at all, as well as the realization that the expectation of every magazine wanting to publish my content just isn't practical.

When you do receive a pickup, it will be your time to announce it to the world. That's when you'll post a link to the article on your website, email the link to your customers and prospects, share it on your social platforms, purchase some reprints of the article if the magazine promises that service, and, of course, calculate the value of the pickup using reach, impressions, CPM, or whatever means necessary so you can prove the monetary value of your efforts.

After you've exhausted every possibility for distribution to the trade press, it's time to take matters into your own hands and begin the content distribution and syndication through your favorite outbound efforts.

DISTRIBUTING YOUR INSIGHTS TO THE PUBLIC BY USING YOUR INTERNAL RESOURCES

What follows is standard marketing fare and I don't need to go into great detail about this because your marketing and public relations teams know how to do this. But now's the time to release the hounds, in whatever tactical manners you choose. It's time to publish your insights and any articles you might have written, including articles that were picked up by publications and those that were not.

Here's one tip to consider and share with your marketing team, but I have no research, no statistics, and no ancient Greek philosophy to support this. I only know that there are ways to expedite the release of critical insights to the industry if for some reason you're on the clock. And I know this only from experience, a sense of what I'm hearing and seeing, and a gut reaction—which many times can result in a gut punch if you're not careful—that you don't always need to wait until all five critical insights have been exhausted by the sales department until you hit the industry with your wisdom. There are certainly going to be instances when your entire sales team has buzzed through the first one or two insights in their Critical Insight Selling process. If that happens, you now have a green light to introduce those two particular insights to the trade. Granted, this might have an impact on pitching a series of five articles to the press, but if you haven't had much success in those types of pickups, it might not matter anyway. The choice is yours. Wait until all insights have been depleted, or flight them so that you're selling and publicly educating concurrently.

When you introduce your critical insight to the industry, it will be shared by your sales team with their customers and prospects. Please refrain from eblasting your critical insight goodness. This is the most valuable content you own, until the next five insights, so treat it accordingly. Each salesperson needs to send an insight every two or three weeks to their customers and prospects and they should take the time to personalize the email. Try something like this:

Joe—as always I'm looking forward to connecting with you at the next ASBO show in Nashville. Until then, I wanted to share the first of five critical insights we've developed over the last twelve months in our expansive research study about the K-12 industry.

As you know, quite some time ago our company took a strong interest in providing valuable information for school districts across the country, and in our effort to share our insights and knowledge about the industry with our customers and friends, we regularly distribute important information that we hope our district partners find meaningful and helpful.

This recent insight is a real humdinger that will absolutely get you thinking about alternative ways to consider increasing administrator longevity by using technology as a catalyst. Hope you enjoy the attachment and please let me know if you have any questions about this insight. See you soon in Nashville!

It doesn't take long to personalize an email, and assuming you have 100 or more prospects (not including customers), this should keep you busy for several days. And that's just the beginning of the syndication initiative.

From there you can develop infographics on each of your five critical insights, or, better yet, make them interactive infographics. You can schedule webinars about each insight, or handle all five in one session, but remember your attendance will dramatically increase if, in addition to a company representative, you have an outside influencer as part of the webinar. I also like to package the five insights into a PDF that resembles a research study; this makes for a terrific prospecting resource for the sales department, particularly at trade shows and industry events. At times, budget permitting, I'll also look to generate leads by participating in sponsored content initiatives with trade magazines. In any event, from pay-per-click to contextual ads, you need to promote your insights full throttle, including video overviews, and when you do, you'll be furthering your position as a thought leader without directly saying it.

I'm all for putting a little razzle-dazzle in my content. Frankly, so much of what is written to support thought leadership can be a snooze fest. And there's no reason it needs to be. As a thought leader, you need to educate and teach. As Plato said, "The purpose of education is to give to the body and to the soul all the beauty and all the perfection of which they are capable." Smart man. The fact is, education doesn't need to be bone-dry, and it doesn't need to be written as a textbook, or even a manual on boredom. Plato did not say to make it suitable for nap time. He said make it beautiful, make it perfect, make it soulful. And by all means, make a good story out of it.

And he should know. He, Socrates, and Aristotle were all wonderful storytellers. Our sense is that Aspasia was, too, but we don't really have many writings or musings from her to verify her storytelling chops. But we can verify this: Our original thought leaders shared the importance of why storytelling was crucial to society, and that's one of many reasons why thought leaders are also great storytellers. It's crucial, plain and simple.

10

LIKE THE ANCIENT GREEKS, ALL THOUGHT LEADERS ARE GREAT STORYTELLERS

Much has been written about the significance of storytelling in sales and marketing. In fact, thousands of people, if not many more, have spoken about the importance of storytelling in everything business related. It's not surprising that this is a favorite topic of professional speakers throughout the country. After all, research tells us that stories are twenty-two times more memorable than facts, statistics, and, you guessed it, sales pitches about product features and benefits.[1] A little online research reveals there are currently eight billion searches for storytelling, which is compounded in its popularity by marketers understanding that there is a 30 percent greater chance of closing a deal if storytelling is part of the sales process.[2]

And this is the tip of the iceberg. Ninety-two percent of people want brands to produce ads that feel like a story, 68 percent of buyers believe that stories influence their purchasing decisions, 20 percent of consumers say that a brand story increases their loyalty to a company, and 64 percent say they make a product purchase after watching a video story on social media.[3]

Want more?

Sixty-two percent of B2B marketers hold storytelling in "high regard" as an effective selling resource,[4] and most likely, there are literally hundreds, if not thousands, of statistics that support the necessity of storytelling in selling your goods and services. But the real doozy about storytelling, the most profound statistic about the bottom line of storytelling's bottom line, was a research study titled "The Significant Object Project," conducted by Rob Walker and Joshua Glenn in 2009.[5] Our two intrepid researchers purchased $129 of near worthless novelties and baubles and then hired storytellers to write compelling narratives about all the trinkets. Next, they placed all the objects on eBay, accompanied by the fascinating stories, and rung up a total sales haul of $3.6 million in net profits for an astounding 2,700 percent increase in sales. From my point of view, not only was the anthropological experiment a validation of how storytelling increases sales, but it was also a cultural reckoning that perhaps my mother's regifting expertise was meant as a lesson that *keeping it in the family* was really an unrecognized revenue stream, and an education that the contents of our "junk drawers" were, in fact, someone else's treasures.

Based on the attention researchers, neuroscientists, and marketers have given the history of storytelling, you'd think it was an invention of the last several decades.

To all of those who have leaped on the storytelling bandwagon—and it's a great bandwagon to hitch your ride to—you're 2,500 years late to the party. That's because all of our original thought leaders—Socrates,

Plato, Aristotle, and Aspasia—were fantastic storytellers, and for the most part superb rhetoricians. It seems to me that the Romans called their gifted speakers *orators* while the Greeks preferred the label of *rhetoricians*. Although the distinction is very real, it's relatively unimportant. What's most important is what Aristotle taught us about the study of rhetoric, and how this applies to classic storytelling.

As you recall, it was Aristotle who told us, "In making a speech, one must study three points: first, the means of producing **persuasion**; second, the **language**; third, the proper **arrangement** of the various parts of the speech." In chapter four, I referenced this in the context of making an oral presentation in determining what discipline of market leadership might suit you best. But let's take a closer review of Aristotle's teachings in the context of the structure and texture of storytelling. In classical terms, this is referred to as the *rhetorical triangle*. It was Aristotle's belief that how well a rhetorician was connecting to an audience was how well he or she was telling a story. Primarily this was based on three different appeals: **Logos**, **Ethos**, and **Pathos**.

Logos, not to be confused with today's icons or service marks, is the appeal of reason. In this case it signifies how well the writer or the storyteller conveys their written or spoken message of their subject matter, or the point they are trying to prove. **Ethos** is more closely defined to be the appeal of the storyteller's character, how legit they might be and if they have any street cred. And **Pathos** is the emotional appeal, what the writer or storyteller makes us believe, or at least imagine. Together, these are the facets that embody the rhetorical triangle that Aristotle insisted comprised the essential parts of writing and storytelling.

When you think about it, it's actually quite fascinating because when you structure a story, or a work of fiction, the structure can be one of many different writing formats, some known as the *classic story structure* defined as exposition, rising action, climax, falling action, resolution, dénouement, and themes; the *hero's journey structure*; the *three-act struc-ture*; the *seven-point structure*; the *snowflake method*; and the *five-act structure*. All of these formats owe themselves, in some shape or another, to Aristotle's rhetorical triangle.

Remember, the persuasion is your discipline, which is now thought leadership. The language is your pitch flow, your proof point, and the critical insight that you developed from the VOC that has now become part of your story, which, incidentally, you've rehearsed time and again. And the arrangement is how you fit all of this together to work in align-ment with your brand, your sales proposition, and the trust you've built by being a sales, marketing, and thought leader.

When I mentioned that most contemporary speakers and writers had hopped on the storytelling bandwagon 2,500 years after the wagon hit the road, it's a matter of fact that's far too often forgotten. What is also a fact is that when it came to rhetoricians, Socrates, Plato, Aristotle, and Aspasia not only knew how to tell a story, but they also knew why it was important.

THEY KNEW WHAT THEY WERE TALKING ABOUT

This time around, let's begin with Aspasia. There are no known writings from her because, as mentioned earlier, during ancient Greek times, women were barely recognized as citizens, and, for the most part, led an exis-tence of despair and servitude. But there is one example of a conversation Aspasia had with Xenophon, a student of Socrates, and Xenophon's wife who, not surprisingly, remained nameless. As the story goes, Aspasia was dissed by the couple when they asked her if she preferred the ornaments she currently possessed, or would she favor the better ornaments from a wealthy neighbor. Aspasia, not one to mince her words, told Xenophon and his wife that her preference would be for the "best ornaments."

Sensing some impending humiliation, Aspasia scolded the couple and said, "Unless you believe there are no better men or finer woman [*sic*] on Earth, you will certainly crave for what you consider as the best. Meaning, you want to be the husband of the very best of wives, and that she wants to marry the most exemplary man."[6] In Greek terms this is equivalent to throwing massive shade on someone as Aspasia ridiculed the couple, in the blink of an eye, for their lack of honesty.

We also know that Aspasia was a gifted speaker and storyteller, and it was Socrates who praised her when he said, "Once made equal to man, woman becomes his superior." Of course, Aspasia seemed to have served as Socrates's speaking coach when he delivered his unexamined life tome at his trial in much the same way King George VI (played by Colin Firth) hired Lionel Logue (played by Geoffrey Rush) in the marvelous film *The King's Speech*.

To say that Socrates was a man who seldom praised anyone is like saying Marcel Marceau was a man of few words. In fact, there are very few known instances where Socrates complimented a single person, so his praise of Aspasia, and her storytelling skills, is more than noteworthy; it's remarkable.

But what about the storytelling chops of Socrates, Plato, and Aristotle? We know by the quotes they delivered that they weren't exactly slackers. More fittingly, they told us why storytelling was important, and it's undeniable.

Beginning with Socrates, it's critical to understand what he was thinking when he said, "Employ your time in improving yourself by other men's writings so that you should come easily by what others have labored hard for." Of course, Socrates was notorious for not documenting in writing much of anything, including his philosophies and teachings, so he believed it was imperative to read the stories of others because that was the primary way we could learn, save ourselves from the agony of mistakes, and become leaders of behavioral ethics rather than followers of evil men like Thrasymachus, a rival philosopher of Socrates, who believed that an enriched life was grounded in power, strength, corruption, and thievery.

In short, Socrates instructed us to read the stories of others because that would help us distinguish what was most important in life—the differences between right and wrong, the importance of introspection and the unexamined life, and the values of listening and asking questions rather than talking incessantly and speaking about ourselves. Most important, when he said, "I cannot teach anybody anything. I can only make them think," suggests he was referring back to our abilities to reason, above anything else, and that we must use those abilities to set us apart from beasts and the mythological Greek gods.

When he told us to improve ourselves by the writings of others, he was telling us to think for ourselves, to soak it all in, to use Socratic Questioning to sort through and form our opinions, and to listen and learn from others just as he did when he walked the streets of Athens listening to the opinions of his elders. Perhaps they tried to teach Socrates their thinking by jamming their opinions down his throat, and that's where he learned that teaching his students how to think was far more important than teaching them a lesson or two.

And where does Plato, the pupil of Socrates, fit into the big picture of storytelling? Well, try this on for size: "Those who tell stories rule society," exclaimed Plato. Now that's some serious shit right there. What Plato believed was that storytelling defined our cultures, that it influenced behaviors, both good and bad, and that it inspired us to lead (hopefully), take action (a necessity), and even build an ideal state (maybe back then). "Books [stories] give a soul to the universe, wings to the mind, flight to the imagination, and life to everything," he said. That's a mighty fine piece of one-sentence storytelling right from the philosopher's mouth.

On to the youngster in the group. Aristotle said, "When the story-telling goes bad in a society, the result is decadence." The ancient Greek meaning of *decadence* is the fall from the ideals of civilization. So, without being overly genteel, Aristotle was warning his flock that the power of stories, particularly bad or untoward stories, can lead to the decay of culture. That's no small opinion and certainly an acknowledgment of how impactful storytelling can be.

Interestingly, it is believed that the very first book of literary criticism was authored by Aristotle in his publication *Poetics*. Much of the work is missing, and some is a bit muddled, but we know that Aristotle wrote quite a bit about storytelling as it relates to the ins and outs of how to write a great story. In *Poetics*, he wrote, "A likely impossibility is always preferable to an unconvincing possibility. The story should never be made up of improbable incidents; there should be nothing of the sort in it." This is superb advice for any storyteller and further evidence that the importance of a good story is nothing new to marketers and advertisers, and shouldn't be a claim that it is. Essentially, Aristotle was saying one of the elements of a good story was plausible implausibility, meaning make it distinct enough to be gripping, but not so distinct that the whole story stinks of something totally unrealistic.

Aristotle went on to say, "The plot, then, is the first principle, and, as it were, the soul of a tragedy; character holds the second place." On the surface, this might be tough to swallow for those of us who put character development ahead of everything else, but this, like most anything else, is open to discussion. Aristotle no doubt believed that even with compelling characters, if the plot sucks, the overall story does, too. I recently saw a pretty lousy movie called *You Hurt My Feelings*. It featured some wonderful characters portrayed by splendid character actors like Julia Louis-Dreyfus; Tobias Menzies, a classically trained English stage actor; and the absolutely fantastic Arian Moayed, who played Stewy in

Succession. Great characters still need a place to go, a plot to take them there, and a story to move them from the beginning to the end. Perhaps, Aristotle was on to something.

When you throw the thinking and the storytelling opinions of Socrates, Plato, Aristotle, and Aspasia in the blender, you're mixing a splendid concoction of storytelling genius and sweetness into one incredibly insightful glass of rhetoric nectar. You really need to take a moment and smile at the speakers who talk about the sudden and new-found importance of storytelling. Certainly, the statistics are new and compelling, and show how the inner workings of a story might fit neatly into an advertisement or a sales pitch, but the attributes, the structure, and the impact are as old as the seven hills that overlook Athens.

IN ACTUALITY, THERE'S A SCIENTIFIC REASON STORYTELLING WORKS

All of the talk about storytelling is really just that . . . talk. But is there a reason people remember stories far more often and with greater accuracy than facts, figures, and the occasional plot of a lousy movie? You bet there is, and it's damn important to know why it works.

It's critical to remember, assuming we humans can actually remember anything, that our brains are like nomads. We're professional wanderers who can't focus on much, and apparently we succumb to as many as 2,000 different miniature daydreams or repasses each day. Stories help to reset our focus by something headshrinkers call *neural coupling*, which means that when we hear a story, the neurons in our brains move into overdrive and begin to mirror the brain of the storyteller, hence, the coupling. So, when we hear a story, our brain—which is on the receiving end of the neurons—reaches some sort of alignment with the storyteller's brain. Yeah, it's sort of freaky.

During this neural process, your brain, and I guess mine, too, releases some very important chemicals that enhance our accessibility and understanding of more complex information while at the same time increasing the memorability of that info. These chemicals include oxytocin, cortisol, and dopamine. According to psychologists, oxytocin promotes empathy and trust, cortisol regulates stress and attention, and dopamine enhances memory and activity. Because I'm not part of the neuroscience community, I can't say this is all true, but *Psychology Today* swears by it, and that's a reputable piece of journalistic integrity.[7]

There's another piece of research I referred to in my speaking gigs that's also of interest. There are two areas of our brains that are important to the science of storytelling. The Broca's area, toward the front of your dome, produces speech, and the Wernicke's area, toward the middle of the brain, processes language. It was determined that mundane words and words that are seemingly overtly familiar do not trigger much emotion; perhaps they don't emit the heavy doses of oxytocin, cortisol, and dopamine that other words and phrases do. But there are other parts of our brains, what I've been told is the limbic system, that trigger emotions in speech. Emrah Düzel, a neuroscientist at the German Center for Neurodegenerative Diseases in Magdeburg, Germany, determined that words with emotion, touch, smell, and texture do release enough dopamine to improve our memory of these types of action-related words, which is why we remember stories, not facts and statistics.[8]

There's a lot of science here, but with close examination, it all makes some degree of sense. In fact, enough sense that it's relatively safe to proclaim that there are five attributes of storytelling that we need to keep top of mind, assuming we can remember five different attributes at one point in time. Actually, I think I'll put these in numeric bulleted format in hopes that it might, in some twisted way, release some added dopamine to help us remember just a little bit more.

1. Dismiss any thoughts from your contemporaries that storytelling is a modern-day notion, and some marvelous newfangled marketing approach. It's not, and that claim is as old as dust.

2. Storytelling works because it's part science and part human condition. The fact that it works is factual.

3. Thought leaders understand the significance and effectiveness of storytelling, but they're not taking credit for it; they know that our thought leader forefathers (just a figure of speech, Aspasia) were the original and probably the best storytellers of all time.

4. We've got some wild statistics that support the claims of exactly how important storytelling is to thought leadership, and to sales and marketing in general. Except, how on earth are we to remember all these facts and statistics without a cocktail of oxytocin, cortisol, and dopamine?

5. And finally, if you desire to stay true to Greek history, and you are a thought leader, start today and tell your pals that you no longer want to be called a great storyteller; politely inform them that you are a great *rhetorician*, but be mindful that their response will be something along the lines of "Yeah, whatever, bro."

So, what's the story about storytelling, and what's the *likely impossibility* to the end of this? Perhaps there isn't one because I'm constantly reminded of the bedtime story my father told us that was originally met with non-stop laughter, and then, over time, was met with the refrain, "Show us some mercy, Dad." To the best of my recollection, the story went like this: *It was a dark and stormy night, and they were sitting around the campfire when someone said, "Captain, tell us a story." The Captain began, "It was a dark and stormy night, and they were sitting around the campfire when someone said, 'Captain, tell us a story.' The Captain began, 'It was a dark and stormy night, and they were sitting around the campfire when someone said . . .'"*

And on and on it went with no stopping my old man, and no stopping his laughter as if he didn't give a rip about the covenants of laughing at your own jokes.

But there's one other significant aspect of storytelling that *is new*, at least it's not part of the storytelling time warp. And that's the interplay of branding and storytelling, and that's a story with a likely ending that's actually worth pursuing, as we'll see shortly. However, one story that's not worth pursuing is who invented branding. I'll spare you the digression. We definitively know the people who were behind writing and telling perfect stories, but with branding, as many marketers and advertisers will profess when their feet are held to the fire—at least after they scream in pain— there are probably as many people in the last century or two who will take some form of credit for inventing branding as there are who actually did invent it. That's why it's not worth the digression.

In chapter eleven, we will discuss how branding is messaging, how messaging is great storytelling, how your thought leadership discipline can break new ground and elevate your company and personal awareness, and how solid, top-tier messaging can further strengthen whatever disciplines you choose to embrace.

Let the neural coupling continue.

11

BRANDS ARE NOTHING MORE THAN MESSAGES, JUST LIKE STORIES

I never thought branding was all that it was cracked up to be. I'm not minimizing its importance, particularly in consumer-facing products, but I always believed, deep down, that it was a bit inflated in its value. At times, I think we overcomplicate branding, over-define it, overinvest in its return, and add more credence to it in hopes we add more dollars to our pockets. There, I said it. Whew.

Actually, as much as I love history, and this you already know, I have no desire to track down who should be credited with inventing branding. In part, that's because it makes little difference to who we are, how we behave, and by what standards we carry ourselves. Truth be told, there's a long line of people who have taken credit for inventing or coining the word *branding*, and others who probably will. All I really know is that companies like Coca-Cola, Ford Motor Company, Jim Beam, JPMorgan Chase, DuPont, Colgate, Macy's, HarperCollins, Pabst, and plenty of others were branding before there was branding. This is one of those instances when the inventor, whoever he or she was, is not significant because history won't get it right, and it just doesn't matter.

What does matter, of course, is what branding is, and how we decide to use it. There are definitions galore, far too many to even count, and I'm content to let people have their say as to how they view branding, and the best way it should be implemented. For my money, I'm delighted that branding is open to interpretation. Unlike VOC where the more people who are involved in the process, the worse the outcome will be, I like the fact that everyone has a definition and a process. It will only help further the conversation and the efficacy of branding as part of an overall business strategy.

I'm of the opinion that brands are nothing more than a series of messages, with the exception of your brand identity, and those messages are best told by transitioning them into stories. In actuality, what fascinates me more than branding is how we really view advertising, although I'm not certain there's really a difference. One of the oldest companies in America is Macy's and that's where I'd like to begin our discussion of branding, advertising, advertising budgets, messaging, and storytelling.

IT WAS JOHN WANAMAKER ALL ALONG

As I mentioned, Macy's is one of the oldest companies in America, but its predecessor to its predecessor to its predecessor before that was a retail establishment named Wanamaker's, Inc. In Philadelphia, Pennsylvania, in 1861, John Wanamaker, along with his brother-in-law, Nathan Brown, opened a men's clothing store called Oak Hall. Five years later, the name changed to Wanamaker's when it moved to a larger location and became America's first department store offering extremely high-end goods including all-wool clothing.

Innovation after innovation followed as John Wanamaker literally reinvented what was any semblance of retail thinking in the United States. In 1874 he produced and placed the first-ever copyrighted print advertisement in the country (okay, do you really want to know who invented branding?), offered the first money-back guarantee, opened a restaurant in his store in 1876, installed electric lights in 1878, and developed a system of elevators in his main Philly location in 1889. And if you think Amazon's one-day Prime sale was the beginning of that sort of promotional whiplash, it wasn't. You can thank Wanamaker for that: His "White Sale" in January 1878, followed by his "Opportunity Sale" in February, which was then followed by his "Mid-Summer Sale" in July, beat Amazon to the punch by a measly 137 years.

There are a handful of advertising quotes I really love. "He who proves too much ends up proving nothing at all," is one of them that my father recited time and again, although I was never certain if that was a quote he coined. At the top of the list was John Wanamaker's statement, "Half my advertising spend is wasted; the trouble is, I don't know which half." Of course, we've come a long way since then and actually do a damn good job of knowing where our spend is going, as well as understanding what's working and what's failing, but for many years, his quote was a fact. It's also a fact that if anyone revolutionized consumerism, and consequently the lead-up to branding, it was John Wanamaker.

And the headline for that first half-page and then full-page print ad? "Full Guarantee, One Price, Cash Payment, Cash Returned." Well, it's not exactly a barn burner, but considering the times, that he wrote his own copy, and believed in a straightforward truth in advertising approach, it was pretty radical particularly for the 1800s.

THE ELEMENTS OF BRAND ARCHITECTURES

Of all the differences and definitions there are of branding, there remains some common ground. The most important is what people call *brand architecture* or *brand structure*. I'm not only a believer; I'm also a user. Classically, a brand architecture can be described as having four components, although it's fairly safe to say that it could be many more. They are **Branded House, House of Brands, Endorsed Brands**, and **Hybrid**.

In the architecture of the **Branded House**, imagine a master brand lurking ever present above a series of descriptive brands all sharing the name of the master brand. It's sort of like the heavyweight boxing champ George Foreman naming all his sons George Foreman, which he actually did. The go-to case example of this is FedEx, which serves as the umbrella brand hovering over its disciples, which have names like FedEx Office, FedEx Ground, FedEx Express, and FedEx Freight.

In a **House of Brands** scenario, there is a single owner with a lot of brands that have their own name under the thumb of the overall company. In many cases, the individual brands don't even acknowledge the owner's existence. The most-often used example of a **House of Brands** is Proctor & Gamble, which owns companies like Crest, Tide, Bounty, Pampers, Dawn, Gillette, and many others. This is pretty much like *Animal House* where the homeowner is almost irrelevant, but the inhabitants and the players—Bluto, Otter, Flounder, Dean Wormer, and Neidermeyer—are not.

In the **Endorsed Brand** architecture, there is one parent owner, but the individual brands are entirely independent with the exception that they pay homage to the parent. For instance, Marriott has many different hotel names under its auspices, like Residence Inn, Fairfield Suites, Courtyard, and Springhill, but they make it clear that the brands are part of the Marriott empire. They are all brought to you by Marriott. This reminds me of the British royals, who include King Charles III; Queen Camilla; William, Prince of Wales; Catherine, Princess of Wales; Anne, Princess Royal; Prince Edward, Duke of Edinburgh; and Sophie, Duchess of Edinburgh. They're all operating out of the House of Windsor and officially endorsed by whatever protocols they still hang on to.

Finally, a **Hybrid** brand architecture is just that, a hybrid because no one can figure out what the hell to call it. And, yes, it's a pretty laughable name particularly coming from people who are supposed to be creative geniuses. This is just a catch-all for companies that have changed their names, had so many mergers and acquisitions that nothing fits neatly into any structure, or businesses who are running from the law (just kidding). For the **Hybrid** structure, we most often refer to Alphabet as one of the best examples, with many diverse business units being tucked under the Alphabet name, including Google, Nest, YouTube, Calico, and plenty of others. Think of this as a junkyard of spare auto parts, badass dogs, random bags of garbage, recycling that wasn't recycled, some faulty windows and doors, and a few barrels of asbestos thrown in for good measure.

I tell you this because there is a possibility, albeit very slight, that you might be working with a consultant who wants to expand the scope of your thought leadership goals and fold it into a much larger reorganization of your brand, messaging, and storytelling aspirations. That's fine, but probably not necessary, because changing your brand architecture won't make much sense, particularly if you're an SMB, but also if you're a Fortune 500 or 1000 company, because you probably would have done this months or years ago. But at least you have a heads-up on brand structure and where you might fit into all of this.

BRANDS ARE MESSAGES

If we really think about it, branding, with the exception of your brand identity (logos, service marks, iconology, etc.), is really a well-thought-out series of messages. That's why people continually refer to a litany of state-ments as brand promise, brand value, brand proposition, brand truth, brand voice, brand slogan, brand vision, brand mission, brand differentia-tion, brand personality, brand archetype, brand position, and I'm probably forgetting a few dozen. But what's the one thing all these statements have in common? Exactly, they're statements, and statements are made up of sentences, and sentences are comprised of words, and all the words strung together are messages, and the only messages that resonate—and that we actually remember—are messages that tell some sort of story; conse-quently, when you strip down branding to what's underneath the maple glaze, it's about messaging and storytelling. And as we know, storytelling from our original Greek thought leaders all the way through today's irre-futable statistics is of critical importance in supporting our discipline of thought leadership.

Again, that's the messaging where we talk about **Wisdom and Insights**, **Trust and Honesty**, and **Ethics and Causes**. That's your thought leader discipline and it's defined by how you talk about it, write about it, and prove it. That's why I'm not sure you'll ever need to be in a discussion regarding brand architecture. It's probably not a framework you'll be working in.

Now, for everyone's amusement, let's take a look at how the heavy-weights define branding and we'll see if thought leadership fits, or doesn't fit, into their contextual descriptors. First up is the textbook used throughout many business schools, *Marketing Management*, by Philip Kotler and Kevin Keller who described branding this way: "Branding is endowing products and services with the power of a brand."[1] Oh boy. That's like saying, "Running is endowing your legs and feet with the power to run." I'm not sure I even know where to begin with this description, but it seems to me that if our product and our service are thought leadership on one level, then I can see how this makes some sort of sense. After all, if thought leadership were a brand, then we would be endowing our product and service with the power of thought leadership, which we already know to be a superpower.

Let's look at a different definition, this one from the American Marketing Association (AMA) who we can assume really know their stuff: "A brand is a name, term, design, symbol, or any other feature that identifies one seller's good or service as distinct from those of other sellers."[2] I can live with this one, too, if only because I'm a member of the AMA. This is a pretty broad brushstroke and I don't blame them. Why get overly definitive knowing that us members want a definition that can lasso just about all of us wild horses? Well, thought leadership is certainly a term, a feature, an identity, and a service that differentiates us from other sellers, so it works for me.

This all makes a ton of sense particularly if you want to make the ultimate leap of faith and exclaim that your brand is thought leadership, but that's not something I would recommend. Again, thought leadership is a discipline that is part of the *21st Century Disciplines of Market Leaders*, not necessarily a brand, and I'm far more comfortable talking about disciplines and how to find them, craft their messages and stories, convert them into insights that are salable, and sustain those disciplines over a decade. This is a discipline that's a cross between an incredibly effective sales tactic and a relevant differentiator as opposed to a brand, which we've seen is a concept that defies definition and some amount of clarity, and certainly defies all types of selling processes and sales motions.

But that's just me. I'd prefer to keep it simple. Working your way down the thought leadership highway is enough to tackle and will probably last you a decade or more until you have to reassess the market and your place in it. That means you'll need about four or five rounds of critical insights to get through the next ten years, and four rounds of stripped-down VOC after the first initial game-changing

VOC research. That's hardly a massive amount of work, so piling on more by trying to work your way through various brand architectures doesn't seem overly relevant to me.

YOU *SHOULD* HAVE A MESSAGING COMPOSITE

I remember when annual marketing plans were 200 pages, housed in three-ring binders, and sat on a shelf until the plastic outercoating started peeling off like scales on a mackerel. Thankfully, now most everything is bite-size as our attention spans have diminished, probably because the amount of noise has amplified. Web text is shorter, one-pagers are more prevalent, blogs are brief, and we've pretty much boiled everything down to emphasizing the first sentence and the last sentence of whatever it is we're writing. To some extent, there are minor exceptions with messaging and storytelling, but it's more than apparent that everyone enjoys a good story—although, not necessarily a long story.

The facts support brevity. One of the reasons I've always found writing websites to be tough sledding is because I know the ending. It's like watching the movie *Titanic*; it sinks. Nielsen Norman Group, the famed UX consultants, spoiled it for all of us with their eye-tracking software findings. Basically, anything we are reading on a website, or a screen akin to that . . . well, we aren't really reading at all. We're skimming at best to the tune of about fifty-five words on a page.[3] So, on a web page we're only looking at 20 percent of the words, and if John Wanamaker were still alive, he'd ask, "Which 20 percent of the words?" Well, John, that's sort of easy. Not surprisingly, we're reading a headline (remember Hed), and we're reading a sub-headline (remember Dek), and maybe a bullet and a link, but thereafter, forget it.

And talk about an impatient public. In an analysis of 4 million Google searches, it was determined that only .063 percent of searchers made it to the second page of Google's queries.[4] We're so pressed for time and so impatient for results and immediate gratification that we no longer even bother going to the second page of a search, opting instead to change our search term rather than clicking to page two or, heavens, the wasteland of page three.

So, we need to keep the telling of information short and digestible. In order to do this, it's best to cut down on the manifesto and forgo the heavy cargo. That's why it's going to be best to tighten up your narrative pitch flows, condense your proof points—both emotional, and factual and statistical—and trash the three-ring binder stored on your shelf and store a few pages on your phone for quick reference when no one is watching, like under the conference room table during a meeting.

I tell my clients to develop a messaging composite that consists of the narrative pitch flows—regardless of which discipline you've chosen to be a market leader in—your proof points, and then any annotations that document the process for the selection of that discipline. So, for instance, if you're a thought leader, you are going to put together a messaging composite that includes your pitch flows for **Wisdom and Insights, Trust and Honesty**, and **Ethics and Causes**. Under each one of those, you'll have the proof points that support those pitch flows, and then under that, you'll cut in your supporting data. You can choose to include some VOC findings, the critical insights that were developed, some stories that support your propositions about your wisdom, your honesty, and your ethics, essentially whatever is in your handbook of goodness. But keep it brief, maybe ten pages, but not 210 pages.

Believe me, you'll be glad you did this. This is the fastest and most surefire way to train a new employee on your team. And you'll need this PDF when you begin the process of implementing a thought leadership campaign into your company. Most likely, you won't be required to develop this messaging composite if you choose to be a thought leader for personal awareness and individual gain because like the professional speaker you are, or will become, this will all be committed to memory.

Please know that committing this to memory is not a hard-and-fast rule of thought leadership, although you're about to learn what some of those hard-and-fast rules are. There's a lot here to memorize, but it's a good idea to understand the ins and outs of this stuff because it sure beats referring to the pages in this book time and again, and that's assuming you aren't going to regift this book to your associate at the next holiday party.

IMPLEMENTING THOUGHT LEADERSHIP INTO YOUR COMPANY AND FOR YOUR PERSONAL SUCCESS

It's official, we're now on to the easy stuff. It makes little difference if your company employs ten people or 1,010; you still need to introduce your new thought leadership position to the entire corporation, and that means every department and every individual. It can also mean every contract employee, if you've headed down that type of employment path, and even your A-plus consultants if they're still engaged with you.

You have only one shot to do this, like a grand opening of a new business, and you want the introduction and the launch to be as close to perfect as possible. You do not want to sell this short, and you certainly don't want to leave any questions unanswered. I have never witnessed any blowback from adopting a thought leadership position, but I have heard questions—good ones and not so good ones—so be prepared and scripted for launch day. I have found that the most pressing questions are threefold.

One of the first has always been, *How can we sustain this?* It's 100 percent legit, but you already know the answer to this because you understand the critical insight development process will happen at a regular cadence as we detailed previously. You should speak to this cadence. In fact, do not be short on details as that will only lead to more questions.

This will invariably lead to question two, *Who will be responsible for leading, contributing, and sustaining our newfound discipline?* The obvious answer is everyone, and this is the point in time when you'll explain that this is a corporate-wide philosophy, a top-to-bottom initiative where sales and marketing are at the forefront, but everyone is part of the process. It might even be a good time to invoke the old American Hospital Supply Corporation motto: "Not everyone is in the sales department, but everyone is in sales." After you've belabored this point, it's time to introduce the people who will be driving the disciplines and what their exact roles and responsibilities are, including the company CEO. Again, spare no details. Tell everyone about Critical Insight Selling and the members of the sales department who will administer and adhere to the selling of wisdom. Introduce your marketing team and their involvement in the formulation and development of the discipline. Have your consultant on hand, and your executive team to signify the highest levels of importance to the thought leadership discipline. In a moment, the following agenda will help you craft the launch introduction.

The third question that you can anticipate is how this will impact the company financially, and what the costs might be. Your answers to this will be dependent upon many factors including, but not limited to, being a public company, how open you are to sharing financial details with your employees, and if you are amenable to sharing one-, three-, and even five-year forecasts. I can't help you in this regard, the variables are too extensive, but for my money, the more you share, the more enthusiasm you'll create. If you invested $100,000 up front, tell them. If you'll be investing another $50,000 each year, tell them that, too. If you are forecasting a payback that's ten times more than the annual investment, by all means share some of that information. If you choose to avoid some of these details, you might be setting yourself up for the next follow-up question, *But if thought leaders are always honest, shouldn't we know everything about this?* Touché.

Your kickoff meeting needs to be an all-hands meeting, a town hall, a come one, come all celebration. And you should tease the living hell out of it. Let your employees know well in advance that attendance is mandatory, that you'll want ninety minutes of their time, and that there will be a celebration after the meeting with food and cake because now we'll have our cake and eat it too. Go big, as in *This will be one of the most important corporate announcements you'll ever hear from us.* But be mindful of the worriers who might think it's a doomsday message. Say in your email invite that you're celebrating *the introduction and launch of a market leadership position that will differentiate us from the competition and make us the best sales machine in the industry, even better than we are (if that's possible). It's a new day, a new business approach, and a huge win for our company!!!!*

You just noticed that I used a series of exclamation points, which, for those of you who know me and my writings, is a punctuation mark I frown upon. As F. Scott Fitzgerald said, "Cut out all these exclamation points. An exclamation point is like laughing at your own joke." But in this case, I'm writing an email invitation . . . so if you're willing, please cut me some slack.

The next step is to plan this event top to bottom, leaving no stone unturned. Make certain the planning involves representatives from the sales and marketing teams, and also make certain the entire executive team, including the CEO, is at the launch. Here are a few suggestions I've implemented in the past, but you'll have wrinkles of your own that you'll need to add to the list:

- Get your planning team together, not too small, but by no means too many.

- Set your all-hands meeting date and make sure you give all employees at least a three-week notice of the event's date, time, and place. For those not in the office, they'll be able to dial into the celebration.

- Plan every minute of the event and allow plenty of time for questions, but let's make sure we avoid any Socratic Questioning.

- Talk with the team about any outsiders who should attend; this could include your VOC and insights consultant, investors, bankers, accountants, and contract employees, perhaps even a few retirees who are still closely aligned to the company.

- Develop the outline for the event. The kickoff of the kickoff should always start with the president or CEO; this will send a strong message about the importance of the entire initiative. Thereafter, I like to begin with the *21st Century Disciplines of Market Leaders*; it's essential to explain why all companies, if they can, need to own one of the disciplines, sometimes even more than one, and the rationale of why thought leadership was selected ahead of price, customer service, and technology and innovation. Don't short shrift the other three. You don't want to alienate any employee who has been working in customer support or technology advancement. You'll want to be straight-up and explain that the most compelling proof points all pointed you in the direction of thought leadership, but certainly not at the expense of other disciplines.

- Next, if I'm involved in the kickoff, and I frequently am, I like to walk through the process; I start at VOC and talk about *market leadership determination.* I'll spend a few minutes discussing some reoccurring themes, perhaps some of my annotations and VOC insights, and then I move into the development of the critical insights and what they are.

- Typically, I would be joined by the sales executive when discussing the ins and outs of Critical Insight Selling, and how it works. This is the time when your sales leader talks about the training, the role-playing, and any workshops the sales reps have been engaged in. I think this is important because it shows the employees that we're beyond the pixie dust, that this isn't ethereal bullshit, and that we're already 100 percent invested—not just as a company but as individuals as well.

- After this, I like to have the CMO discuss the marketing team's involvement, how we're launching this internally, when the sales department will begin Critical Insight Selling (if they haven't already), how we're going to sustain this over the next few years, and why this is important to our long-term viability and success. At this time, I like to sneak in a sales rep who already bagged a new customer using Critical Insight Selling (or is really close). It adds authenticity when they tell their story, and it adds legitimacy to the discipline, verifying its effectiveness before there's any head-scratching.

- Just as the open was stage time for the president or CEO, the same holds true for the close. This is where your leader describes the importance of **Wisdom and Insights**, **Trust and Honesty**, and **Ethics and Causes**. It's also the time when they talk about the qualities of thought leaders as if the expectation is that all employees will do their best to follow suit. This can be the perfect time to address the rules that thought leaders follow (see the next chapter).

Again, this is the fun stuff, but do not let the pilot light flicker. You own the momentum, and it's imperative you keep the juices flowing even after you have devoured the celebratory slice of cake. For this, I suggest some next-day, next-week, and next-few-months activities. These include sending all employees the first content asset you've created about wisdom, trust, or ethics. Do this the next day after the meeting. Do it again, and then again so they can see what thought leadership looks like and how it will be an integral part of the company moving forward.

Turn the pilot light into a beacon. For the first few months don't lose sight of the fact that this is new, that the *21st Century Disciplines of Market Leaders* is unknown to almost everyone in the company, and just as Critical Insight Selling is a new approach for your sales team, thought leadership is new to the company and will require a little bit of gentle selling itself. But rest assured, the enthusiasm will grow, particularly when you begin notifying your employees about the success the sales team is having with Critical Insight Selling. It will be important to share every sales win with all the employees for a few months, and don't forget to add a little detail about the victory; perhaps what other companies were in the hunt, how you relevantly differentiated the company from the competitors using thought leadership, or what the new customer might have said about the process. Put some extra froufrou on the revenue with some storytelling because, well, you know what your employees will remember most.

If you take the time to implement many of the suggestions on the list, you'll have a successful launch (and post-launch) of your new thought leadership initiative, and furthermore, you'll gain the necessary momentum to keep the discipline firing on all cylinders for the first year of the campaign. This will ensure that thought leadership will find its traction, mojo, and long-term resting place in the organization.

NOT JUST A THOUGHT LEADER, AN EDUCATOR

The ancient Greek philosophers, every one of them, believed in education. They might have disagreed on how it should be delivered, what the best context and lesson plans should be, and how it benefitted an individual, but there was consensus around the importance of education. As a thought leader, you must remember you are also an educator, and that's the right mindset to have when introducing thought leadership into your company, or into your life.

Socrates said, "Education is the kindling of a flame, not the filling of a vessel." He was pretty adamant about this. He thought that education was a process of collaboration where the teacher was far less effective lecturing students, and talking at them, than discussing various topics with them. The goal is to not fill the student's vessels (minds) with all the answers—whether the teacher has the right answers or not. It's far more beneficial to teach wisdom as a lifelong vehicle for learning—and how to pursue knowledge—than it is to simply provide the information. Many educators and philosophers also contend that filling the vessel does little for retention and comprehension. It merely provides an outlet and a framework for a lecture rather than an understanding of concepts, imagination, and both the unexamined life and the examined life. Remember, it was Socrates who said, "I cannot teach anybody anything. I can only make them think."

Not surprisingly, Socrates believed we needed to educate our adolescents to be more mindful of the significance of introspection and examination—which is exactly what business leaders are now appreciating and understanding—and that they must practice introspection to be better corporate leaders, more complete humans, and better ambassadors in the hunt for a life of quality. This is now who you are, and it's a valuable part of being a thought leader from the time you launch the initiative in your town hall until the time you pass the torch.

Plato received the typical education of a Greek youth, as long as you were a male. He learned to read, write, and study the poets. He reflected upon his schooling from the age of eight to sixteen in his work *The Republic* where we become familiar with his beliefs about education. Plato was only a few years old when his father died, and shortly thereafter, his mother remarried an acquaintance of Pericles—the intellectually gifted Athenian statesman—so it was expected that Plato would be educated and well versed in politics, military science, swimming, and gymnastics.

Unfortunately, if you were a woman in Athens, your education was limited to domestic training and occurred only within a home. But rest assured, Plato believed that education should be for all, and was most influenced by the educational equality found in the learning system south of Athens in Sparta.

Plato said, "The direction in which education starts a man will determine his future life." And that's not too different from what it takes to begin the implementation process of thought leadership into your company. It's the beginning of your future. Overall, to ensure your standing as an educator, in addition to being a thought leader, it's important to understand Plato's insights about education. He admired intellectualism, civic engagement, and an open-minded teaching environment based on dialogue and conversation. Generally, his approach to education was holistic. His admiration for the world, humanity, his students, and education was centered on order and discipline, but he believed it needed to be a two-way street, not a complete free-for-all of open dialogue. In much the same way you listened to the respondents in VOC and respected their insights, Plato rationalized that some type of order would always be needed to make sure that education and various disciplines wouldn't entirely fall off the rails. You've already accomplished this by instituting many processes and protocols that drive your efforts in becoming a thought leader, and that's why it's important to detail your pathway in the pursuit of your thought leadership discipline at the kickoff announcement. That way, there's no chance that anything is going to fall off the rails. I might have helped you a bit in outlining some of the formalities, but you've graduated far past that and customized your outcomes and insights, all of which are now valuable in a disciplined sort of exercise. That's why you're going to appreciate either being a thought leader or working for a company that has embraced thought leadership.

Aristotle also believed in a holistic approach to education. For him, a well-educated mind was the only way to become a satisfied human being. Although we have only a few tidbits from Aristotle's writings about education, we do know he categorized education into three parts: theoretical, practical, and technical. He also stood firmly in his belief that teachers should provide a well-balanced schooling grounded in the mind, body, and soul, and that teachers should possess the characteristics and accomplishments to provide a clear understanding of ethics. It sure sounds to me that he was describing *you*.

In his philosophies, Aristotle believed that educators must teach the virtues of courage, justice, temperance, and wisdom so that individuals could be strong contributors in the making of a better society. He wrote that education should fulfill the potential of an individual and nothing less. He said, "Excellence is never an accident. It is always the result of high intention, sincere effort, and intelligent execution; it represents the wise choice of many alternatives; choice, not chance, determines your destiny." That's why choosing a thought leadership discipline was an act of choice; you didn't throw darts at the board and idly say, "We're going to be thought leaders today. We will now be the most thoughtful of all thought leaders in our industry." This was not an accident; this was intended, it was your destiny, and that needs to seep through the town hall like water through a basement (hopefully not your basement). And it needs to keep flowing through your company; don't muzzle the thought leadership spigot, but keep it streaming all year long. And if you want to have an annual thought leadership wellness check, I'm 100 percent in favor of that, too. It makes perfect sense to recap the year, highlight the sales successes, call attention to the content victories, and tell some stories of what your customers have said. By all means, give the whole ball of wax a thumping heartbeat.

Congratulations on your thought leadership with an extra F. Scott Fitzgerald exclamation point because you're also an educator!

USING THOUGHT LEADERSHIP TO DRIVE YOUR PERSONAL SUCCESS

I believe in personal branding. And not just for one-saddle Sams who need it the most like real estate agents, writers, professional speakers, fine artists, commercial models, photographers, and so on. But also business leaders need a personal brand—under the right circumstances, of course—and that's only when they do not become a distraction (or an oxygen hound) from the company they're leading, or the company they are working for.

Depending on the industry you're involved with, you could choose a personal brand that mirrors some brand archetypes like the more comical examples of the *magician, outlaw, revolutionary,* or *rebel.* Perhaps you'd like to choose a more traditional archetype, say, the *ruler, hero, innocent, everyman, sage, caregiver, lover, explorer,* or *creator,* but these are all pretty much cartoon characters, too. And that's not a trapdoor you want to fall into. The one archetype that's not even listed, or even defined as an archetype, that you want to hitch your personal brand wagon to is obviously the *thought leader.*

There are quite a few differences in the protocols of becoming a thought leader as a company as opposed to a thought leader as an individual. Obviously, if thought leadership as your personal brand is in your sights, and if it makes professional career sense, then you should pursue it with as much gusto as your grandfather did when he grabbed a can of Schlitz (the beer that made Milwaukee famous). Whether it makes sense or not is not for me or others to decide. That's your call and you'll understand better than anyone if it's the right decision or not, but there are some necessities and a few pitfalls to be aware of along the way.

Obviously, you don't need to weave your way through the processes of *market discipline determination,* or lengthy VOC discovery, or the preparation of pitch decks, and town hall kickoff meetings, but after that, there aren't really many shortcuts. There are still activities to attend to, lessons that need to be learned, and practices of sustainment that need to be deployed. Most people think it's as simple as "my personal brand is going to be that of a thought leader and I'll publish some insights to prove my wisdom." If it was that simple, and that easy to succeed, we'd all be thought leaders, and that would mean none of us would be a thought leader.

So do what Drucker advised us to do and do "the right things" in your effort to adopt thought leadership as part of your brand. First, you'll need to determine what type of thought leader you're going to be, and that begins, not strangely, with the unexamined life from our dear friend, Socrates. It's time you rolled up your sleeve and willingly accepted the introspection injection; it's time you transitioned from the unexamined life to the examined life, and found the light that Plato told us to follow. Will you be a sales thought leader, a futurist, a management efficiency expert, a historian and scholar, a health and wellness influencer, a parenting skills specialist, or one of hundreds of other possibilities? The choice is yours, but you need to define and then refine your personal thought leadership position in much the same way we whittled down our options from price-cutter to customer service provider to innovator and then to thought leader. However, the primary difference with your personal brand is that you have far more options for specialization than a business that is confined to the *21st Century Disciplines of Market Leaders.*

"To be yourself in a world that is constantly trying to make you something else is the greatest accomplishment." Boy . . . did Socrates get that right. We will always be pigeonholed into something we're not. That's just the inner workings of everything from the human condition to existentialism, and from the malice of social media to the jealousy of others. There's no way around it, which is exactly why you need to choose a definitive subject for your thought leadership position and stick to it, no matter who is trying to unstick your landing. If you are really good at motivating people to go the extra mile, that's your highway. If you can make people see beyond the obvious, that's your vision. And if you can offer people the secrets to be better listeners, that's going to be your microphone. The pitfall for almost anyone who positions themselves as a thought leader as part of their personal brand is that they swerve from their highway lane, they become more peripheral in their vision, and they drop the microphone in favor of a Harman Kardon sound system. Stay focused on who and what you are as a thought leader and the expansion into other like-minded territories will occur organically.

That's the first hurdle: Pick your poison and stay with it. The next hurdle will be determining all the ways you're going to prove it, long before you try to prove anything at all. Because of my years on the professional speakers circuit, and my obvious familiarity with it, I'm going to use the circuit for some telling examples for the next steps in your pursuit of a solid personal brand.

There are two types of speaker bureaus: There's the traditional variety where there are agents who work with convention planners, company HR employees, event coordinators, and those types of people who book speakers for whatever purpose and reason they might have. Most of the speakers in the stable of traditional bureaus have quite a bit of street cred, and a lot of name recognition. These are active and former politicians, celebrities of all stripes, athletic heroes, famous authors, and a handful of CEOs. It would not be unusual for these well-known speakers to command a six-figure payday (plus first-class travel) for a one-hour speech.

A tier down from that are some fairly renowned business professionals who have made a name for themselves talking about customer service, quality control, managing corporate aspirations, and various motivational virtues. Even the tier two speakers can haul in $30,000 for a one-hour talk, which by the way has been whittled down to fifty minutes in some cases. This fee does not include first-class travel and any merch that is sold at the gathering. The merchandise is usually a book or two written by the speaker that is either purchased by the event coordinators and distributed free of charge to the attendees, or sold to the participants at a discounted rate, but with the promise of receiving an autographed copy. In many cases, it is not unreasonable to think that a tier two $30,000 speaker is really a $40,000 speaker.

There's no doubt about it: It's a really good hustle.

Many traditional speaker bureaus have fallen by the wayside, and the pandemic had a lot to do with it. In fact, from 2020 through 2022, the business of public speaking was all but shuttered. However, there are many successful digital bureaus, probably too many to even list on the next few pages. This is where most of the other pros reside. No matter which type of bureau you're aligned with, there's an unspoken rule when it comes to your bio and the list of topics that are on your soap box: *The more is not necessarily the merrier.* Planners and coordinators are a little suspect when you offer multiple disparate topics. If they're looking for a customer service expert, they don't want to see a speech titled "You Are the Fuel that Drives Your Children." Similarly, if they want a convention keynote about world affairs, they won't be turned on by a speech titled "A Managerial Kick in the Ass Is All They Need." It's best to stay focused on whatever your personal brand will be and keep the attributes aligned with your overall pitch flows. So, if you are a sales thought leader, keep your expertise to selling, but broaden the subject matter to motivating sales teams, driving incremental sales, and using your existing customers as added sales bait.

That's your next step. Just like we did before, take note of your level 1, level 2, and level 3 narrative pitch flows, and then begin to develop your factual and statistical proof points, as well as your emotional proof points. Obviously, we're not in a workshop setting, so this should move pretty quickly. Ultimately, you will need to cut this into your bio as you set appointments, schedule speaking gigs, write articles that require a byline, and on and on. Many years ago, this was my speaking gig bio that also doubled in brass as my workshop bio:[1]

As has been said, Thomas R. Marks is where sales and marketing thought leaders go for their thought leadership. Over the course of his more than four-decade career, Tom has counseled Fortune 500 companies, and other organizations of all shapes and sizes, on the 21st Century Disciplines of Market Leaders; *how to use Critical Insight Selling, his revolutionary selling approach that uses knowledge and insights to sell goods and services; and how to implement thought leadership positions into a company to distance themselves from the competition more decisively and with more dynamic narrative pitch flows and messaging.*

Tom founded TMA+Peritus, a nationally recognized marketing consulting firm, more than 40 years ago, and over time has worked with leading clients including McDonald's, Foot Locker, Honeywell, Finish Line Sports, American Family Insurance, Rakuten, Bombardier, Associated Bank, PowerSchool, FIS Global, California Avocado Commission, National Mango Board, CUNA Mutual, and countless others. Tom is the former president of the American Advertising Federation (Wisconsin Chapter), and with TMA+Peritus, is a 65 time winner of the American Advertising Awards.

Tom is the author of hundreds of articles, white papers, and sto-ries including Of Socrates, Plato & Aristotle: How Thought Leadership Drives Stronger Sales, Marketing & Ethics; How to Put the ROI in Your URL; The Fall of Harvey Weinstein: Lessons in Screwing-Up an Already Screwed-Up Mess; *and* Is the Bankruptcy of Trust Diluting Brands?

Tom is also considered to be a master storyteller, understanding the art, science, and neuroscience behind why storytelling increases both recall and recall accuracy in your sales messaging. His speeches and workshops are educational, insightful, and bring practical and useful knowledge to any organization.

The first thing Tom did when he began researching thought lead-ership's history including the philosophies of Socrates, Plato, Aristotle, and Aspasia, along with Tom's own 21st Century Disciplines of Market Leaders *and* Critical Insight Selling, *was to make certain there were no direct online search results for his topics. Zero. As a meeting planner, you can be certain that your clients and their audiences have never heard anything like Tom's insights before. If you want true originality at your next meeting, you'll want Thomas R. Marks.*

Aside from the fact that this is totally embarrassing as I look back on this, even though this wasn't written by me, I do realize that to some extent I probably heeded my own advice and stuck to what I knew best. It doesn't appear that I swerved too wildly from my lane on thought leadership. Again, I suggest you do the same.

Upon further digging, I also found this write-up of my pre-speech bio that is generally publicized in some type of convention booklet or trade publication:[2]

Thomas R. Marks is an acclaimed marketing, sales, and storytelling thought leader. He's a prolific author and has written hundreds of articles, white papers, and e-books on diverse topics ranging from the great philosophers, Socrates, Plato, Aristotle, and Aspasia, to assorted works on trust, corporate ethics, and the neuroscience of storytelling. Tom was also the Sunday Marketing Columnist for Gannett Newspapers.

*Tom is a graduate of the Claremont Colleges, the same institution where his mentor, Peter Drucker, was a professor. Tom also studied creative writing and historical fiction overseas, spending time with the great English Working Class authors including Alan Sillitoe (*The Loneliness of the Long-Distance Runner*), John Wain (*Hurry on Down*), John Braine (*Room at the Top, Life at the Top, The Crying Game*), Kingsley Amis (*Lucky Jim*), Arnold Wesker (*The Kitchen, Chicken Soup with Barley*), and Ann Jellicoe (*The Sport of My Mad Mother*). In recent years, Tom is notable for his efforts implementing thought leadership positions in corporations throughout the U.S. as well as teaching clients Critical Insight Selling, the technique of using knowledge and insights for sales success rather than the tired approach of selling product and service features and benefits.*

Feel free to use these as templates, or, more appropriately, as recycled waste in the nearest county landfill.

Next up in your pursuit will be the actions you'll need to consider in order to launch your thought leadership quest toward creating personal awareness and being "yourself in a world that is constantly trying to make you something else." The easiest default advice I can give you is to start writing your first book, with heavy emphasis on *first*. That's because your second book—as is the case with most thought leaders who are trying to build their consulting businesses, advance their speaking careers, or up their hourly consulting fees—should do better in unit sales than your first book. Because this will be the most time-consuming part of enhancing your personal brand, there's no time like the present to let your fingers do the talking (and walking). Don't be overly concerned about finding a publisher just yet. Presently, there are over 2 million self-published books each year, many of which are business books. It's not easy finding a publisher, but that shouldn't hold you back. In fact, I would advise that you think about your writing career—all in the effort of advancing your personal thought leadership career—as a two-part book series, maybe even three parts if you have a foolproof plan.

This is a better strategy than relying solely on writing and syndicating articles, blog posts, social content, and whatever else the content du jour is of the times. But while you're toiling away on your treatise, you will still need to keep writing articles, connecting with the media, designing and writing infographics, and shooting videos for your YouTube series. As I mentioned before, my video series was called *Front Lobby Confessionals* and I shot it on Sundays in our front reception area. A good cadence for your series would be one video every two weeks; a weekly commitment is just too grueling.

Let's spend a moment focusing on a few reasons I'd like you to drive your personal thought leadership brand through a video series. Most importantly, YouTube is the second most prolific search engine after Google, which isn't surprising since Google (Alphabet) owns YouTube. Over time, you'll want to work your way onto the first page of search, particularly in whatever your specialty is within the thought leadership discipline. A video series is a good method to do that, plus you can imbed the videos on your website, use them on your social platforms, share the videos easily, and let people get a glimpse of you and your expertise.

But there are other reasons to invest in a video series. In an article published by *Blogging Wizard*,[3] 86 percent of marketers use videos, 84 percent of businesses indicate that videos have increased lead generation, 94 percent of those marketers believe videos improved customer knowledge and understanding of their products, videos drive 82 percent of all web traffic, 83 percent of people prefer watching videos to reading instructional content, and 54 percent of marketers say that videos build customer trust. Maybe it's not *video killed the radio star*, but perhaps it's *video killed the writing star*. But that doesn't win you a get-out-of-jail-free card; you still need to write your first book, and think about your second book while you're at it.

And one last thought about your thought leadership video series. Don't invest much money in it. Purchase a tripod for your phone, a phone mount, and an external microphone. There's nothing else you need. Use any number of apps to shoot your video and off-load them to your desktop or your YouTube account (currently I'm using the app ProMovie that I forked over $1.99 to download). That's all you need to produce your video series.

As you continue to work on your book, keep producing and distributing your other content, and continue to pitch your content assets to the media, newsletters, online publications that chew up content faster than a Great Dane or an English mastiff (as in "My dog ate my homework."), local newspapers (some still exist), and other industry websites. Give your followers a break and mix things up with a savory blend of videos, infographics, e-books, articles, co-written blogs, and social posts across as many platforms as you can tolerate. And when you've settled in after six months or so, consider starting your thought leadership podcast, but not before you line up eight to ten guests in advance, and only after you've learned the ins and outs and the myriad technicalities, equipment, and partnership requirements to get in the podcast game. Spoiler alert, it's nowhere near as easy as you think it is.

If your personal brand is going to be the thought leadership discipline, and I'm hoping it will be, the rewards can be everlasting and the risks only miniscule, financially speaking. Beyond what you invest in time, the investment is not significant, so that shouldn't even be a consideration. What you need to consider, ahead of anything else, is the effort. Can you do most of the activities I have previously outlined? Let's face it, the upside to all of this is that you'll be investing in yourself, and there's no greater investment than that.

I know . . . perhaps investing in yourself sounds a little self-absorbed, but think about it this way: Because you're a thought leader, caring for others is something you'd be doing regardless of any outlying circumstances, and let's not forget that because you are also an educator, you are naturally going to take time to care and teach others, not necessarily by filling their vessel, but by engaging in conversations, teaching the process of acquiring wisdom, showing everyone that leading a life of quality is the best type of life to lead, and understanding that transitioning from the unexamined life to the examined life is a guiding principle that defines you.

With your thought leadership personal brand intact, and the introduction to thought leadership firmly grounded in your company's culture, it's time to discuss the rules of the game.

13

THE RULES THAT ALL THOUGHT LEADERS NEED TO FOLLOW

On the speaking circuit, I would always spend the last few minutes discussing the seven rules of thought leadership you need to follow. I didn't have much time to elaborate on all seven decrees, but I'm going to highlight the rules of thought leadership, just as I would have in my speeches, and then circle back and further explore each one of them. Of course, as a thought leader you'll probably have the tendency to be a rule-breaker, as often as you would be a rule-follower, and that's great with me. Just remember these are suggestions, and as time goes on, you'll be able to pile on a few rules of your own when you're passing the baton to your next thought leaders.

These are the seven thought leadership laws of the land you should consider following:

Rule Number One: You don't need to be promotional to be promotional.

Rule Number Two: You're not the only thought leader who's a thought leader.

Rule Number Three: Don't confuse thought leadership with being the smartest person in the room.

Rule Number Four: Thought leadership is like saffron—a little goes a long way.

Rule Number Five: Thought leaders know how to tell and write great stories.

Rule Number Six: What's really, really ancient is really, really new again.

Rule Number Seven: Thought leaders look at the world differently; they forgo the obvious in favor of the obscure.

And now the bonus rule: Never call yourself a thought leader, not even as a pickup line.

Let's take a closer look at all seven rules beginning with **Rule Number One:** *You don't need to be promotional to be promotional.* You don't, and it shouldn't appear that you're overtly pushing your thought leadership, because there's no need to do that. Unless you're the greatest of all time, like Muhammed Ali, who famously said, "There's not a man alive who can whup me. I'm too fast. I'm too smart. I'm too pretty. I should be a postage stamp. That's the only way I'll ever get licked. I'm so mean I make medicine sick." This isn't just cocktail hour talk, mano a mano chest pounding, or haphazard bravado, but it's damn serious that you don't get too absorbed in your self-absorption, unless, of course, you're the greatest of all time, which ultimately you might be, but not quite yet.

Don't let it seep through your writings, musings, new video series, interviews with other influencers, new book, and blog posts. And by all means try your best not to outdo the social media doers who find it necessary to write in terms of one-upmanship in an effort to be hip in their courtship of being blue chip. It's okay to be hip, but not hypocritical.

And if you're a business that has successfully taken advantage of the thought leadership discipline, essentially the same holds true for you. You don't need to be grandstanding just because you're outstanding. And that's a temptation I see regularly—that as much as we try to hold back our promotional tendencies, there's a natural propensity to promote. The only suggestion I have is to keep a watchful eye on how much hawking you do and to invoke some Socratic Questioning to make certain you don't overstep the boundaries of being overtly promotional.

As I've mentioned many times, one of the advantages of the thought leadership discipline is that it's a nearly benign investment compared to the disciplines of price and value, customer service, and technology and innovation. Part of that reason is you won't be advertising your thought leadership in a way that a company might promote their products and services, the benefits of their technology, their award-winning customer service, or their special pricing during the month of May. You will certainly continue to advertise, that's an aspect of marketing that few companies have the luxury of avoiding, but generally you will not need to push thought leadership. Although there was one instance, long ago, when I broke my own rule, and I'm glad I did. Don't forget, I did say you will break some of these rules and I'd be fine with that.

A print ad we wrote and designed for SunGard K-12 was a blatant promotional, full-page endorsement of our own thought leadership. The headline read, "We're using our thought leadership to develop the nation's next thought leaders."[1] And the copy, under an alluring photo of two students shouldering their backpacks, read:

We're more than K-12 software innovators, more than school information system providers, and more than ERP and district partners. We're student success thought leaders, and we're committed to making your students the next great thinkers, tinkerers, and doers. Let us show you how we have helped K-12 school districts nationwide become leaders in their community. Contact SunGard K-12 for a copy of our new white paper "Redefining District ROI: Return on Value as the New Benchmark," and learn more about the SunGard K-12 Success Ecosystem that explains how we can help students in your district lead with thought.

It's been many years since I revisited this ad, but for some reason, I still seem to be okay with it. Our design department did a wonderful job with the ad's look and feel, and the results were second to none. I don't recall hearing or receiving a single untoward response from the ad's placement, which was in the top education journals. But I'm not sure I'd base an entire campaign on this, let alone move too far past a print publication and go full monty with digital, social, broadcast, and public relations. In any event, keep the muzzle on, not to the extent the Greeks hamstrung their women, but be a bit temperate with your bullhorn.

And now let's move graciously to **Rule Number Two:** *You're not the only thought leader who's a thought leader.* And I do mean graciously because there are other members of the flock you are now part of. It's a brotherhood and sisterhood that recognizes thought leaders. It doesn't pit them against one another in a WWE cage match until someone surrenders. It shouldn't be about you because there will always be others involved, including the possibility of another thought leader or two. As I say, there is no "I" in "we" unless you're French, of course, and what Peter Drucker said was:

The leaders who work most effectively, it seems to me, never say 'I.' And that's not because they have trained themselves not to say 'I.' They don't think 'I.' They think 'we'; they think 'team.' They understand their job to be to make the team function. They accept responsibility and don't sidestep it, but 'we' gets the credit. This is what creates trust, what enables you to get the task done.[2]

So, in addition to not being the only thought leader in your industry's universe, you shouldn't be the only voice in it either.

It's doubtful that it might happen, particularly if you have a solid leg up on your competitors and you've been flexing your muscles in the thought leadership gym, but it's possible another company will envy your thought leadership success and try to grab the medicine ball from your clenched grip. There aren't many times when I think it's all right to take your ball and go home, but this might be an instance when it's okay to do it. If it gets a little feisty, take your ball, walk away, don't turn back and tell someone where to go, and, by all means, make no hand gestures. If you have a competitor who claims they are a thought leader, they will make you a better thought leader, but there's no rule that requires you to be their best friend. Acknowledging their intellect is the high road.

When you get to a trade show, or some sort of industry event where there's more than one thought leader—hell, there might be a handful—it's permissible to make a bit of noise. Not only because these types of events are decibel-aggravating, but also because you can certainly count on other thought leaders not subscribing to my classic rules. Expect the unexpected, like book signings, breakout panels inhabited by your thought leader brethren, keynotes, and the dreaded in-booth thought leadership demo replete with what the trade calls *writing and lighting instruments*, but you know as promotional items. Nothing spells thought leadership quite like a monogrammed ice scraper at Orlando's Orange County Convention Center. But all of these types of platforms for sharing your industry knowledge are more than fair game and you should book yourself into them as much as you can, including your own book signing.

You'll probably be the only thought leader in the neighborhood, but I want to warn you that there's a possibility you might need to share the limelight. The good news is that another company won't be as prepared as you, and they certainly won't have transitioned from the unexamined life to the examined life, which makes you a better educator and rhetorician, among many other attributes.

And not surprisingly, this leads to **Rule Number Three:** *Don't confuse thought leadership with being the smartest person in the room.* This is a rule that is both behavioral and contextual. I'm not suggesting you should maintain a non-strategic spot in the corner and hydrate yourself like the wallflower you aren't; on the other hand, it's not always befitting to act like the smartest person in the room, which is most often in the conference room. It's not often I quote Apache proverbs. In fact, I know only one Apache proverb and it goes like this: "It's better to have less thunder in the mouth and more lightning in the hand." Don't you love that? I do and I've always cherished it.

The third rule probably applies far beyond thought leadership, which is the contextual part of the equation. It's also the behavioral part because it's solid advice for just about everyone. As you know, I've cautioned all of us to act more like Socrates, who was a great listener, because that's what you do as a consultant, as an educator, and as a thought leader. In other words, don't launch into Socratic Questioning overdrive until you've composed your thoughts and listened to the drumbeat of whatever is rumbling in the bedrock. I like really smart people, but my jets cool when really smart people tell me how really smart they are. In fact, on the pro speaking circuit, you will never hear thought leaders and educators say anything remotely close to reminding the audience that the person on the stage is a blue-chip intellectual. They don't need to. You won't hear a speaker talk about their accomplishments; that's almost always reserved for the sponsor who delivers the intro and bio of the speaker. And you'll never hear the words *I was recently awarded*, or *I've been cited for*, or, the most cringeworthy, *as a Greek scholar, award-winning philosopher, and sales and marketing thought leader . . .*

Obviously, I don't need to explain the finer parts of **Rule Number Three** to you, but if you're getting into this stuff for the first time, it's important you understand some of the rope-a-dopes. Plus, it never hurts to remind people that working a room doesn't always translate to being the center of intentional attention. "Humility," Aristotle said, "is a flower that does not grow in everyone's garden." Let's cultivate humility together, whether we're stuck like a wallflower in the corner of the room or we're behind the podium delivering a keynote to 1,000 people.

And that leads effortlessly into **Rule Number Four:** *Thought leadership is like saffron—a little goes a long way.* I like saffron; it ferries me to some weird place where I'm running through a field of wheat grass with a honey stick in my hand. But a little does go a long way, and from time to time, it does have a tendency to turn the food I'm cooking yellow. And that's what's so terrific about the fourth discipline of market leaders—you don't need a lot of it to prove your point.

Let's take a closer look. You have three disciplines within the discipline of thought leadership to focus on: **Wisdom and Insights, Trust and Honesty,** and **Ethics and Causes**. I believe the development and syndication of two content assets each month is plenty of ammo to support your thought leadership qualifications. Weekly seems too heavy to me, but if someone was steadfast in their belief that it should be three per month, who am I to stand in their steadfast way? But assume two assets per month is the proper weight. That's twenty-four assets each year, or eight assets per year, per discipline within the discipline. That's not a heavy load to carry; in fact, it's relatively lightweight compared to the midnight candles you'll need to burn if you're going to be a price-cutter, a customer service advocate, or a technology and innovation leader.

If you commit to being a price leader, you'll be working around the clock to stay true to yourself, not to mention the fact that it makes for a lousy personal brand. The price leaders whom I've worked with, after long periods of time, tend to begrudge the discipline. Once you're a price-chopper, clawing your way out of that whack-a-mole hole is a tough duty, and if you can make the ascent to a more profitable discipline, it can take years to replenish your stamina and find new footing.

Customer service leaders have it easier, but it's no cakewalk. You are also on call every day of the year, and just as a price leader will never have a low enough price, your customer service will never be good enough. And if you operate a call center or a help desk, even with the advent of AI, you'll still burn through employees, spend loads of time training new ones, and need to deal with the never-satisfied prototypical blockhead, week after week.

And the only way you can be a technology and innovation leader is to throw a lot of R&D money at it because that's what's going to keep the discipline afloat. I like the technology and innovation leadership discipline. I always have. That's why I've spent decades working with technology companies and integrating thought leadership into their cultures. Tech companies are fast-paced, are forward-thinking, have eager employees, and have a change-the-world attitude that's always been appealing to me. But it isn't for the faint of heart, and it takes time to build a solid and profitable foundation.

If you're looking to be a technology and innovation leader as part of your personal brand, you'll need to expect ongoing education costs, new certifications, training on new product and software innovations, investments in hardware and software applications, and a lot of trial and error. That's just part of the drill. But for thought leadership, it never seemed to be a drill to me, never an uphill battle, and rarely an investment that was under pressure from shareholders, stakeholders, and the sales prevention departments.

Rule Number Five: *Thought leaders know how to tell and write great stories.* We know this beyond a shadow of a doubt. From statistics about the importance of storytelling in the sales and marketing process to the neuroscience and chemical releases that make us remember stories far beyond our abilities to remember facts, statistics, tables, and figures, there's no denying the value in having the capabilities of telling a good story. As long as it's on the shorter side, of course.

Like saffron, it is possible that storytelling can be too much of a good thing. We've all seen and heard it before, not necessarily from a thought leader, but certainly from people who might not know when to stop; it's part of life, but not part of a thought leader's life.

As Aristotle reminded us in his work *Poetics*, "A likely impossibility is always preferable to an unconvincing possibility. The story should never be made up of improbable incidents; there should be nothing of the sort in it. The plot, then, is the first principle, and, as it were, the soul of a tragedy; character holds the second place."

In my speeches I always began with a story (not one of improbable incidents), and truth be told it was the same story whether it was summer or winter, Omaha or Oklahoma City, at a car wash convention or a convention of marketers. It went something like this:

I arrived a day early in Des Moines for a speech to several advertising, marketing, and public relations associations, and I pulled into a diner in my rental car. I took the only seat available well within earshot of four ROMEOs (Retired Old Men Eating Out) having a late breakfast. As much as I tried to keep my distance, it was impossible to not overhear their conversation. Between the clanking of dishes in the diner and the hearing aids worn by the ROMEOs, their conversation was loud, but it was also amusing and engaging.

They were talking about the winter of 1959 when the snow was so high it eclipsed their adolescent torsos. They talked about building a giant snow fort in one of their backyards that remained intact for most of that brutally cold winter. And they remembered in vivid detail how excited they were to play in that snow fort after school, how they had been dressed in layer over layer of clothing, how much fun they had laughing and smiling, and how rosy their cheeks would be with the cold stamped onto their bare skin. And then they'd go inside the house to warm up and they'd be greeted with a cup of steaming hot cocoa with marshmallows and the entire house smelled of chocolate.

They had obviously just played nine holes of golf, probably at the local Muni, and probably not more than thirty minutes ago, and they switched their conversation to their scores on hole number eight. It was easy for me to listen in and hear our four guys trying to remember what they shot on the eighth hole, what that number was, but they just couldn't remember, even though they remembered what happened over sixty-five years ago.

I'd usually end this story with a closing sentence about friendliness, how our ROMEOs had obviously known each other from grade school, and little had probably changed in how tight they were. It was a segue into my next slide which called attention to the fact that there were 95 million searches about storytelling that week, and I was delighted to be able to share this story with my audience; it gave me a good feeling about life.

And then I would proceed with the ancient Greeks as thought leaders, how they listened far ahead of talking, why thought leadership was the most important discipline in the *21st Century Disciplines of Market Leaders*, and so on. When I hit the section of my speech about why storytelling worked, how the Broca's and Wernicke's areas of the brain process language, how dopamine enhances memory, and how action words with emotion, touch, smell, and texture actually release more dopamine than common words, I picked up the story of our four gents, without missing a beat, roughly forty minutes after I started telling the audience about the winter of 1959 . . .

And you can see how we can remember words like steaming hot cocoa and marshmallows *(smell),* laughing and smiling *(emotion),* rosy cheeks on bare skin *(touch), and* layers of warm clothing *(texture), but our four ROMEOs couldn't even remember the scores they shot on the eighth hole at the local Muni only thirty minutes earlier.*

I can't even remember how many times I told that story, so many times that it got harder and harder to tell, but it hit home each time, and furthered my theories about storytelling. All told, that one story, the only story I really told in my speech, consumed about three minutes of my sixty-minute discussion. Length does not make for a good story, but as Aristotle reminded us, plot first and characters second rules the day, although I'm not completely convinced of that.

In the case of sales and marketing, storytelling might be one of the top three most important attributes of getting the deal done. As the highest-paid copywriter in history, Gary Halbert said, "And do you know what is the most-often missing ingredient in a sales message? It's the sales message that doesn't tell an interesting story. Storytelling, good storytelling, is a vital component of a marketing campaign."[3] Thank you, Gary.

Rule Number Six: *What's really, really ancient is really, really new again.* Time and again, we want to convince ourselves that the latest discovery might be authentic, without any roots or origins in the past. I'm as hopeful as the next person that this is true, but oftentimes, it doesn't measure up. There are so many foundational principles of today that owe their existence to discoveries and authentic thinking of the past. If we're going to educate—regardless of it being schooling, business philosophies, or life lessons—then we need to give credit where credit is due. Obviously, without much history to reflect on, Socrates,

Plato, Aristotle, and Aspasia wrote about their own history by creating their own future, but we tend to dismiss or simply are not aware of it because we aren't overly attentive to history. It's understandable when our focus is almost always on what's in front of us, what's around the next corner, and what next year will bring. But history is incredibly important to study, not just because we learn from the mistakes of the past, but also because it allows us to formulate opinions and approaches based on facts and occurrences, which is far more pragmatic than formulating opinions out of thin air.

A significant problem with business in general, and sales and marketing in particular, is that there's very limited study of the history of business, and that includes formalized education in business schools and even at the corporate level. It's a shame because there's so much to learn from our Greek scholars, from John Wanamaker, from Peter Drucker, and the list goes on. That's why it will always be important to remember, in any context, what Eduardo Galeano told us: "History never really says goodbye. History says, 'See you later.'" One day, perhaps when you least expect it, history won't just say, "See you later," but it will also say, "Hello again," or as John Prine sang to us in "Hello in There,"

> *So if you're walking down the street sometime*
> *And spot some hollow ancient eyes*
> *Please don't just pass 'em by and stare*
> *As if you didn't care, say, "Hello in there, hello."*

For me, those "ancient eyes" are none other than the classic Greek philosophers; for you, they might be Thomas Edison, George Washington Carver, Marie Curie, or Steve Jobs. Whoever it might be, take the time to dig a little deeper into the past; it just might shed some light on the future. And I know for certain that sort of curiosity is an unrelenting characteristic of all thought leaders.

Rule Number Seven: *Thought leaders look at the world differently; they forgo the obvious in favor of the obscure.* There's a lot of truth in this rule, and I've seen it firsthand. I can't count the times listening to thought leaders I thought to myself, *Where on earth did that concept come from? That's totally and wonderfully beautiful.* It's like "Hello in There." I want to know what's making that person tick. For the most part, and most often, it's a curiosity that thought leaders possess that causes them to view the world differently, beyond the obvious, in favor of digging deeper and looking for astonishment and wonderment between the lines, which is exactly what you did so wonderfully in your VOC research.

I remember working with a terrific company in Cleveland, Ohio, known as OverDrive. They are a digital distributor of e-books, library services and software, content management, and other contributions to a life of quality. At the time of my thought leadership work, OverDrive was owned by Rakuten, but was later purchased by Kohlberg Kravis Roberts & Co. of Claremont Colleges and Peter Drucker fame.

I guess what goes around, comes around.

In any event, during a thought leadership content discussion, I noticed the sales and marketing teams were focused on developing case studies regarding K-12 libraries in the largest school districts in America. That was fine, but I asked if there wouldn't be more interest, more curiosity, and therefore more chewability in doing a case study about the smallest school district in America.

At the time, that was Sheridan, Wyoming, where the entire district had about seventy students, where there were no school buses because of the gnarly terrain, and the students were all picked up and delivered in Chevy Suburbans. It was a much better case study than focusing merely on the largest school districts. And a much better story.

The seven rules of thought leadership are considerations for any of us to chomp on. You can choose the rules that most apply to you and trash those that aren't worthy of attention. These are my self-inflicted rules, but there are plenty of others. In the bonus department, there could always be many other rules, including *thought leaders are always good listeners*; *thought leaders will always focus on the what-if, not just the why*; *thought leaders must always believe that the more we know, the more we need to know*; and *thought leaders understand the ins and outs of the unexamined life*. The list builds from there, but it will always be important to set some ground rules when developing the rules of thought leadership.

Here's to you abiding by the rules, and breaking them, too.

14

BEING THOUGHTFUL IN LIFE
(SORT OF AN EPILOGUE)

I had a pretty successful career counseling businesses how to be thought leaders and corporate ethicists, and how to make money by selling wisdom ahead of anything else. But I shy away from advising anyone about matters of life and matters of the heart. It's not my lane on the highway, not my vision—straight or peripheral—and certainly not my microphone. But there are lessons to learn from the Greek scholars and they're not exclusively about business and thought leadership. They are about the Greek notions of soul, humility, stoicism, education, the examined life, listening, doing the right things, and searching for a life of quality. You don't need to understand every translation of teleological, deontological, and *Nicomachean Ethics* to know that we need to be creating a better society for all, not just for one, as Aristotle taught us, and you don't need to get lost in every conversation Plato wrote in *The Republic*, but we do need to know that our pursuit of a life of quality—in business and in life—shouldn't be hijacked by corporations and people who don't give a damn. The evidence, the research, and the statistics overwhelmingly support the idea that consumers, and that's all of us, want goodness.

So goodness it shall be, but goodness to others is the real difference maker. And that's not any sort of directive from me, because it was Socrates who said, "For who is there but you? Who not only claim to be a good man and a gentleman, for many are this, and yet have not the power of making others good? Whereas you are not only good yourself, but also the cause of goodness in others." These ancient scholars are the gifts that keep on giving. We all owe it to ourselves to get acquainted with them, even if it's for a short time.

And when you do take some time to know Socrates, Plato, Aristotle, and Aspasia a little bit better, you will discover that the key to an excellent life, according to Plato, is that it takes practice, and that's no different from being a thought leader in business and in sales. That's why your sales director asks you to role-play, that's why I suggested you write a book to further your personal brand, and that's why you need to produce pitch flows and proof points—not just one or two, but several—because it takes practice to get things right, and to make your efforts excellent. Plato said, "Excellence is not a gift, but a skill that takes practice. We do not act 'rightly' because we are 'excellent,' in fact we achieve 'excellence' by acting 'rightly.'" That's not only true in your business life, but it makes perfect sense in your personal life, too. Drucker also told us to act rightly and do the right things. I believe companies like Mister Car Wash, Marten Machining, WEA Trust, Avante Properties, M3 Insurance, OverDrive, ArbiterSports, and many others do, or did, the right things because the people who work there do the right things when they aren't working there.

I have no idea if our Greek philosophers were happy or miserable. Perhaps it was a little of both. But they did teach us to think about happiness, and that, according to Aristotle, was the initial foothold to a better life. He told us that true happiness wasn't a feeling that came and went, and what we needed to search for was *eudaimonia*, a sort of euphoric life that was the highest order of human good. I think Aristotle teased us a bit when he mentioned that the highest human good was a combo, or maybe it was a trombo, of a life of pleasure (I'm down with that), a life of political activity (for me that's a life of involvement and engagement, not necessarily politics), and a philosophical life (an existence of thought, examination, education, virtue, and honor). Who's to say if any of this is wrong? Assuredly I cannot because it sounds very right to me.

"Happiness is the perfection of human nature," said Aristotle. "Since man is a rational animal, human happiness depends on acquiring a moral character, where one displays the virtues of courage, generosity, justice, friendship, and citizenship in one's life," he continued. Going once, going twice, going three times, sold to the highest bidder, which should be all of humankind.

The perfection of human nature seems to me to be *eudaimonia*. Our highest order of human good. And that also seems to me to be *pulchritudinous*, very beautiful in so many ways. Here's to your excellence, the perfection you bring to your work and your life, to your courage, generosity, the *just* way you treat people, friendship, and citizenship, to your examined life, to the education you bring to others, and to the thought leadership you bring to yourself, your family, and others in your world who rely on your ethics, wisdom, and insights.

AFTERWORD

As a chief marketing officer, I need to surround myself with a topflight team of co-workers and also a steady stream of research, both quantitative and qualitative. It's research that allows us to make decisions that are timely, informative, offer validation of what is happening in the field, and what is happening in our customers' minds.

Most often, we are defined by the people who work with us and the information that is provided to us. Over the last few years, I've found gratification in knowing that Tom Marks was working *with* me and providing information *to* me.

But not just any type of information. That's because if you've rubbed shoulders with Tom, you already understand that you'll receive more than you ever asked for. More insights, more research, more strategy, more stories, more history, and more lessons on ethics. And in spite of what Tom might tell you or write about the importance of brevity, he's not exactly an adherent to the art of writing a short brief, or anything else for that matter. In fact, he's the only marketer I've ever worked with who consistently delivers briefs that are twenty to thirty pages long; that's because he has so many insights, so many thoughts on what makes people behave the way they do, and a perspective on marketing that's a unique combination of being a stickler for the fundamentals while at the same time wanting to explore strategies that have never been implemented before.

I've been in the marketing business for twenty-five years with much of it in the marketing of food. With my years at Jack in the Box, QDOBA, and now El Pollo Loco, I've learned a lot about trust, the value of hard work, and the creative process. But I never imagined the detail, the cadence, and the insights that can result from exquisitely orchestrated VOC research. There's a reason people call Tom the VOC King and it has a lot to do with his abilities to produce groundbreaking findings by communicating with people in a manner that makes them feel they're the center of the universe, that their feedback is an essential path to a company's improvement, and that their voice—regardless of its size and reach—is the most important voice to be heard. I'm not suggesting that you read just one chapter of *The Second-Best Business Book Ever Written: The Pursuit of Thought Leadership in Sales, Marketing, and Life*, but if you are searching for the definitive step-by-step process of how to conduct VOC research, chapter seven is a gift to all of us; it's the most complete and detailed guide to VOC I've ever seen. It's important to treat yourself to every chapter in this book (if you haven't already) because you'll learn a lot more than VOC; in fact there's something for all of us—marketers, salespeople, executives, consultants, and those new to business—to learn on virtually every page.

After reading Tom's book, I'm still struck by the combination of his commitment to practicing the fundamentals of sales and marketing with pushing strategic, tactical, and creative boundaries; I've seen it firsthand for several years, so I know it well. It's just a different perspective when you read about it. It makes the combination even more unique, rare, and valued.

And for anyone who hasn't learned yet, Tom really is a great storyteller. Sure, some are too colorful to tell here, but stories flow from him without missing a beat in their clarity and their relevance to whatever we're discussing at the moment. It's delightful, educational, and will take you away to places you can only imagine.

Although Tom asked me if I'd write the afterword to this particular book, I'm secretly hoping that this is far from being the last afterword he asks me to write. As you now know, words flow from Tom, one after the other, and I want more of them.

With fondness and appreciation,
Jill Adams
Chief Marketing Officer, El Pollo Loco
Costa Mesa, California

NOTES

CHAPTER 2

1. Willy Stern, "Did Dirty Tricks Create a Best Seller?," *Bloomberg Businessweek*, August 7, 1995.

2. Violation Tracker, "Violation Tracker 100 Most Penalized Current Parent Companies," https://violationtracker.goodjobsfirst.org/top-100-parents.

3. "December 2000—Nucor Corporation, Inc. Multimedia Settlement," United States Environmental Protection Agency, https://www.epa.gov/enforcement/december-2000-nucor-corporation-inc-multimedia-settlement.

CHAPTER 3

1. First Insight, *Consumer Holiday Shopping Trend Report 2022* (Warrendale, PA: FirstInsight, 2022).

2. Neil Canty, "How Erica Fiedner [*sic*] Sold 41 Million Dollars in Pianos," LinkedIn, https://www.linkedin.com/pulse/how-erica-fiedner-sold-41-million-dollars-pianos-neil-canty/.

3. Nordstrom, "The Nordy Pod: The Truth about Nordstrom's Legendary Tire Story," Nordstrom Now, https://press.nordstrom.com/news-releases/news-release-details/nordy-pod-truth-about-nordstroms-legendary-tire-story.

4. Albert Mosby, "33+ Amazon Prime Statistics 2023 (Users, Revenue & Trends)," Yaguara.co, August 9, 2023, https://www.yaguara.co/amazon-prime-statistics/#:~:text=Amazon%20generated%20%2435.22%20billion%20in%20revenue%20through%20prime%20membership%20in%202022.

5. Gennaro Cuofano, "Is Amazon Profitable without AWS?," FourWeekMBA, https://fourweekmba.com/is-amazon-profitable-without-aws/.

6. Abbas Haleem, "Costco Ecommerce Sales Improve Compared with Previous Quarters, but Still Down Overall," Digital Commerce 360, September 27, 2023, https://www.digitalcommerce360.com/2023/09/27/costco-ecommerce -sales-q4-2023/.

7. Abbas Haleem, "Target Online and Total Sales Decline in Q3," Digital Commerce 360, November 16, 2023, https://www.digitalcommerce360.com/ article/target-online-sales/.

8. GovInfo, "About National Institute of Standards and Technology (NIST) Publications," https://www.govinfo.gov/collection/nist.

9. Marten Machining, "About," https://martenmach.com/about.

10. Office of Advocacy, "Frequently Asked Questions about Small Business 2023," US Small Business Administration, March 7, 2023, https://advocacy.sba .gov/2023/03/07/frequently-asked-questions-about-small-business-2023/.

CHAPTER 5

1. NCR, "NCR Announces Full Year and Fourth Quarter 2022 Results," February 7, 2023, https://investor.ncr.com/news-releases/news-release-details/ncr -announces-full-year-and-fourth-quarter-2022-results.

2. "Keebler: A Pioneering Approach Establishes a National Brand," Rosica Communications, https://www.rosica.com/case-study/keebler-famous-amos -cookies/.

3. Cone Communications, *2017 Cone Communications CSR Study* (Boston: Cone Communications, 2017), 11, https://www.cbd.int/doc/case-studies/inc/cs-inc -cone-communications-en.pdf.

4. Harry Lang, "From Hero to Zero: Why Loss of Trust Is So Damaging for Premium Brands," Marketing Week, April 12, 2023, https://www .marketingweek.com/loss-trust-damaging-premium-brands/.

5. Gitnux, "Must-Know Cause Marketing Statistics," October 15, 2023, https://gitnux.org/cause-marketing-statistics/.

6. Havas, "New Havas 2023 Global Meaningful Brands™ Report," p. 2. www.adcgroup.it/static/upload/hav/0000/havas_mb_whitepaper.pdf.

7. Linchpin SEO, "The Power of Branding: How to Create a Strong Brand Identity," updated October 10, 2023, https://linchpinseo.com/blog/the-power -of-branding-how-to-create-a-strong-brand-identity/.

8. Zeno Group, "2020 Zeno Strength of Purpose Study," June 17, 2020, https://www.zenogroup.com/insights/2020-zeno-strength-purpose.

9. Diana Kaemingk, "Online Review Statistics to Know in 2022," Qualtrics XM, October 30, 2022, https://www.qualtrics.com/blog/online-review-stats/.

10. James Anthony, "62 Customer Review Statistics You Must Learn: 2023 Market Share Analysis & Data," FinancesOnline, n.d., https://financesonline.com/ customer-reviews-statistics/.

11. Podium, "22 Online Review Statistics Every Business Can Leverage in 2023," March 16, 2021, https://www.podium.com/article/online-review-statistics/.

12. Dominique Jabbour, "3-Star Reviews Result in a -70% Decrease in Trust [Data Study]," *Go Fish* (blog), April 7, 2023, https://gofishdigital.com/blog/3-star -reviews-result-in-70-decrease-in-trust-data-study/.

13. Myles Anderson, "87% of Potential Customers Won't Consider Businesses with Low Ratings," Search Engine Land, August 25, 2015, https://searchengineland .com/87-percent-customers-wont-consider-low-ratings-228607.

14. Jameela Ghann, "59 Product Review Statistics Every Online Store Needs to Know," Fera A.I., n.d., https://www.fera.ai/blog/posts/online-product-review -statistics-ecommerce-stores-need-them.

15. Jessica Bruce, "How Positive and Negative Reviews Affect Business Revenue," *Reputation X* (blog), August 3, 2023, https://blog.reputationx.com/how -positive-and-negative-reviews-affect-business-revenue.

16. Tim Stobierski, "15 Eye-Opening Corporate Social Responsibility Statistics," *Harvard Business Review*, June 15, 2021.

17. John Elsasser, "14 Views on When a Company Should Speak Out About a Social Issue Today," n.d., *PRsay* (blog), https://prsay.prsa.org/2021/04/15/14 -views-on-when-a-company-should-speak-out-about-a-social-issue-today/.

CHAPTER 6

1. Havas, "New Havas 2023 Global Meaningful Brands™ Report," p. 2. www .adcgroup.it/static/upload/hav/0000/havas_mb_whitepaper.pdf.

2. Brooklyn Museum, "Aspasia," https://www.brooklynmuseum.org/eascfa/dinner_ party/place_settings/aspasia.

CHAPTER 7

1. Darin Gerdes, "Peter F. Drucker's Wit and Humor," The Leadersmith, https://www.daringerdes.com/peter-f-druckers-wit-and-humor/.

2. "Culture Eats Strategy for Breakfast," Daily Agile, https://dailyagile.com/culture-eats-strategy-for-breakfast/.

CHAPTER 8

1. Ian Hawkins, "12 Classic Quotes from Peter Drucker," Process Excellence Network, July 23, 2019, https://www.processexcellencenetwork.com/lessons_from_peter_drucker/articles/12-classic-quotes-from-peter-drucker.

2. Peter F. Drucker, "The Age of Social Transformation," *The Atlantic*, November 1994, https://www.theatlantic.com/past/docs/politics/ecbig/soctrans.htm.

CHAPTER 9

1. Steve Martin, "7 Reasons Salespeople Don't Close the Deal," *Harvard Business Review*, August 2, 2017.

2. Edelman-LinkedIn, "How Thought Leadership Impacts B2B Demand Generation," Edelman, June 1, 2017, https://www.edelman.com/research/how-thought-leadership-impacts-b2b-demand-generation.

3. RAIN Group, "What Sales Winners Do Differently," https://www.rainsalestraining.com/sales-research/what-sales-winners-do.

CHAPTER 10

1. Jennifer Aaker, "Harnessing the Power of Stories," Stanford University VMWare Women's Innovation Leadership Lab, https://womensleadership.stanford.edu/resources/voice-influence/harnessing-power-stories.

2. Toby Nwazor, "How to Use the Art of Storytelling to Boost Content Marketing Results," Search Engine Watch, December 20, 2019, https://www.searchenginewatch.com/2019/12/20/how-storytelling-boosts-content-marketing/.

3. Tumisang Bogwasi, "Brand Storytelling in 2023: The Latest Statistics and Trends," *The Brand Shop* (blog), March 27, 2023.

4. Nwazor, "How to Use the Art of Storytelling."

5. Jeanne Grunert, "How Brand Storytelling Increased ROI by 2,700%," Seven Oaks Consulting, January 13, 2021, https://sevenoaksconsulting.com/how-brand -storytelling-increased-roi-by-2700/.

6. Simply Knowledge, "Aspasia," http://simplyknowledge.com/popular/biography/ aspasia.

7. Manfred F. R. Kets de Vries, "How Storytelling Makes You a Better Leader," *Psychology Today*, July 11, 2023, https://www.psychologytoday.com/us/blog/ from-the-classroom-to-the-boardroom/202307/how-storytelling-makes -you-a-better-leader.

8. "Feel-Good Hormone Helps to Jog the Memory," EurekAlert, November 8, 2012, https://www.eurekalert.org/news-releases/735187.

CHAPTER 11

1. Philip Kotler and Kevin Keller, *Marketing Management*, 15th ed. (Upper Saddle River, NJ: Pearson Prentice Hall, 2016).

2. American Marketing Association, "Definitions of Marketing," https://www.ama .org/the-definition-of-marketing-what-is-marketing/.

3. Jakob Nielsen, "How Little Do Users Read?," Nielsen Norman Group, May 5, 2008, https://www.nngroup.com/articles/how-little-do-users-read/.

4. Brian Dean, "We Analyzed 4 Million Google Search Results—Here's What We Learned about Organic Click Through Rate," *Backlinco* (blog), May 28, 2023, https://backlinko.com/google-ctr-stats.

CHAPTER 12

1. Thomas R. Marks, "About," https://thomasrmarks.com/about/.

2. Thomas R. Marks, "Meeting Planners," https://thomasrmarks.com/meeting -planners/.

3. Adam Connell, "60 Latest Video Marketing Statistics for 2023: The Complete List," *Blogging Wizard*, October 17, 2023.

CHAPTER 13

1. SunGard K-12 advertisement, *Ohio School Boards Association Journal* 60, no. 3 (June 2016): 23.

2. "Peter F. Drucker Quotes," Goodreads, https://www.goodreads.com/quotes/ 167298-the-leaders-who-work-most-effectively-it-seems-to-me.

3. "10 Quotes that Prove Brand Storytelling Is the Future of Marketing," 22 Group, https://www.22group.co.uk/news-events/10-quotes-that-prove-brand -storytelling-is-the-future-of-marketing.

INDEX

ABOUT THE AUTHOR

TOM MARKS survived forty-seven years in the advertising business and has lived to write about it. He's the founder of TMA+Peritus, one of the leading marketing, thought leadership, and corporate ethics firms in North America, and has won the American Advertising Awards more than sixty-five times for his writing, including TV commercials, print ads, and magazine and newspaper articles. He spent many years on the professional speakers circuit and apparently survived that, too. His thought leadership workshops for Fortune 500 companies, as well as for SMBs, have brought him national acclaim, and his love of the original thought leaders, the ancient Greek scholars, has made him a favorite among CEOs who want to learn about corporate ethics and its origins.